KANTISHNA

MINERS, MUSHERS, AND MOUNTAINEERS

KANTISHNA

MINERS, MUSHERS, AND MOUNTAINEERS

THE STORY BEHIND MT. McKINLEY NATIONAL PARK

TOM WALKER

Copyright © 2005 Tom Walker

All rights reserved.

Library of Congress
Control Number 2005937936

ISBN 1-57510-124-6

FIRST PRINTING February 2006
SECOND PRINTING August 2007

PRINTED IN CANADA BY FRIESENS, ALTONA, MANITOBA

COVER PHOTO BY TOM WALKER

The early formation of a lenticular cloud over Mt. McKinley's summit signals the beginning of a vicious high-altitude storm like the one in 1912 that defeated Belmore Browne and Herschel Parker just a few feet below the summit.

FRONTISPIECE BY MATT UNTERBERGER

PUBLISHED BY
Pictorial Histories Publishing Company, Inc.
713 South Third Street West, Missoula, Montana 59801
PHONE (406) 549-8488, FAX (406) 728-9280
EMAIL phpc@montana.com

CONTENTS

Acknowledgments vii

Prologue ix

1	Gold and Ice	1
2	Eureka!	15
3	Kid Karstens	33
4	Sheldon on the Toklat	51
5	Market Hunters	69
6	Quigley of Kantishna	81
7	Community in Isolation	97
8	The Glen Creek Boys	111
9	Frontier Justice	125
10	Mountain Men	135
11	The Deacon and the Sourdough	153
12	The Summit at Last	165
13	Down the Trail	179
14	Mt. McKinley National Park	189

Epilogue 204

Appendix 205

End Notes 211

Bibliography 227

Index 232

ACKNOWLEDGMENTS

The first halting steps on this planned two-volume project began in the 1980s, continued through the 1990s, and accelerated in 2000. Needless to say I owe many people for their help.

Megan Holloway and Nan Eagleson gave able research assistance. Mike Brown, of the BLM, provided vital research data. Candy Waugaman offered her photographic files and suggestions for further enquiry. Rex Fisher provided a few noteworthy era newspaper clippings, friendly advice and diligent research. My long-time friend and author Jim Rearden detailed market hunting activities and made available to me his collection of taped interviews with Frank Glaser. Historians Terrence Cole, Ann Kain, and Frank Norris commented on parts of the manuscript. Dr Steven Rogers supplied information about his relative Jack Haydon. David M. Dean, Hudson Stuck's biographer, answered numerous questions. John Hewitt reviewed a second draft as did Kathy Hennigan. Climbers Dave Johnston and Brian Okonek commented on a section of the book. Susan B. Adams read and commented on the final draft.

Bill Nancarrow, the park's first naturalist, gave generously of his time. He and his wife, Ree, offered unflagging support. Denali National Park's Cultural Resource specialist Jane Bryant provided research assistance, and waded through the original rough draft offering numerous vital suggestions. I am grateful for her continuing support and help.

My daughter Mary Anne, currently with the Smithsonian Institution, edited the final manuscript with a critical eye and attention to detail.

The author has taken every effort to insure accuracy. Every important detail has at least two sources, others have more. Some wonderful stories were deleted due to insufficient documentation. To offer corrections, additional information, old photographs, or comments, please contact the author at Post Office Box 146, Denali Park, Alaska 99755.

PROLOGUE

The great chain of gold rushes that began in the Klondike in the late 1890s filled the North with people hooked on the Next Big Thing. When on July 17, 1897, the steamship *Portland* docked in Seattle with "68 Rich Men" on board and "Stacks of Yellow Metal!" the news raced around the country and the world and sparked an unparalleled stampede north. While a handful of wealthy Americans enjoyed the luxuries of the Gilded Age, countless thousands of others struggled to eke out a living in a time of economic depression, caused in part by the American economy's ties to the gold standard. Many immigrants labored in squalid sweatshops and lived in rat-infested tenements. In 1890, 11 million of the nation's 12 million families earned less than $1200 per year; their average annual income $380. Following the financial "Panic of 1893," violent strikes and riots wracked the nation throughout the era glamorized years later as the "Gay '90s." North in the Yukon, literally, was a "golden opportunity" to get rich and escape the bonds of perpetual poverty. Thousands left everything, homes, wives, and children, sometimes even their real names, and rushed north.

This last grand adventure of the nineteenth century actually began in 1896, with the discovery of gold on Rabbit Creek, a small tributary of the Klondike River in the heart of Canada's Yukon wilderness. Word to the Outside leaked out and by mid-summer of 1897, the news had spread and the first stampeders began arriving. In the spring and summer of 1898, between 40,000 and 50,000 people arrived in the Klondike gold fields. Many gave up and headed back home when they found that the majority of the ground was already claimed and food in short supply. Most of those who stayed labored in the creeks for wages, but others fanned out across the Yukon and into Alaska to prospect for gold.

The Klondike Rush was one of the first in a series of northern gold strikes. The first rush to Nome in Alaska began in the fall of '98, just as the exodus from Dawson City peaked. Two years later, thousands more stampeded north to yet another Nome discovery. Other strikes would be made in the Territory of Alaska but none as accessible as Nome's golden beaches. Gold and gold seekers, profoundly changed Alaska and its people. As hopefuls sought riches, Alaska's white population grew from 4,298 in 1890 to 30,293 in 1905. Many of them believed that the next Bonanza lay right over the ridge and they would be the ones to find it.

With the influx of gold seekers, and others seeking to mine the miners, the federal government worked quickly to establish the rule of law. First on the scene were garrisons of U.S. soldiers, followed by civilian law enforcement and members of the judicial system.

Exploration of the Alaska Territory and an inventory of its mineral wealth were of paramount importance to the United States Government. Military and scientific expeditions were dispatched to not only explore the region but tighten Federal control.

Alfred Hulse Brooks' seven man United States Geological Survey (USGS) expedition arrived at Cook Inlet on May 27, 1902, with provisions to last 105 days. D.L. Reaburn served as expedition topographer and Louis M. Prindle, assistant leader. This was to be the first USGS expedition to traverse the unexplored northern slopes of the Alaska Range around Mt. McKinley. The group traveled by horseback west through the Alaska Range, naming Rainy Pass as they passed through. (Horses packed supplies in sufficient quantity to avoid the starvation and privation that earlier foot expeditions had suffered. Less than half the horses survived the journey.)

On the west side of the Alaska Range the expedition turned and proceeded northeast, subsisting on sheep and caribou. "There was no sport in hunting such innocently tame creatures, and we never molested them except when we needed meat," Brooks said while providing the first description of the region's animals.[1]

Brooks' party came closer to Mt. McKinley than perhaps any other Euro-Americans before them. Brooks lamented the fact that he had neither the time nor supplies to attempt a climb. He contented himself with a hike up the mountain's flanks. A sheer ice wall stymied him and turned him back. "I gazed along the precipitous slopes . . . with a thrill of satisfaction at being the first man to approach the summit," he wrote. "No white man had ever before reached its base and I was far beyond where the moccasined foot of the roving Indian had ever trod." On the way down, he built a cairn and cached an expended rifle cartridge that contained a brief account of his hike and the party roster. (Fifty-two years later, Park Ranger Grant Pearson and J.C. Reed, of the USGS, found the shell and note.)[2]

From the mountain's slopes, the survey party traveled east to the mouth of Yanert Fork, a tributary of what was then called the Cantwell River (now the Nenana.) Then they retraced their steps westward to the 149th meridian, which they followed, more or less, north to the Tanana River. In three and one-half months, they traveled 800 miles through uncharted country and became the first to cross west to east through the center of what would one day be Denali National Park. Geologists and geographers considered their 105-day journey, especially Reaburn's continuous plane-table survey of the entire trip, one of the grandest achievements of northern exploration.

Geologist Brooks did not view his endeavors as particularly incredible. After finding a blazed trail on the northwest side of the Alaska Range, Brooks wrote: "Who were these lonely travelers of this wild region? . . . Often these pioneers make journeys that would put to shame the widely advertised explorations of many a well-equipped government expedition. . . . Unfortunately their ideas of where they have been are often almost as vague as of where they are going. Many a life has been lost on these hazardous journeys, and only too often are bleaching bones the sole record of unproclaimed and unrewarded heroism."[3]

No one will ever know who left the blazed trail Brooks found but the region was not entirely unexplored by gold seekers. In 1878 the famed traders Al Mayo and Arthur Harper poled a boat up the Tanana River from its confluence with the Yukon, and then up the Kantishna River on their way to the Kuskokwim River. The two may have been the first Americans to sight the mountain from the north. A few years later Frank Densmore and two partners traversed the Minchumina–Kuskokwim portage after poling up the Kantishna. The 225-pound Densmore, who came north in 1882, was described as the most powerful man in all the Yukon. He once backpacked a 250-pound pump over the summit of Chilkoot Pass. He was a partner in Densmore, Spencer, and McPhee, owners of Dawson's *Pioneer Saloon* where Densmore so gloried in his tales of the mountain Athabascans called *Denali* that for many years it was known along the entire Yukon River as "Densmore's Mountain." He was an energetic and early explorer of the Tanana wilderness until the time of his death in 1898.

Besides mapping this unexplored region, one of Brooks' major goals was to identify any likely mineral-bearing formations and prospects. Consequently, the Harvard-educated Brooks was one of the few Federal Government men who throughout his life enjoyed the respect and praise of Alaskans. His courage and strength of character won over skeptical Alaskans. His popular writings on gold, coal and other minerals brought the public the kind of information they wanted and treasured. To Alaskans he was simply "Our George."

His death in 1924 brought genuine grief to residents of the Territory. The Seattle Chamber of Commerce passed a resolution expressing the "sense of loss that is felt throughout Alaska and the Pacific Northwest," adding, "To the mining men, he was known also as a personal friend, endeared to them by his fine character and lovable traits. His place will not be filled as the counselor and friend of all who seek the welfare of the Northland."[4]

Throughout his life, Brooks reflected on his time on the slopes of the great mountain. "Were the day clear I could see Mt. McKinley from [my] window. As I picture in my mind its stupendous height, I compare it to our science," he wrote shortly before his death on November 22, 1924. "Many have assailed its flanks; some have proclaimed untruths about it; some have climbed by great effort well up the slopes; a very few, the best by natural selection, have reached the summit and there attained the broad vision denied those at lower altitudes. As for me, I am satisfied to have been able to traverse the great lowland to the base and to climb the foothills."[5]

Alfred Hulse Brooks' impact on the McKinley region did not end in 1902. The year following the pioneer expedition, he published a plan to climb Mt. McKinley. This small side note to an epic exploration ultimately lured climbers to the mountain.

Brooks' reports of "game animals" also attracted the attention of hunters. "In fact, the abundance of sheep, bear, moose, and caribou found along the north slope of the Alaskan Range rank it as one of the finest hunting grounds in North America," Brooks wrote.[6]

"But the very reason of this abundance lies in the inaccessibility of the field, which must deter most sportsmen. The fact that it can not be reached without the organization of an expedition prepared for a campaign of at least two to three months makes it beyond the purse and time of the average hunter."[7]

Brooks' comments and writings about the mountain and wildlife were just side notes to his expedition's main purpose. As often is the case, however, these incidentals had unexpected impact. Brooks's fantastic journey inspired three exceptional men, Federal Judge James A. Wickersham, hunter–climber–artist Belmore Browne, and hunter–conservationist Charles Sheldon, to journey to the region. Ultimately, the trio would be instrumental in helping to carve out Alaska's first National Park.

1

Gold and Ice

Judge James A. Wickersham sat on the summit of Chitsia Mountain and stared southwest toward his prize, the white dome of Mt. McKinley. His two companions left him to his thoughts. One of them dozed; the other prospected for quartz. In the three years that Wickersham had been in Alaska, he had developed a powerful urge to climb North America's tallest peak. Finally in early June 1903, he was on his way. He was still too far from the 20,320 foot mountain to pick out a route, but his eyes traced the distant ridgelines. Although he was the only member of the expedition with climbing experience, he had chosen as companions trail-hardened men used to Alaska's harsh climate. He trusted that they would follow his lead, no matter the difficulties encountered. As he stared at the glistening summit, his eyes once again sparkled with the thought of the fame that would be his by being the first man to climb the mountain. He stood up, brushed off his pants, and after calling to his partners, started back down to camp with renewed purpose.

Wickersham's trail to Mt. McKinley was long and circuitous. He was born in Patoka, Illinois, on August 24, 1857. Although he had only an eighth-grade education, he passed the Illinois bar exam in 1880 and soon married Deborah Susan Bell. Four years later, the couple moved to Washington Territory to a small crime-ridden and corrupt town near Tacoma. Gambling halls, bordellos, 30 saloons, and a brewery competed with the town's seven churches. Wickersham worked as a roofer and carpenter to make ends meet but eventually served as probate judge, Tacoma's city attorney, and later a member of the Washington State House of Representatives. A large American Indian population in the area required Wickersham to develop innovative decisions integrating their customs with white man's laws.

An avid outdoorsman, Wickersham took his family on extended hiking and climbing trips into the Olympic and Cascade Mountains. He climbed all the major peaks in the Olympics, walked the entire peninsula, and was the first to champion an Olympic National Park.

At the urging of a friend, U.S. Senator Addison G. Foster, Wickersham won appointment to the federal bench in Interior Alaska and took the oath of office on June 12, 1900. In preparation for his new position Wickersham hired George A. Jeffery, his stenographer, and Albert A. Heilig, a Tacoma attorney, to serve as court clerk. Just one week before the Judge assumed his duties, the U.S. Congress reworked the Alaska criminal and civil codes, dividing the Territory of Alaska into three judicial districts with headquarters in Sitka, Nome, and Eagle.

Wickersham's Third Judicial District sprawled over a 300,000 square mile wilderness stretching from the Arctic Ocean south to the Aleutians and Prince William Sound. His constituency included Inupiaqs, Athabascans, and fewer than 1500 white residents. In the

COURTESY OF U.S. ARMY, ALASKA, #431854

Eagle, near the Alaska/Yukon border, was the site of Wickersham's first home and judicial headquarters. Fairbanks, on the Chena River, eclipsed Eagle as the most important city in Interior Alaska.

entire district, there were no schools, courthouses, jails, or other public buildings, and no money to build them. The competent manner in which Wickersham turned his backwater post into a position of integrity remains an enduring legacy.

Eagle, 100 miles west of the great Klondike gold fields, and just six miles from the Alaska–Yukon border, served as a supply point for the Fortymile mining district. In 1900, it boasted a population of 286, only 22 of them female. The town consisted of two mercantiles, two churches, a hospital, two restaurants, and five saloons. Numerous small cabins and the U.S. Army's Fort Egbert completed the scene. In many ways, the Judge's stint in Tacoma prepared him for what he found in Eagle. Not only did he have experience dealing with pioneers and Native Americans, he was no stranger to hard labor.

Although most of the community greeted the Wickersham and Heilig families when they arrived on the steamer *John Cudahy* on July 15, 1900, their arrival provoked little celebration. Area residents, the majority veterans of the Klondike stampede, were an independent lot and viewed the government with suspicion and open disdain. To them, Wickersham represented the Federal government's unwanted attempt to establish civil authority over the prospectors flooding downstream into Alaska from the Klondike.

When introduced to the new judge, the proprietor of a roadhouse replied: "Well, the thing for you to do is get right t'ell out of here. We don't need any of your kind . . . We've got a great country here and we don't need it spoiled with lawyers and judges."[1]

Prior to Wickersham's arrival justice was often administered at "miner's meetings," which doled out efficient and swift justice, sometimes ordering miscreants to leave the territory for good. Woe to the man who ignored the group decree.

Wickersham hired a crew to cut logs then set to work building a log home for Deborah and son Howard, 7. By mid-winter he had laid in a supply of moose and caribou meat. He even found time to do a little prospecting. Wickersham's concern for the comfort and safety of his wife, who suffered with tuberculosis, and young son, remained uppermost in his mind.

Early in 1901, the pioneer judge faced the brutal realities of Alaska. It took 45 days for Wickersham to make his 1200-mile circuit by dogsled and snowshoes, at temperatures often -50°F, or colder.

Wickersham, a tireless worker endowed with great physical strength and extraordinary mental capacity, proved equal to the hardships of the trail.

Professionally, he was challenged by one enduring trait of Alaska juries—verdicts were lenient and jurors open to bribery, blackmail, and intimidation. Many juries refused to return indictments except in the most grievous breaches of "sourdough law." Over the next few decades, this traditional laissez-faire attitude would vex those charged with enforcement of Alaska's new hunting and game laws.

Corrupt judges, politicians, and lawyers helped turn the great Nome gold fields in 1901 into riotous anarchy. In mid-September, Wickersham was ordered to replace Arthur H. Noyes on the Nome Bench and he went there without delay. Many of his rulings, even his tenure, proved controversial, but he carved law and order out of chaos.

The Judge buried himself in work to assuage his longings for his family in Eagle. In March 1902, a telegram from Heilig in Eagle brought stunning news. Wickersham's son Howard had died on January 11, as a result of typhoid fever. Grief-stricken and unable to comfort his wife, Wickersham wrote: "He was my pride, my love . . . His death almost killed his mother and quite destroyed one half of my life—hopes and happiness." [2]

Huge gold strikes on the Tanana River transformed Wickersham from a minor federal judge into the tsar of Alaska's Interior. After leaving Nome and vacationing Outside with Deborah for four months, Wickersham returned to Alaska, sold his furnished cabin in the abruptly deserted town of Eagle, and joined the stampeders headed downstream toward Felix Pedro's fabulous gold strike near the confluence of the Tanana and Chena Rivers. Wickersham located his new headquarters at Rampart on the Yukon River, but in 1904 moved it to Fairbanks. Wickersham loved the Tanana Valley, which he called the garden spot of Alaska.

Looming over all of Interior Alaska stands North America's highest peak, which the Athabascans called *Denali*, but which is known widely by another name. In 1896, prospector W.A. Dickey named it *Mt. McKinley* for the future president, then Ohio's Governor and champion of the gold standard. Dickey, a Princeton man, sent the New York Sun a 4,000-word account of his exploration of the south side of the Alaska Range. While ascending the "Sushitna" River,

Dickey said, "we had many glorious views of Mt. McKinley and an unnamed companion southwest . . . Mt. McKinley is in this valley as ubiquitous as the Washington monument in the city of Washington. Everywhere you go in clear weather you can see its glorious summit dominating the northern landscape." He learned only on his return home that he had been hailed as the "discoverer" of the mountain.[3]

Wickersham loved climbing and his obsession with the mountain was predictable. He drew inspiration from Dickey but more importantly from the accounts of Alfred Hulse Brooks' and D.L. Reaburn's pioneer surveying expedition along the north side of the Alaska Range.

When word got out that the Judge planned to climb Mt. McKinley, he was besieged with applicants. The Judge had his pick of companions and with one notable exception picked long-time acquaintances. He chose Charley Webb, a packer, hunter, boatman, and guide; lawyer Morton I. Stevens, a boatman and all around athlete, and his stenographer; and his secretary George A. Jeffery, an accomplished photographer.

Although in his book, *Old Yukon: Tales-Trails-Trials*, Wickersham writes that his companions picked the last member of the expedition, in reality he actively recruited Canadian John McLeod, 26. McLeod was not some "Cheechako" new to the North. (A Cheechako was a newcomer poorly prepared for the northern conditions.) His father, Murdock, was a Hudson Bay factor at Fort McPherson, and his mother, Laura, the "beautiful" daughter of an aristocratic Virginia plantation owner. McLeod was born on the Liard River and spent most of his life on the lower MacKenzie River. McLeod accompanied Professor Andrew J. Stone, for whom the Stone's sheep and a sub-species of caribou are named, when he collected wildlife specimens from the Mackenzie to the Arctic for New York's American Museum of Natural History. McLeod came to Alaska in 1902, over the "Rat Portage" and floated down the Porcupine to Fort Yukon and ended up in Circle City.

McLeod spoke several Indian languages and dialects and his success as a trapper–trader stemmed in part from his ability to communicate. McLeod grew up around Indians and lived like them, trusting to his rifle, fish lines, and traps. He lived strictly on meat and fish and spent winters alone, which he preferred to society. McLeod, it was said, "knows the wilderness life as well as his foster brothers, the Indians."[4]

"We have accepted him as a philologer, philosopher, and friend," Wickersham said.[5]

Wickersham was pleased with his chosen companions. " . . . [A]ll four [men] strong and sound in heart and lungs," he remarked at the expedition's outset, unaware of the conflict and challenges ahead.[6]

Two additional, but essential, members of the expedition were the pack mules, Mark and Hannah, which the Judge hired from May 18 to July 20th for $50. In addition, he promised to pay each member of the expedition $100.

To raise funds for the expedition, Wickersham wrote and edited the first newspaper ever published in the Tanana Valley. The one and only issue of the *Fairbanks Miner*, all seven copies typed by George Jeffery, appeared on May 9, 1903, and sold for $5 each. Thirty-six ads were sold at $5 apiece and public readings were held in saloons with a charge of one dollar per person.

A crowd of well-wishers from the two rival boomtowns of Fairbanks and Chena cheered Wickersham's departure. The steamer *Tanana Chief* pushed a barge with the expedition members and gear down the Tanana and up the Kantishna River, then also known as the Dugan River, after a U.S. Army officer.

At the time he finally set off in late May, Wickersham, due to his judicial position, was arguably the most powerful man in Interior Alaska. The Judge, politically ambitious, knew that a successful climb would bring him worldwide acclaim and open many avenues for advancement. He was anxious to get under way but ice jams and floes caused delays. One day, while waiting for the ice to clear, McLeod salvaged a derelict, but well-built, 16 foot double-ended boat big enough to carry the entire outfit, less the mules. They dubbed their new vessel *Mudlark*. The very next day, the ice quit running and the *Tanana Chief* forged upriver into "splendid virgin country." Above the confluence with the Toklat River the expedition's primitive maps proved unreliable. Leaving the steamer behind, the group split up with two men and mules going overland while the others lined and poled the *Mudlark* upstream. They rendezvoused at intervals along the route. Wickersham's companions at once proved their worth, leading him to note that "Webb and Johnnie are fine river men and understand boats and their uses."[7]

Supplied only with the meager rations typical of prospecting excursions—bacon, beans, salt, sugar, and flour—the expedition lived

Gold and Ice 7

ALASKA STATE LIBRARY #PCA 277-18-43

Judge James A Wickersham pauses on a river bank during his 1903 climbing expedition to Mt. McKinley.

off the land. They spent two days encamped, smoking and drying the meat of two bull caribou that McLeod and Webb killed. To procure fish, McLeod would fire a rifle into the water, then wade in and toss the stunned fish out. "What would Izaak Walton say to that?" the Judge asked wryly. [8]

They were not, as Wickersham supposed, the only white men on the river. Rounding a bend one day, they saw a boat floating downstream with a single occupant. Butte Aiken said he had been in the wilderness for eleven months without seeing another white man. His canoe was loaded with furs he planned to sell when he reached civilization. On another occasion, trappers/prospectors Frank Peterson and C.G. Lundeen boated downstream into their camp. They also displayed a bundle of furs from the headwaters of the Kuskokwim and the "big lake at the head of this river." [9] These three men likely were the very first white trappers to exploit the fur riches of the Lake Minchumina region.

Upstream, the men encountered Athabascans and visited their villages. Wickersham dutifully recorded place names and a lengthy creation story. The Natives, according to the Judge, called Mt. McKinley, "*Dee-na-thy*" (meaning father). "One man was called Che-ah, his name means to eat," Wickersham wrote, "at lunch, he did not fail to live up to the highest tradition of gastronomic nomenclature."

Che-ah gave Wickersham the names of local rivers—"*Hun-teth-na*" instead of Kantishna and "*Too-tlat*", which he said meant headwaters. Other names recorded were "*Chid-zey-ah*" (the hills to the north), "*Chid-zi-ah-na*" for Moose Creek, and "*Chet-siah*"—the Heart Mountain—for the prominent 3862' dome the men would eventually climb for sport. When he heard their plans, Che-ah spoke a few phrases that provoked rude laughter from his fellows. McLeod translated for Wickersham: "You are a fool." [10]

As they drew closer to the mountains, the men climbed promontories to better view the dramatic massif. The Alaska Range scythes east to west across central Alaska before turning southwest. Countless snow-capped summits serrated by immense rivers of grinding ice spear the horizon. Even in mid-summer, snow persists above 7000 feet. Where the range wrenches southwest, the giant mountain dominates and overwhelms the sea of summits. Mt. McKinley looms above all, one of the highest vertical rises from basal terrain of any mountain in the world. Wickersham and his cohorts could only stare at the mountain's stupendous bulk and wonder if Che-ah was right.

While forging upriver, Wickersham upheld the European tradition of ignoring Native names and naming landmarks for various non-indigenous people. He named "Webb Creek" for Charley Webb

—likely today's Moose Creek—and "Alma Lake" in honor of Mort Stevens' sister. (Alma Lake was for a short while also called "Roosevelt Lake" but gained renown as Wonder Lake.) On June 14, 1903, the Judge named McLeod Creek for his friend "on account of the fact that it does things early and late." He named the 17,400 foot peak west of McKinley, Mt. Deborah "in honor of my good wife, whose pure clean mind and heart are fairly typified by the white snow ever resting upon its 16,000 feet." Later Wickersham was disappointed to learn that the peak already had been named Mt. Foraker after an Ohio senator. (Today another peak in the Alaska Range to the east of Mt. McKinley honors his wife's memory.)[11]

The men hired Native guides to point out sections of the route but once the party left the river and started overland, they were on their own. Instead of bee lining for the peak, the men prospected the intervening range of hills. Alaskans of that era held the search for gold foremost in their thoughts. On a cloudy June 4, they prospected "Chit-siah" Creek and found good color. Wickersham staked the Discovery claim and the others staked claims above and below—in all, 11 claims for themselves, family, and friends. This find near the creek's tributary "Two Bull Moose Gulch" would have a greater significance than any of them could have imagined.

The great ice-bound mountain loomed ever closer as the expedition left the hills behind and crossed the wide McKinley River valley. Wickersham found the country compelling. "A more beautiful game country does not exist than this fine large mountain-backed mountain meadow region . . . with a background of Switzerland magnified 100 times," he wrote. These particular comments would be avidly absorbed by other adventurers already piqued by Brooks' reports of the region. As the expedition approached the mountain, tensions within the party boiled over. "Johnnie McLeod has cold feet and is going to desert us," Wickersham wrote in his diary. "He has been entirely scared out by the Indian stories about the inaccessibility of the mountain."[12]

For days, and despite the Judge's disapproving glare, his companions had teased and taunted the rustic McLeod. They delighted in venting their own animosities on the hapless Johnnie. They knew he was afraid of bears and told him countless horror stories. Everyone but Wickersham enjoyed torturing McLeod with tales of the mayhem mules could wreak. McLeod avoided the two mules as if they were grizzlies. Johnnie threatened to quit a dozen times but each time the Judge somehow persuaded him to stay with the expedition.

Near the very base of the mountain, the undercurrent of dissension exploded into open rebellion. "Hells to pay," Wickersham wrote. "Webb got mad at Stevens this morning packed up and left us . . . [but he soon] came back and asked me for a statement which I gave him in this form: 'Mt. McKinley, June 17, 1903: To whom it may concern — Very much to my regret Mr. Charles Webb has this day voluntarily left my party to go home. Respectfully, James Wickersham.'" After long negotiation, the Judge convinced Webb to remain but the expedition was close to implosion.[13]

Although McLeod and Webb sorely tested the Judge's leadership, the real challenge would come from an unexpected quarter, his old friend George Jeffery. Stevens and Jeffery had formed a mutual admiration society and their scheming and dislike of McLeod and Webb undermined the expedition's already tenuous cohesion.

With tensions simmering, the expedition pressed on. During the arduous cross-country travel, the Judge stopped several times to study the mountain. He recognized that the towering ice wall ahead, which Brooks had described, was an insurmountable obstacle and so he veered course slightly to the southwest. Eventually, the party camped near the base of the mountain and scouted for a route upward.

At ten o'clock in the evening of June 19, Wickersham set out for the summit with Webb, Jeffery, and Stevens. McLeod stayed behind to guard the camp. Armed with alpenstocks, ropes, and knapsacks filled with four days worth of chocolate, bread, and caribou jerky, the climbing party turned southwest and ascended five miles up the Peters Glacier. Here they climbed a side glacier—now named Jeffery Glacier—to a high spur on McKinley's western slope. The roar of giant avalanches had disturbed their sleep the previous night and they moved cautiously and roped together. "Immense masses of snow and ice high on the mountainside broke loose with the report of a cannon," Wickersham wrote. "It sent a shiver of fear down every back and warned us to keep clear of the avalanche path." The Judge led, picking his way around crevasses, over tenuous snow bridges, and across icefalls. His past climbing adventures in the Cascades proved invaluable on these volatile slopes. Eventually at 8100 feet on an icy knife-edged ridge, rising to nearly perpendicular, the climb reached its end. [14]

"Avalanches . . . by the hundreds and hardly a moment goes by without the thunderous noise of one tearing its way down the mountain sides," Wickersham wrote. "We recognize that we are inviting destruction by staying here." [15]

The climbers returned to camp on June 21. With their food running out, the heat triggering ever more avalanches, and the mosquitoes simply hell, the men held a council. Their unanimous decision: further effort was futile.

"We returned to our labors without any feeling of failure but with a glow of satisfaction that we had done so much with so little. We acknowledge our unpreparedness, both through inexperience and want of equipment, but at least we blazed the trail to the great mountain's northern base, mapped its approaches . . . and bore back to waiting prospectors the hint of gold in Chitsia gravel bars." [16]

Rather than being a failure, Wickersham's assault is a tribute to the party's daring. The expedition pioneered the northern approach to the mountain, navigated the Kantishna River, explored a route up the Peters Glacier, and proved without a doubt that summer, the peak avalanche season, was *not* the time to attempt a climb of Mt. McKinley.

As Wickersham retreated from the mountain, another party, led by Frederick A Cook, a then-respected polar explorer, was approaching it on the trail blazed in 1902 by Brooks. This party, too, was defeated not far from where Wickersham had turned back. Although Cook completed the first "circumnavigation" of Mt. McKinley, he was not satisfied. He would come back in three years and provoke a controversy that persists to this day.

Instead of retracing their steps, Wickersham and his men headed for the McKinley River, where they planned to build a raft to float down to the Kantishna River. The boggy tundra was difficult to cross and the mosquitoes nearly drove them crazy. En route, and low on food, they surprised a cow moose and, despite Wickersham's protests, McLeod shot it. By now the Judge had endured enough. "It was a brutal waste of a big fine animal by a man who ought to value them for he lives on them from year to year. It will be wasted and was a wanton exhibition of his brutal savage nature." [17]

On the McKinley River, they built a log raft. Wickersham and

Jeffery were unwilling to trust it and took the mules overland. Webb, Stevens, and McLeod loaded their gear and pushed off. A short distance downstream, the raft crashed on rocks in the whitewater of Eagle Gorge and the men and gear tossed overboard. Gone was Webb's gun, ammunition, all of the bedding and cooking utensils, two axes, and all of their provisions except for a two-day supply of flour. "McLeod was nearly hysterical after the wreck—laughing and crying—he lost all his little belongings except his gun—and this seemed a ray of sunshine to him for without it he is lost, but with it never. He sleeps with it, never allows it beyond reach of his hand, and is now cleaning and talking to it," Wickersham wrote.[18]

Jeffery sided with Stevens and the two verbally lashed Webb for the disaster. Stevens boasted of his own skill and nerve until Wickersham exploded and told him that his nerve was wholly in his mouth. Clearly the expedition was falling apart.

In fairness to all, it should be pointed out that the Judge himself was not an easy man to get along with either. "James Wickersham is no saint . . . A man as impulsive, hot-tempered and combative as he, is sure to make mistakes . . . But his faults are of that sturdy, rugged character that rather endear him to an Alaskan," wrote one acquaintance. [19]

McLeod wisely refused to set foot on the raft again, and accompanied Wickersham and the mules overland while the others continued by raft. The two men waded and swam river channels, avoided quicksand, fought the torturing mosquitoes, and would have gone hungry without McLeod's woodsmanship. "He cooked 'bannocks' and one night shot a goose," Wickersham recounted, "McLeod gave an exhibition of his cunning in killing rabbits . . . placing the back of his hand to his mouth [he] made a kissing sound for a minute, when here came the rabbit on the jump toward him. The shot was easy." [20]

In what Wickersham called the finest moose country in the world, Webb shot and killed a bull moose. The reunited party feasted on fresh meat. Wickersham's acceptance of this shooting was pragmatic—shoot or starve.

When the party again separated, Stevens warned McLeod that, because of the lack of provisions, he would wait at the designated downriver rendezvous point for only two-and-a-half days. If Wickersham and McLeod did not show up by then, he would leave them. "I realized that if they did desert us," Wickersham wrote, "or putting it more liberally, if we were unable for any reason to find them at the mouth of the Kantishna we would be 150 miles in the bush and wilderness with no boat or raft and no means of making one."[21]

Alarmed by Stevens' comments, Wickersham and McLeod insisted upon taking the guns, ammunition, and axe with them on the mules. "I felt they would be more careful and certain to wait if we kept the guns . . . and events proved that we did right . . . for they informed me plainly when we found them below the mouth of the Kantishna that they had intended to wait only 10 hours or 8 hours [more], before leaving us," Wickersham said. "We had not been gone from them but 24 hours . . . I hate a deserter!!" [22]

At the rendezvous, McLeod, still distrusting the raft and mules, built himself a canoe out of spruce bark while the others repaired the raft. The next day, another violent quarrel broke out between Stevens and Webb but the Judge intervened, forestalling violence. Eventually, they recovered the *Mudlark* and their meager supplies. They boiled beans in an old tin bucket to add to their moose meat. Loading the mules into the *Mudlark*, they once again proceeded as a group. Periodically they rowed to hasten their voyage downstream.

Late on July 5, they reached Belt and Hendricks' trading post near Manley Hot Springs on the Tanana River. "We have been starving for 8 days—four days on moose meat, straight . . . the last four days on flour and beans straight without meat or salt."[23]

Wickersham then walked 50 miles across country and reached Rampart, and his beloved Deborah, late the next evening. Before greeting his wife, Wickersham bathed, shaved, and donned clean clothes borrowed from a friend. The friend stepped "gingerly to the bank of the Yukon and threw my cast-off clothing, with my hundred-dollar gold watch . . . into the river . . ."[24] The loss of the gold timepiece was an ironic punctuation to an expedition that's most enduring legacy was the incidental discovery of gold.

The rancor, conflict, and deprivation experienced by Wickersham and his men were quite typical of the Gold Rush era. These traits were on abundant display in Alaska's pioneer expeditions and in mining camps, especially in the remote Kantishna.

News of the expedition's failure to reach the summit sparked little disappointment. The great ice wall that had stymied Wickersham's drive for climbing fame seemed unclimbable. (The towering 14,000 foot tall ice wall is now known as the Wickersham Wall.) In fact, the wall would not be conquered for another 60 years. On his return, Judge Wickersham told reporters that "no one would get to the top [of the mountain] except by flying." [25]

Although the ground Wickersham and his companions staked proved of little value, their discovery would ignite a stampede to the Kantishna hills, which eventually resulted in the establishment of Mt. McKinley National Park.

2

Eureka!

Time and again, Joe Dalton dipped his pan into an eddy and swirled away the gravel and sediment until only a thin covering of black sand remained. One last time, Dalton submerged his pan into the stream and gently washed away the sand. When he finished, he rocked back on his heels and stared at a mound of glittering flakes and tiny nuggets. He looked upstream a short distance and saw his partner, Joe Stiles, cradling his gold pan as tenderly as a babe. They had found "colors" before, but here, on this small, clear stream flowing into Moose Creek, was a genuine strike.

"So, it's true," Dalton thought, "the Wickersham boys were right. There is gold in the range." He put down his pan, leaped up, and pumped his fist into the air. "Eureka!"

Dalton and Stiles did not know it then but they were not alone in those hills. Piqued by Judge James Wickersham's enthusiasm for his strike on Chitsia Creek and other more lurid reports, several prospectors had slipped out of Fairbanks and Rampart in 1904 and headed for the Kantishna region. Wickersham's promotion sparked the initial excitement but another report heaped fuel on the fire. In the October following the Judge's summit attempt, two miners returned to Nome after a year's prospecting trip into the region. They had staked eight claims and found gold "bright and coarse, closely resembling Dawson gold." This electrifying news spread quickly. *Dawson gold!* [1]

Dalton's big strike was the product of a year's prospecting. Late in the summer of 1904, he and Matt Regan had found colors on a

U.S. GEOLOGICAL SURVEY, L.M. PRINDLE COLLECTION, #526.

Joe Dalton made his big strike on Eureka Creek, the richest in the entire district. The majority of the placer gold was found in the first quarter mile of the stream above its confluence with Moose Creek. This photo of claim #2 Above Discovery shows the rock and slabs that made mining difficult and labor intensive.

Toklat River tributary. Almost a year later, on July 21, Dalton and his new partner Stiles, hit the jackpot on Eureka Creek. At nearly the same time, two other prospectors, Jack Horn and his partner Joe Quigley, following up on trappers' tales, found gold on nearby "Trapper Creek," which they re-named "Glacier Creek."

Farther up Glacier Creek, at its confluence with Yellow Pup Creek, two more prospectors, A.J. "Gus" BenBenneck and Joseph H. Benson, made a major find. Their claim #14 Above Discovery, would develop into one of the richest placer gold claims in the entire district. The two partners excitedly pounded in their stakes. After all the years of searching they'd found their bonanza.

To establish a legal claim, a prospector had to place four corner posts over a section of creek or land. On one corner post, called the discovery stake, the prospector placed a location notice which contained personal identification and a brief description of the claim.

Each placer claim was limited to 20 acres, usually 660 feet long by 1320 feet wide, straddling a creek. Those claims staked upstream of Discovery were called Above, and those downstream of Discovery, Below. Before a claim could be legally recognized, however, it had to be officially recorded. The nearest Recorder's Office for what would be soon designated as the Kantishna Mining District was in Fairbanks, 250 or more river miles away. After staking their claims in June, Horn and Quigley built a raft at the mouth of a river they named Bearpaw and floated down to the Tanana River, where they caught a sternwheeler to Fairbanks. As word of the new strike raced through town, saloon-goers hoisted drinks to toast Horn as "father and discoverer" of the Kantishna.[2]

While even a mere rumor of gold could ignite a rush, Horn and Quigley's samples of coarse gold sparked intense excitement. Some of the miners who saw the pokes claimed that the new district would surely rival Nome's fabulous "Portland Bench." Wild rumors circulated that men were already panning 26 ounces of gold per day, then equal to roughly $500. A few Klondike veterans did not believe that the Kantishna would prove as rich as claimed. Some skeptics believed that the stories were "wild fabrications made out of whole cloth . . ." For the most part, at this juncture, they were right.[3]

Many Fairbanks-area residents paid little attention to the naysayers. They viewed the Kantishna as the Next Big Thing, and they were determined not to miss out. Almost every businessman in Fairbanks grubstaked prospectors or bought trade goods bound for the new strike. By mid-July, at least 60 poling boats loaded with men and supplies labored up the Kantishna River. By early August, the Bearpaw was "lined with tents." A genuine stampede was underway.[4]

"Kantishna or bust!" was the cry of those dashing to the Bearpaw.[5] Here was yet another chance to get rich.

Back in the hills, and unaware of the hullabaloo, Dalton and Stiles continued to prospect Moose Creek tributaries. A few days after their find on Eureka Creek they made another strike on Friday Creek. Neither man could believe the amount of gold glittering in their pans. For the Canadian-born Dalton this was the dream of wealth that had tantalized him ever since he stampeded in 1898 to the Klondike.

Dalton made a mistake that he then believed would cost him

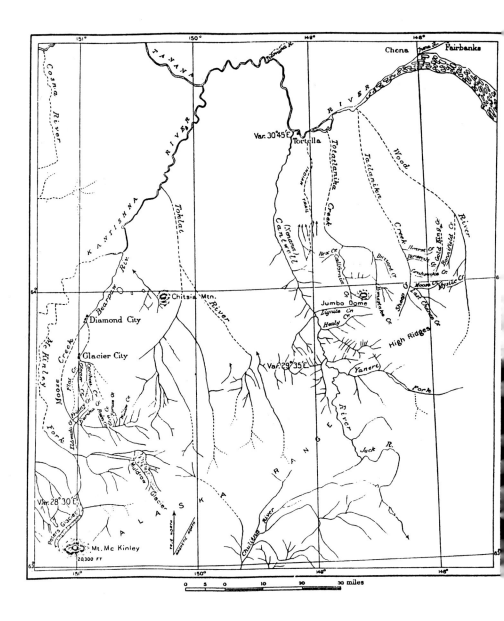

U.S. GEOLOGICAL SURVEY BULLETIN 314, PLATE IV

L.M. Prindle, of the U.S. Geological Survey, prepared this 1906 map of the Bonnifield and Kantishna mining districts. The present day town of Nenana is identified on the map as "Tortella." The "Cantwell" River is now the Nenana River. White quartz gravels on Glacier Creek, which resembled Klondike's famed "white channel" gravels, thrilled veteran stampeders who expected to find rich deposits of placer gold.

dearly. Each miner was allowed to stake the Discovery claim as well as adjoining ones. Dalton and Stiles erroneously thought that they were alone in the hills and consequently staked only Discovery claims on the two streams before moving on to other creeks. On July 25, 1905, they met a prospector who told them the sobering news of the stampede. They rushed back to Eureka Creek and found a few people already there. Dalton and Stiles staked the "Eureka Group" for themselves and their brothers. A few days later, their friend Matt Regan pounded in his stakes on Eureka's "Lucky Gulch" tributary just ahead of the arrival of dozens of treasure seekers.

Most of the stampeders from Fairbanks headed for Glacier Creek, the most publicized strike, but quickly fanned out to nearby Caribou Creek. As the numbers swelled, others poured into the Moose Creek drainage where they encountered Dalton and his friends.

Dalton knew many of the men he met. As a gold rush veteran, he also knew that most of them would leave empty-handed or end up working for wages. The best ground was already staked even before the first stampede peaked.

When Dalton and Regan returned to Fairbanks that fall to record their claims they each carried a dazzling display of coarse gold. Some men who assayed the gold called Eureka Creek "probably the richest creek the country has ever seen." Another prospector soon arrived in town with an eight-ounce baking powder can filled with gold but he kept his mouth shut about his find. After he and his partner re-supplied they tried to sneak out of town but were followed. They slipped their pursuers on the Kantishna trail. Their secrecy only intensified the craze.[6]

"News of a gold strike has wings," old-timers said. Word of the new discovery sped out of the Interior to the Klondike and beyond. People came by boat and sternwheeler and, after freeze-up, they came by foot and by dogsled.

The small paddle-wheelers *Jennie M* and *Tanana Chief* were among the first to take passengers and freight up the rivers and as close to the strike as they could get ". . . the present trip of the [two] steamers will be in the nature of a prospecting trip . . ."[7]

The boats found the McKinley River unnavigable and took their passengers back to the Bearpaw. Soon a half-dozen steamboats loaded with supplies and stampeders were headed for the new diggings. "It don't seem natural [to see women and children on the trail]. It's too tame like," one old-timer said. "You ride almost to the diggings in upholstered seats . . . and find petticoats all along the line . . . it was hard to realize that I was on a real stampede, such as we used to follow in the old days." The grandest of the "old days"—the Klondike rush—was just seven years passed.[8]

The *Luella* transported a town site party but low water dashed their plans for a McKinley River camp. Instead, the steamer dumped the men and their supplies at the mouth of the Bearpaw. The men quickly laid out a site and started building.

The stampede peaked in late September when low water ended navigation. As the river dropped and winter approached, fierce arguments broke out at the Calderhead and Hall dock in Fairbanks, with shippers demanding that their freight be sent on the last vessel. In late September, the *Florence S* made the last voyage of the year and reached the mouth of the Bearpaw with 28 passengers and tons of supplies.

At the end of September the Kantishna—"Kantish-i-naw" they called it—seethed with activity. Within a few short weeks, almost every creek and bench in the hills had been staked from source to mouth. Expectations ran high. "It is my honest belief that the Kantishna will be one of the best camps in the north," reported William A. Boss, who had visited every great mining camp in the world—California, Nevada, Mexico, British Columbia, and South Africa. He added that he had no fear of sparking a greater stampede because every tributary within a radius of forty to fifty miles of the strike had been staked. His words carried great weight but may have been self-serving since he had staked claims on Glacier Creek, with interests in others.[9]

"There can be no doubt but that Eureka is an exceedingly rich creek . . . Doherty and Stiles, old Klondike miners, were taking out $1,000 a day at the mouth of Eureka," he said. "They only have a few men working so that will give you an idea of the richness of the ground . . . The claim above them Jim Dalton sold a half interest in for $10,000 cash," Boss expected Dalton to take out $20,000 before freeze-up, estimating that Dalton would reap $100,000 from Discovery.[10]

How many people actually joined the stampede is a matter of conjecture. "As many as a hundred declared their intention of going," a newspaper reported, "but when it came to putting up the money for freight and fare the number thinned considerably . . . Old-timers realize that great opportunities are offered to the first ones who get near the pay ..." and none to stragglers.[11]

Fannie McKenzie, who later married Quigley, arrived in the Kantishna in 1906. Years later, she told a visitor that the Eureka camp bustled in "1905 with 2,000 people," a gross exaggeration according to one historian. By late fall, however, hundreds of people were in the Kantishna. The upstart towns of Bearpaw, Roosevelt, Diamond, and Glacier City hummed with the activity necessary to mine and survive the approaching winter.[12]

Bearpaw, the first town to develop, was located at the confluence of the Bearpaw and Kantishna Rivers, a point slightly northwest of Chitsia Mountain. At low water, large steamers dumped their freight and passengers here and the small settlement developed by default. A few early stampeders quickly staked most of Chitsia Creek, where Wickersham had made his find, and prospected the surrounding area with disappointing results.

Roosevelt—sometimes called "Square Deal" after President Teddy Roosevelt's slogan for the common man—sprang up on the Kantishna River, about 10 miles below the mouth of the McKinley River and roughly 30 miles above the Bearpaw. From Roosevelt, it was 35 miles overland to the creeks.

Diamond, at the confluence of Moose Creek and the Bearpaw River, was the nominal head of river navigation for even small sternwheelers. A large "pretentious" saloon, one of the first buildings erected, dominated this town and was one of the first businesses to open.

Navigation upstream from Diamond to Glacier City, at the confluence of Glacier Creek and the Bearpaw, was limited to boats drawing no more than two feet of water. Often there was not enough water to float vessels even that size. The small steamer *Dusty Diamond* regularly carried Tanana Trading Company's goods to Hamilton's Store there. Eventually, several winter trails converged on Glacier City, and it remained in use well after the other towns were abandoned.

Each settlement boasted at least one trading post, restaurant, and saloon. Food, fuel, and supplies were scarce and expensive, a situation typical of the early days of a strike. Flour sold for $15 per 100 pounds and salt pork between twenty-five and fifty cents a pound, large sums in those days. Commercial hunters sold the meat of Dall sheep, caribou, and moose that they killed, barely meeting demand.

Early in the winter of 1905–06, the tent camp of Eureka, at the confluence of Moose and Eureka Creeks, bustled with as many as 400 people. As in every other northern boom camp a tent saloon and gambling hall entertained stampeders. Soon after freeze-up, logs were hauled in by dog team and a few cabins started. A restaurant there charged $4.50 per day for board alone, almost half-a-day's wage for laborers. At least one prostitute, working out of a large tent, "absorbed a large share of the miners' wages."[13]

As winter tightened its grip on the land, more stampeders arrived via dog team and snowshoes. The first winter travelers followed frozen waterways or made their own trails to the strike. By trial and error, good routes were found, cleared, and marked. A regular winter trail was explored from Fairbanks to Eureka that "followed the Tanana River down to the mouth of the Nenana, ascended that stream to

U.S. GEOLOGICAL SURVEY, L.M. PRINDLE COLLECTION, 1922, #531

Long after the stampede fizzled, and other haphazard gold rush towns decayed into ruins, portions of Glacier City, the intersection of many trails, remained important to the region's transportation and trading enterprises.

the base of the foothills a distance of 20 miles, and thence proceeded westward along the base of the foothills to Knight's Roadhouse on Toklat River, north of Chitsia Mountain. The trail then followed up the Toklat and its tributary Clearwater Fork to Myrtle Creek, up Myrtle Creek and across a low divide to Spruce Creek and down that stream and Moose Creek to the mines . . . The total distance by this route from Fairbanks to Moose Creek at the mouth of Eureka Creek is about 165 miles." In good weather, the trip took 27 hours by dog team or a week or more in bad weather. [14]

A series of roadhouses along the trails were spaced a day's travel apart. These first "roadhouses" were tents offering food and basic shelter. Some of the early winter stampeders left Fairbanks shockingly ill-prepared for the trail and climate. Gold fever exacted a terrible toll on many of those infected. In the coldest weather, these simple roadhouses saved the lives and limbs of those suffering from frostbite and exhaustion.

Before the first dog team freighters made it to the new diggings, supplies grew perilously scarce and were sold at extortionate prices for gold only. Long-time partners Henry P. "Harry" Karstens and Charles "Mac" McGonagall, both Klondike veterans, arrived in the Kantishna in late autumn of '05. They found the camps short of supplies and saw an opportunity. In the fall, they blazed a winter trail into the diggings and at freeze-up promoted an express service for passengers, mail, and light freight.

Karstens and McGonagall staked a few marginal claims and divided their responsibilities. McGonagall took charge of the diggings and Karstens ran the private mail service. At each town, Karstens arranged for a post office and charged 25 cents per letter that he carried. Karstens later said he started his mail service in the fall with a dog team and $1,000, ending in the spring with "$500 and a lot of knowledge."[15]

While winter-freighting, Karstens saw numerous Dall sheep carcasses brought into the camps from the nearby mountains. Professional hunters reported thousands of these animals feeding on the hills and mountains. This simple observation would impact Karstens' life in an unsuspected way and have a profound impact on the region.

The indiscriminate slaughter of wildlife for food was only one consequence of early mining. Miners netted fish by the thousands to use for dog food. Creeks were dammed, re-routed, and muddied, which killed more fish and ruined spawning grounds. Miners cleared swaths of forest for lumber to build cabins and miles of sluice boxes. To facilitate removal of the overburden and get at the ore, miners burned the vegetation off their claims, which often started uncontrolled wildfires. The fires and slaughter of animals brought famine to many Athabascan Indian villages where people lived solely off the land. Many stampeders treated the Athabascans with open disdain and sometimes violence.

The Kantishna strike attracted men associated with many of the Interior's other gold rushes. One of them, pioneer trader Gordon C. Bettles, planned to stake and plat a town site on the Kantishna River and open a trading post. In late July, he and his partners ordered supplies for immediate shipment to the new diggings. Low water in late August hampered navigation and Bettles' crew and outfit were unceremoniously dumped on the riverbank at the edge of a swamp. Their town of "McKinley City" was quickly abandoned for the new town of Roosevelt, 12 miles upriver.

Bettles was no Cheechako. In 1887, when he prospected the Fortymile country, he was reportedly one of only 70 white men in all of Interior Alaska. Later, he built trading posts in the Koyukuk District. His first one in Bergman, one of the toughest mining camps in all Alaska, was famed for drinking, fighting, and nightlife. In 1900, he platted a town site—now named Old Bettles—on the Koyukuk River. He stayed there two years, mining and trading, before selling the two-story *Pickarts, Bettles, & Pickarts* trading post to the Northern Commercial Company. Bettles planned to conduct his brand of "business as usual" in the Kantishna.

While in the Koyukuk District, Bettles was involved in a brutal incident of "frontier justice." On the Hogatza River in 1888, an Indian allegedly murdered John Bremner, one of the Koyukuk's first prospectors. A posse, including Bettles, caught a 20-year-old Athabascan man in possession of Bremner's goods. (Mere possession was no real proof of involvement in a crime. A significant amount of equipment was left behind by prospectors as they moved from strike to strike.) After the man allegedly confessed to the murder, the miners declared him guilty and hung him from a tree at the mouth of the Koyukuk. Several men then fired a volley into the body and left it hanging as a warning to others.

Life was hard in the semi-lawless frontier mining camps. Many stampeders had little or no money and were desperate to make a strike or earn a wage. Men like Bettles understood the transitory nature of the camps and worked hard to "mine the miners" before the pay gave out. Gambling and drinking emptied many pokes.

Bettles probably envisioned the Kantishna as another of his lucrative ventures but that dream faded quickly. His "Bettles Group" association claim produced very little. The claims he purchased on Eureka and Moose Creek also fared poorly. A little more than six months after his arrival, Bettles sold his Eureka Creek holdings to trader John "Jack" Hamilton and moved on.

In August of '05, Wickersham appointed Lee Van Slyke to serve as U.S. Commissioner for the Kantishna Mining District and ordered him to establish his headquarters in Roosevelt. Federally-appointed Commissioners acted as coroner, judge, and recorder, handling everything from murder to mail sorting. Often these Commissioners were the only duly appointed authority in a vast region. Instead of receiving a fixed salary, they charged a fee for each transaction—the larger the volume of activity, the greater the income. Van Slyke's appointment enabled prospectors to forego the long trip to Fairbanks or Rampart and record their claims in Roosevelt.

Van Slyke arrived in September and found 50 people at work building the town. At first, Van Slyke made good money handling a variety of transactions, most notably the recording of claims. Often he had to settle conflicting claims for the same patch of ground. "Mr. Van Slyke is well liked by the miners, generally speaking," wrote one miner. "He has shown a disposition to be fair and impartial . . ."[16]

Small sections of Glacier, Eureka, and Friday Creeks produced substantial quantities of gold right through early winter when preliminary mining was curtailed. Claims on other creeks proved worthless, prompting their owners to quit the district. For those who stayed, there was a lot of work to be done prior to the resumption of full scale mining the next summer. The first order of business was the construction of winter quarters. The sawmill in Diamond ran full tilt and the hills echoed with the sounds of hammers and axes. Money was tight and jobs few. Many people labored for room and board. Others hunted or cut cabin logs, lumber, and firewood. Once the winter trails opened, dog teams began freighting between the towns and Fairbanks.

Even after freeze-up, with temperatures dropping well below zero, many stampeders frantically searched for promising unstaked ground. As winter deepened many of the "Argonauts" (as they were called)—their grubstakes gone—called it quits and headed for Fairbanks. Some vowed to acquire a new grubstake and return in spring. Others simply quit the district forever. Tellingly, at least three disappointed prospectors had headed back to Fairbanks in the middle of *August*. As rivers froze, making overland travel easier, the trails were filled with more people going out of the Kantishna than into it.

Even in the darkest, coldest days of winter, a few prospectors continued to work their claims. Some spent the winter building fires to thaw frozen ground and hand shoveling "glory holes" down to the shallow bedrock. The recovered gravel was piled in mounds for spring sluicing. Even in winter, some of these glory holes suddenly filled with water and promptly froze, snuffing out weeks of labor. Because "the conditions in the Kantishna [are] not favorable for winter working," said Billy Abramskey, "the winter residents who do not hunt, trap, or cut wood, hibernate." [17]

By February 1906, some prospectors began to describe Eureka and Glacier Creeks as "freak formations." Even the pockets of the best ground, they said, would be quickly worked out. "In many ways," said one stampeder, "the district has proven a frost. There is no use in trying to gloss over the facts . . ." [18]

Intense searching turned up gold only in limited places. "The character of the gold is the same [in all the creeks], the pay being found only on bedrock that has not been disturbed . . . the real pay will be found [only] at the mouths of the streams." Such pessimistic reports effectively ended the stampede.[19]

The shape and texture of gold varies from drainage to drainage and the nature of Kantishna gold puzzled veteran miners. They believed that the rough, unworn character of gold from Eureka and Friday Creeks indicated that a mother lode had to be nearby. They scoured the benches, ridges, and creeks in an attempt to find the source. It just didn't seem possible that the coarse gold just "appeared" without washing down from somewhere. Despite winter conditions the hardy, and foolhardy, kept looking.

Miners and prospectors faced daunting hazards: cosmic cold, isolation, hunger, wild animals, and terrain. Add accidents, disease, and violence to the mix, and any gold rush "romance" fades into jousts with implacable, deadly foes. The sub-zero reality of Interior Alaska exacted a terrible human toll on those who ventured into the wilderness.

That first winter, the Kantishna District reported its share of tragedies. Men lost fingers and toes to frostbite and suffered other terrible accidents. Frost injuries were so common that they were referred to as the winter "harvest." Moose Creek's Joseph Brochu got lost during a heavy snowstorm and wandered for four days before being found. His frozen feet were amputated, "the first of the harvest . . ." [20]

Some men who ventured into the silent, sullen hills never came back. In the spring of 1906, miners found the decomposed body of a man lying face down near a prospect hole on Caribou Creek. His heavy clothing indicated that he had died the winter before. He was unidentifiable and papers found in his clothing gave conflicting information. A hole was dug and the nameless man buried, just another "who laid down his life while working in that isolated region." [21]

In their search for gold, men literally hurled their youth into a grave. One death that hit the people of Interior especially hard was that of John W. Johnson, a Tanana pioneer who had assisted in the construction of E.T. Barnette's trading post on the Chena River, the forerunner of Fairbanks. Late in the winter of 1905–06, the barking and whining of Johnson's dog led searchers to his body. "John Johnson dug his own grave at Kantishna," read one headline. "His body was found near the six-foot hole he had scooped to bedrock on Caribou Creek and [he] was buried in it the next day. It is believed that old age and exposure caused his death." Johnson's dog had stood guard over his master for at least a month. [22]

Owners of the best Kantishna claims greeted the spring of '06, with high expectations. This would be the year the district would prove its worth or go bust. Spring saw frenzied activity on the diggings. Placer mining here was labor intensive, employing pick and shovel, pan, rocker, and sluice box. On the best streams, miners removed shallow overburden and then shoveled the foot or so of gravel above the bedrock into their rockers and sluices. The process was exhausting work. Claim owners expected their laborers to work hard and steady for $6 a day plus room and board, or one dollar an hour for a 10-hour day

Dalton initially hired 15 men to work his claims and at peak production he and his partners employed almost 50 workers. As the summer wore on and the "pay"—as miners called gold—began to accumulate, Bob Mann, a respected prospector, told newspapers that "I don't believe that the Kantishna deserves the bad reputation it appears to bear." While it was true that a few Kantishna claimants were getting rich, most people scoffed at Mann's report. For every success story, they said, there were a hundred more disappointing ones. [23]

By late summer of 1906, the clean-up was about complete. The brothers Jim and Joe Dalton, along with Joe and Simon Stiles, had hit it big with their "Eureka Group," which produced the bulk of the Kantishna gold. The first half mile above the mouth of Eureka Creek was the richest in the district. Boulders and slabs added to the work of mining there but the partners recovered almost 10,000 ounces of gold. By summer's end these claims were largely exhausted.

With low water bringing an end to the 1906 mining season, claim owners headed to Fairbanks. The Daltons and Joe Stiles brought in flakes and nuggets worth $86,000, at the official U.S. Government average gold price of $18.90 per troy ounce. The Discovery claim yielded two large nuggets, one weighing 11 ounces and one weighing 43 ounces. The latter, called the "Queen of Eureka," was put on display in a Fairbanks jewelry store. In all, the partners netted a reported $120,000 (over $2.6 million in 2004 dollars).

BenBenneck and Benson, full partners on Glacier and Caribou Creek claims, brought into town nine huge nuggets, which they displayed in a store window, and a $10,000 poke of gold from #15 Above on Glacier Creek, a claim said to be worth "a half-million dollars" (almost $11 million in 2004). [24]

James Chronister and Abramskey, who worked the adjoining claim on Glacier, had the second richest ground in the Kantishna after Eureka Creek. Chronister, a veteran of every strike from Ketchikan to Kobuk, and a former partner with Bettles, described his claim as among the richest in the entire Tanana district. Although the partners would not say how much they had found, their "pokes would choke an elephant." Fellow miners hailed Chronister as the "Kantishna King."

Abramskey also reported another new strike on Yellow Pup where he said two partners were getting up to $30 of gold—one-and-a-half ounces—per shovel of gravel. The two Kantishna Kings banked their gold and headed Outside—as Alaskans called the lower 48 states—to spend the winter.

Sections of Eureka and Glacier Creeks produced small fortunes, but other streams quickly played out. Intense prospecting in the two years after the first strike found gold widespread but in insufficient quantity to be economically viable. It seemed strange to many of the miners that all there seemed to be was Discovery and #1 on Eureka Creek and two or three Glacier Creek claims. The diehards believed the source would be found in time. In a sense, the Kantishna was a freak formation, as a critic had dubbed it. Hot spots at stream mouths held very rich deposits but quickly played out up stream. The richest creeks drained from two neighboring peaks, Glacier and Spruce. A few people would spend their lives there looking in vain for the mother lode.

Less than a dozen men struck it big. The vast majority of Kantishna claims were worthless. For hundreds of people the headlong dash to the hills, the deprivation and danger, was all for naught. Mining outfits and claims sold for next to nothing and the losers left before freeze-up. "The whole thing was a bust," Karstens said.[25]

A few men refused to leave empty-handed. In every mining camp in Alaska, there were dangerous and desperate men who, if they could not find their own gold, would steal it. The Kantishna was no exception.

On September 17, 1906, Glacier City storekeeper H.T. Fleming, known as the "Hunchback," drifted down the Kantishna River with 116 ounces of gold and $1,000 in currency and right into an ambush. A few miles from the confluence with the Tanana, a masked man stepped out of the woods and at gunpoint ordered Fleming to row ashore. With an oath, Fleming grabbed his rifle and began shooting. A second thief opened fire from the timber. Suddenly, Fleming cried out in agony and slumped over. The thieves cut loose with a fusillade in an attempt to stop his drifting boat.

A few miles downstream, Fleming dragged himself up the bank and into Charlie Swanson's empty trapping cabin. By a stroke of Providence, someone happened to be passing this remote spot and found Fleming bleeding profusely from his wounds. The passerby helped Fleming as much as he could and then rushed off to alert the U.S. Marshall. Later, in Tanana, doctors extracted a .30-30 slug from Fleming's shattered hip and a .22 slug from his shoulder. His boat was riddled with 40 bullet holes. Fleming barely survived and spent almost three months hospitalized. Doctors attributed his survival to his excellent physical condition.

Deputy Marshall Vautier quickly captured Calvin Swift and Samuel Tansy near the scene of the shooting. The Marshall theorized that the men knew that Fleming had sold his store and when to expect him on the river. Both men hotly denied any involvement, even though they had been accused a month earlier of stealing $500 and clothing from Fleming's store. They claimed they were hunting far up the Kantishna at the time of the shooting.

The suspects were transported to Fairbanks and jailed. In mid-October, Swift was released on $5,000 bond and traveled to the site of the shooting to "procure evidence of innocence." Despite Fleming's positive identification of Tansy, the case was dismissed in April 1907.

Theft took several forms. In the summer of 1906, Louis Bono took a "lay" on Hamilton and Ott's claim. (A "lay man" works someone else's claim for a share of the proceeds, in this case 50% of all the gold recovered.) Just after clean-up, Bono absconded with the claim's entire output. He then brazenly sold his lay in the claim to someone else. Bono was arrested on a charge of embezzlement the following February in Carson City, Nevada, and extradited.

As placer claims played out, prospectors searched for lode deposits. In late autumn of 1906, Tom Lloyd and Billy Taylor chartered the *Florence S* to haul in hard rock mining equipment. The two men believed that with the right capital and equipment they could find the mother lode. Early freeze-up wrecked their plans and the *Florence S* returned to Chena with their equipment still on board. Undaunted, the partners made plans to haul their freight in over the ice, claiming that their quartz prospect would prove to be one of the biggest mining propositions in all of Interior Alaska. They never said what they had found to warrant such optimism.

U.S. Commissioner Van Slyke, worried about his wife's health and with his revenue in sharp decline, left Roosevelt in August 1906, cutting the population there in two. Before leaving for Washington State, the dispirited Van Slyke reported to Wickersham that only 20 men were left in the district and the towns abandoned. In reality, 60 to 70 miners still grubbed the ground. There were 20 men working on Glacier Creek alone and Grant and Anna Courtney kept their store and boarding cabin at Glacier open all winter to serve them.

Ernest I. Foster replaced Van Slyke as Commissioner and shifted his headquarters to Glacier City. Foster was not new to the Kantishna.

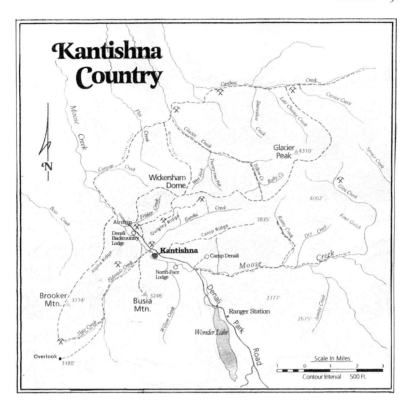

COURTESY, KANTISHNA ROADHOUSE.

This "Kantishna Country" map shows the major drainages of the mining district as they relate to the modern-day developments at the end of the Denali National Park road.

He and his wife Gertrude had managed the Hamilton freight station at Diamond during the stampede's peak. The Fosters' daughter Elizabeth, 5, was perhaps the only child in the camp. She may not have had other children to play with but she was fawned over by grizzled miners. To all too many of these men the child was a poignant reminder of their former life, and the family and identity left behind.

The impressive returns brought into Fairbanks in the autumn of 1906, coupled with the Yellow Pup find, sparked another, but much smaller, stampede. Some prospectors just would not give up, no matter the doom-and-gloom reports. In mid-winter the reports of a strike on the benches above Glacier Creek pushed hibernators out of their cabins to join the mini-stampede. "A number of miners rushed to the place and staked everything in sight," Karstens reported.[26] That winter over 100 men prospected in the Kantishna.

The Kantishna strike, which engendered high hopes of another Klondike bonanza, fizzled rapidly as the pockets of gold played out. On more than one occasion the Kantishna would tease the faithful few who clung to the search for the mother lode. In 1909, two Glen Creek miners, James Mulville and Frank Hagel, brought to Fairbanks a nugget weighing 81.33 ounces, worth about $1,537 (over $33,750 in 2004). This nugget eclipsed the famed Dome Creek nugget as the largest found in the Fairbanks District.

By mid-winter, 1906–07, the Kantishna was all but deserted. In December, the population of Glacier City was 12, Diamond 4, and Roosevelt 1. For a few of those that stayed behind the Kantishna was the last stop on the trail. They had had enough of the crazed scurrying from place to place and these hills seemed a good place to settle in. Game was plentiful, gardens productive, and trapping good. Also, a hard worker could mine enough gold for a fair income, maybe even a little more. This was their last stampede. "How many times in the great romantic Northland," said Charles Sheldon, a hunter who visited the camps in the autumn of 1906, "has the history of Eureka been enacted!" The answer: too often to count. Some of the dispirited stampeders who left Kantishna merely re-supplied and rushed off to a new strike at Iditarod, then after that to Ruby, Wiseman, and Livengood.[27]

The Kantishna strike was typical of the boom and bust cycle of the great northern gold rushes. This strike offers a look at some of the best in human nature—courage, perseverance, loyalty—as well as the worst—avarice, duplicity, violence—also typical of the history of northern exploration and exploitation. This gold rush, however, would spawn a quest for a new land ethic—one based on resource protection—one that would change dramatically the future of this region. The consequences of a side note to the Kantishna strike, the visit of the hunter Sheldon, would far transcend the region's gold and mineral wealth.

3
Kid Karstens

WIND-DRIVEN SLEET pounded mail carrier Harry Karstens and his two trailbreakers. Earlier in the day, a sudden deep snowfall in the Alaska Range at the head of the Delta River had buried the trail, forcing the men to abandon their dog teams and plunge ahead on snowshoes in an effort to establish a trail. Darkness overtook them far from camp and without shelter of any kind.

The skies cleared overnight and the weather turned bitter cold. By morning one of the trailbreakers was unconscious, his feet badly frozen. Karstens did all he could to ease the man's suffering, then hurried back alone for the dogs. Karstens, fighting fatigue and hypothermia, retrieved the dog team and evacuated his companions to the village of Gakona. In a cabin there Karstens built a roaring fire in the wood stove and bundled the injured trailbreaker in blankets. When the man awoke, he began to writhe and scream in agony as his feet thawed.

Once assured of the man's survival, Karstens left the two trailbreakers at the cabin and set out alone with his load of mail. A wicked blizzard dogged his journey north but he eventually reached Fairbanks.[1]

Carrying the mail in frontier Alaska was no job for the inept or weak. "So far as there is anything heroic about the Alaskan trail, the mail-carriers are the real heroes," Episcopal Archdeacon Hudson Stuck wrote. "They must start out in all weathers, at all temperatures; they have a certain specified time in which to make their trips and they must keep within that time or there is trouble. The . . . Canadian Yukon has a more humane government than ours. There neither mail-carrier nor any one else, save in some life-or-death emergency ... may take out horses or dogs to start a journey when the temperature is lower than 45 below zero; but I have seen a reluctant mail-carrier chased out at 60 below zero, on the pain of losing his job, on the American side."[2]

A typical contract paid carriers $75 a month to make 13 trips a winter on a schedule of six days on, one day off. The mail carrier provided his own dogs and sled. Mail loads varied from next-to-nothing to over 700 pounds ". . . the virtually empty pouches must be transported from office to office through the running, or over the rotting ice, just the same, on pain of the high displeasure of a department without brains and without bowels," Stuck said.[3]

If the Kantishna was typical of the boom and bust cycle of the northern gold rushes, Karstens was the archetype of the era's stampeders. His early life exemplifies the struggles and obstacles overcome by these pioneers. The cold, demanding wilderness transformed the inexperienced young Karstens into one of the toughest of the tough. Harry Karstens' redoubtable reputation was made hauling the mail.

Henry Peter Karstens, one of seven brothers and sisters of immigrant parents, was born in Chicago on September 9, 1878. Karstens traced his family roots to both Germany and Denmark, but he always said that he was a Dane.[4]

Karstens' father owned a feed store and Karstens spent his youth working around animals. The experience would later prove invaluable. A tragic incident played a pivotal role in his eventual migration to Alaska. In 1895, Karstens, then 17, fought with his brother in the barn behind the family home. Somehow his brother fell, wounded. Karstens saw people rushing from the house. He knew his brother would receive help. Out of fear, horror, or shame, he ran away.[5]

After wandering for two years, Karstens eventually surfaced in June 1897, in Vaugnes Restaurant in Billings, Montana. There he met Windy Bill, just down from Alaska, and learned of the "excitement" up in the Klondike and tales of the rich claims. Windy Bill's story stirred the whole town and ignited Karstens' gold fever.

Perhaps Karstens would not have been so excited if he had known Windy Bill's penchant for tall tales. In some mining camps, almost all exaggerated stories were known as "Windy Bills." A favorite one that made the rounds described Windy Bill lost on the trail and starving. Desperate, he began to kill and eat his dogs. One by one, his team went into the cook pot. Finally, only his favorite lead dog was left. Windy Bill hesitated to kill his old friend, but in desperation he chopped off the dog's tail to boil for food. The very next day the tailless dog and master stumbled on a cabin and were saved.

Two days after listening to Windy Bill, a train loaded with 11,400 ounces of Klondike gold rolled into Helena, Montana. Newspapers claimed that this was merely a sample. A 125-pound ingot was displayed in the window of the American National Bank. Windy Bill's stories paled in comparison. Karstens and an Irishman named Tom Cavanaugh quickly left Montana bound for the gold fields.

"The train was full of parties going to the Klondike and all terribly excited," Karstens recalled. "At Seattle, the crowd was tremendous . . . We tried everywhere to get passage [to the Klondike] but it seemed hopeless. We heard of the old [steamship] *Al-ki* being taken out of the Bebe [ship] yard where she was condemned. We looked up the operators and made a deal to pay passage and help handle freight." [6]

Karstens and his partner had a total of $200 when they boarded the *Al-ki*. From this grubstake, and the one dollar an hour they were paid for handling cargo, they bought supplies, clothing, and their tickets.

Twenty steamers, sailing under the cry "Hurrah for the Klondike," left the Pacific coast in the first five weeks of the stampede. On July 19, the *Al-Ki* set off, loaded with 350 tons of supplies, 900 sheep, 65 cattle, 30 horses, and 110 people. One thousand more had demanded passage.

The two young partners had lucked out. By fall, the cost of steamship tickets had skyrocketed—one sold for $1,500, 10 times its face value. Over 100,000 people set out for the Klondike in 1897–8, with an estimated one million more planning to do so as soon as they could find passage.

When Karstens and Tom stepped down from the *Al-ki* on August 25, 1897, they found the streets of Skagway jammed. The new town, built around steamboat captain William Moore's cabin at the mouth of the Skagway River, was a hodge-podge of tents and shacks in use as boarding houses, restaurants, stores, saloons, and "sporting houses." Thieves and con men of all kinds, the most notorious being Jefferson Randolph "Soapy" Smith, preyed on would-be miners. "The town of Skagway was conceived in lawlessness and nurtured in anarchy," wrote one historian.[7]

Beginning in Skagway, the White Pass Trail, a route "that brought out the worst in men," led 45 miles through the Coast Mountains to the headwaters of the Yukon River. The town grew in part because hundreds turned back due to deep snow and harsh trail conditions. Five thousand stampeders attempted White Pass that fall, but relatively few made it to Dawson before freeze-up. Of 3,000 horses used on the trail that first year, likely none survived the route that became known as the Deadhorse Trail. The situation repelled Karstens. "We heard there were over 1,700 dead horses and mules on the trail at that time." [8]

Forsaking the White Pass route, the partners took a boat three miles west to the town of Dyea, built around John J. Healy's trading post at the start of the Chilkoot Trail, a Native trade route to the Interior. Just a few weeks earlier, Dyea had consisted solely of Healy's lone log cabin but Karstens found it as rambunctious as Skagway, although without the same type of bottleneck. The Chilkoot Trail, though steeper and 600 feet higher than the White Pass, was ten miles shorter and ended at Lake Bennett on the headwaters of the Yukon River. A series of camps had sprung up along the trail, with the biggest, Sheep Camp, at timberline and four miles from the summit. Here were crude hotels, restaurants, and shacks.

To prevent famine in the gold fields, the Northwest Mounted Police required each person entering the Yukon to possess a year's supply of food, about 1,150 pounds. In total, each man needed a ton of food and equipment. Some stampeders took three months or more to relay their required supplies up and over the 3,525 foot pass, slogging more than 30 times up the steps—the so-called Golden Stairs—carved in the almost perpendicular ice and snow.

Packers were in high demand. Karstens and Tom, short of supplies and money, hired out to pack gear over the Scales—the place where goods were weighed. The money was good. Alaska Native packers had formed a block and set prices that ranged from $5 to $15 per hundred pounds, the standard load size. A few desperate men paid packers one dollar a pound. In lieu of cash, some packers bartered for goods. In time, the two young partners had accumulated enough food and gear to enter the Yukon.

With the short northern summer quickly passing, the partners relayed their outfit to Lake Lindemann, above Lake Bennett, where they met two old Germans who had the tools for boat building but knew nothing of boats or boating. Karstens struck a deal: equal shares in the entire outfit in return for helping the older men get to Dawson.[9]

While the young partners set to work hewing out boat ribs, Karstens put the Germans to work building a sawpit and whipsawing lumber. "It took some time to get the hang of it," he said, "but we eventually turned out lumber at a satisfactory rate."[10]

By the time the four men pushed off in their new boat, it was late September with shore ice forming. They floated past boats that had swamped, killing some passengers. The survivors "offered us all kinds of inducements to help them through but we could not handle more than we had."[11]

Karstens, the only one of the four with boat-handling experience, was appointed steerman. Under a tarp in the middle of the boat, the men kept a stove and hot coffee going at all times. As steerman, Karstens sat in the cold the entire journey. He proved equal to the challenges of Miles Canyon, perilous Squaw Rapids, the Lewes, and the twisting Thirtymile, a treacherous stretch of the Yukon that would claim many boats. Karstens navigated Five Finger Rapids above Dawson with little difficulty.

The partners found the Yukon above its confluence with the Klondike River thick with ice floes but on November 1, they landed safely at Lousetown, on the opposite side of the Klondike from Dawson. The boat was so heavy with ice that it could not be pulled ashore. The following day the river froze completely. Karstens' boat was one of the last down the Yukon that fall.

After unloading the boat, Karstens and Tom went into Dawson to see the sights. Shacks, tents, and cabins of every description housed and catered to the 4,000 hungry people jamming the town. Dawson boasted ten saloons replete with dancing girls, gambling, and free-flowing liquor. To maintain order, the Mounties manned a large barracks and jail.

To their surprise the two young men found the boom town's population much diminished from its solstice peak. Many of the stampeders who had made it to Dawson, took one long around, and despite the hardships endured, sold everything and headed back home. Others had stampeded to a new strike down river. In autumn an outbreak of Typhoid scared away still more. When the news broke in early fall that unseasonably low water had stranded sternwheelers 250 miles downstream, and that vital supplies would not arrive before freeze-up, it sparked a panicked exodus.

Karstens and Tom, who had envisioned themselves as "Klondike Kings," learned, to their great disappointment, that every creek for miles around had been staked from source to mouth. In addition, Dawson faced famine. Since many of the stampeders had reached the Klondike prior to the Mounties edict requiring each person to bring a year's supply of food, there was not enough to go around. Scarcity brought high prices. Flour cost $125 a sack, milk was $2.50 a can, a glass of milk $5.00, and butter cost $5 to $10 a pound. ("Butter" was often straight lard.) A meager meal in a saloon cost $3.50.

The very next morning, river ice crushed the boat, leaving the partners with just a small tent, four bearskin blankets, scant clothing, 50 pounds of food, and no stove. Karstens and Tom went a short distance up the Klondike River and built a small flat-roofed shelter. They found work in the mines and struggled to survive the winter. At the end of November, the temperature dropped to minus 67° F. In midwinter, Karstens and Tom went their separate ways. "Some of the rustling to get by, was amusing and others tragic," Karstens recalled.[13]

One place in Dawson that caught Karstens' eye was Bill McPhee's

TOM WALKER PHOTO

By the time Harry Karstens reached Dawson City in the autumn of 1897, the town faced famine. The once well-stocked stores had little food left and what they did offer sold for exorbitant prices. A glass of milk in a restaurant cost $5.

saloon where, after the place quieted down late at night, men slept on benches and tables for want of any other shelter. McPhee came north in 1888 and wherever there was a strike and miners to mine, the bear-like McPhee soon opened a bar. It was in McPhee's old saloon at Fortymile in 1896 that George Carmack first broke the news of his Klondike discovery. The *Pioneer* was a veritable gold mine itself and over the years "Grizzly" McPhee used some of the proceeds to grubstake dozens of prospectors, including Clarence Berry and Frank Densmore. (Berry took almost two million dollars from his claims on the Klondike's Eldorado Creek and struck rich ground a second time on Ester Creek, near Fairbanks.)

The 19-year-old Karstens' attempts to record claims on Skookum Hill failed. He staked claim #31 Above on Henderson Creek, just downstream from Jack London's claim, and that of Elam Harnish who London immortalized as *"Burning Daylight."* Soon disillusioned with Canada, Karstens set out for Alaska. He later said that his two disallowed bench claims on Bonanza Creek proved very rich. "I guess I looked pretty young to be taken seriously," he said.[14]

Karstens teamed up with Soren Sorensen and, in late February or early March, they headed downstream pulling their own sleds, bound for Alaska and the reputedly rich diggings on Mission Creek. About 100 miles downstream from Dawson, Karstens and Sorensen ran into another group of prospectors from Dawson. The men fanned out to test and stake several creeks in the area. Karstens explored several drainages, including the Seventymile River. (Rivers here derived their names from their distance below old Fort Reliance located six miles downstream from Dawson City.)

At a miner's meeting on the bank of the Yukon, V. E. Bevington was elected recorder and a town site laid out. After considerable debate, the new town was named Eagle, eventually becoming the first incorporated city in Interior Alaska.

During one of many miner's meetings, Karstens loudly proclaimed the wonderful riches of the Seventymile. The gathering listened to the baby-faced Karstens with ever-growing humor and when he finished, Lyman Burrell nicknamed him the "Seventymile Kid." The name would last a lifetime, and even into his 70's old-timers called Karstens "Kid" or "Seventy," though by then the nickname had taken on a more heroic cast.[15]

TOM WALKER PHOTO

Jack London's cabin on Henderson Creek was located just a short walk from Harry Karstens' claim. Nearby, Elam Harnish, who London immortalized by his nickname "Burning Daylight," worked another claim on the creek.

Karstens returned to Dawson penniless and without supplies. He sold a half interest in his claims there for a year's grubstake and used $200 of it to buy an outfit, a scow, and food for a year. He recalled that the Dawson waterfront, extending a mile up and down the river, was four to five deep with sunken scows. The men Karstens bought his outfit from "expected to shovel the gold up like gravel, but even at the very rich mines they had to work very hard to get it," he said.[16]

As soon as the ice went out Karstens floated downstream to his diggings on the Seventymile River where he would spend parts of the next two years. In May, he helped build a big cabin on Great Bear Bar, 35 miles up the river and above a waterfall. From here prospectors panned gold from the exposed bars and did "fairly well" until the color played out in fall. Karstens' companions quit and left him all interest in the claims. He continued to "run a cut" in the main bar and "got pretty fair results."[17]

When the river froze again, Karstens headed to Eagle for supplies. By then, the town had grown considerably. The Alaska Commercial

Company had built a large store, and the U.S. Army had started Fort Egbert. The huge influx of stampeders had swamped territorial services and the authorities scrambled to develop reliable mail service. In summer, riverboats hauled the mail and in winter, dog teams and horse-drawn sleighs took over.

With construction of Fort Egbert well under way, the government let a mail contract for the route from Eagle to Valdez. It was a "thing that I believe changed my whole life in the north and filled me with the wanderlust," Karstens remembered. [18]

Karstens became a mail carrier almost by default. Jim Fish, owner of the Valdez Hotel, won the government contract and hired a carrier in Eagle. Fish supplied the carrier with money and a dog team. Since there was no mail to carry yet, the idle carrier drank and gambled away his expense money. Now broke and without work the man grew despondent and tried to hang himself.

"For a week a number of us took turns staying with him as he tried to hang himself several times," Karstens said. "At the end of the week he seemed to be rational, wrote a few letters, so we let him alone. That night he hung himself from a crossbeam of his cabin."

Karstens volunteered to become the new mail carrier. Although woefully inexperienced, he did have a small dog team. He had no money and his boss was a long way off and out of communication. "I knew some supplies were left at the Tanana Crossing," he said, "so I borrowed in debt but got enough to pull out with the mail on time. Me, 20 or 21, out of a big city, my only experience one dog and a sled on the Seventymile and four days with a nine-dog team on the Yukon."[19]

The young man had no idea what he was getting into. Remote mining camps received mail monthly in winter, if at all. Government contracts detailed load sizes and schedules. Carriers were required to keep a journal detailing each day's travel, pace, mileage, weather, and trail conditions. Most pioneer mail carriers used teams of eight or fewer dogs. In a few instances, teams of up to 25 dogs pulled two huge, overloaded freight sleds. Only the stout-hearted and resolute succeeded as mail carriers. During one cold snap on the trail to Tanacross, U.S. Army Lieutenant Billy Mitchell found a mail carrier sitting on his sled, frozen solid, a pile of wood in front of him and a match in his hand. [20]

Eventually, mail carriers garnered high status, legal trail right-of-way, and preferential treatment. Roadhouses provided them with

COURTESY, U.S. ARMY ALASKA, #52545

Lieutenant William L. "Billy" Mitchell, fresh from West Point, prepares to leave the parade grounds of Fort Egbert, Eagle, Alaska. Harry Karstens supported Mitchell's troops building a portion of a telegraph line that would eventually stretch from Valdez to Nome.

the best bunks, food, and animal care. Status, however, did not translate into money.

When Karstens left on his inaugural trip, there was no snow and the Yukon River was not yet frozen, forcing him overland on foot, across the highest point of land. Without a trail to follow, Karstens bushwhacked, wading creeks running with ice and enduring dropping temperatures and bitter winds. He pioneered a route over the hills to the Fortymile River, across the Ketchumstuck Flat, and eventually to the Tanana River. At the Tanana, he met the carrier from the south, exchanged loads, and headed back to Eagle via Circle City. The Eagle Trail, as it became known, led along the Copper River, across Mentasta Lake, to Tanana Crossing and Lake Mansfield, up the Mosquito Fork of the Fortymile River to Jack Wade, then across country to Eagle.

Karstens carried the mail over his 250-mile route for about a year and a half. He said he got enough experience—and caution—to last a lifetime. By taking the carrier job, which bound him for its duration, Karstens lost all his mining claims for lack of required assessment work. "I thought I would make a trip or two and get out of it and go up to my claims," Karstens said, "what a lovely dream." [21]

Later, he looked back on those early mail runs and compared them favorably with other northern epics. Once, while carrying the mail on foot, Karstens encountered a cold snap that froze Steel Creek solid overnight. He fashioned a toboggan from a cowhide and broke trail for 40 miles while pulling the makeshift sled. Another time, while using only three dogs, he traveled 170 miles in three days. After his mail contract expired, Karstens hunted caribou at Mission Creek for the troops at Fort Egbert. The boat bringing in their ration of beef had frozen in coming up the Yukon and the soldiers were desperate for fresh meat.

On May 26, 1900, the U.S. Congress appropriated $450,000 to establish a military and commercial telegraph line in Alaska. The project, known as the Washington–Alaska Military and Cable Telegraph Service (WAMCATS), would link far-flung military posts to Valdez, where an undersea cable would link Alaska to Seattle. The Army Signal Corps, under the able command of Brigadier General Adolphus W. Greely, was given the responsibility of building the line across the wilderness of Interior Alaska. Supplies for the project arrived in Valdez in July 1900, and at Nome in August. 150-pound coils of wire, insulators, tools, dunnage, and food of all types needed transport over mountains, across rivers and vast stretches of muskeg. Local freighters were contracted to haul the tons of supplies.

In 1901, Lieutenant Mitchell, fresh from West Point, arrived at Eagle to take charge of the construction of the line from Valdez to

Eagle. Karstens hired on to guide Mitchell's troops as they strung wire and built line cabins out of Eagle.

Food, medicine, and supplies were often inadequate. Soldiers and officers toiled in the seasonal extremes of heat and mosquitoes and bitter cold and darkness. Little over a year after they started, solders completed the 420-mile Eagle to Valdez segment of the line. Within two years, WAMCATS stretched 1,396 miles, connecting 54 Alaska locations. Karstens described guiding the army construction teams as "exciting times" but it took a toll on him and his health suffered. He returned to Eagle in "pretty bad shape with pains across the shoulders." [22]

After a few days rest, Karstens decided to return to Chicago for the first time since his tragic departure. From Eagle, he walked up the frozen Yukon River to Dawson. From there, he caught the train to Skagway, where he then boarded a steamer to Seattle. His first visit home lasted six or eight months and was difficult. "I had been away five or six years," he recalled, "everything was strange, and I didn't fit in. I held out as long as I could, then went north to Valdez in the fall of 1903." [23]

Back in Alaska, Karstens' former employer Fish, had a contract to transport mail from Valdez to Fort Gibbon at the confluence of the Tanana and Yukon Rivers. Fish hired Karstens and Charles McGonagall to haul mail over the northern portion of the route.

In McGonagall, Karstens found a partner and friend to rely on. McGonagall was an experienced mail carrier and musher. He came north in 1896 and, with two partners, floated the Yukon to the Fortymile strike. On the journey, McGonagall and his partners camped on an island near the future site of Dawson City, just a short distance away from the yet-to-be-discovered bonanza.

That following winter, McGonagall carried mail from Fortymile to Fort Yukon. Over the next two years, he freighted between Dawson and down river camps. During the winter of '98, McGonagall hauled the mail and on one trip spent 34 straight days outdoors when the temperature never rose above -50° F.

When he heard of the Nome strike in 1900, McGonagall charged off with a two-dog team. Near Topkok—less than 50 miles from Nome's "Golden Beaches"—he and his partner were quarantined through the entire summer because of a smallpox epidemic. Once released, and his chance at riches again missed, McGonagall turned around and went back to Dawson. [24]

Karstens and McGonagall spent their first summer together driving Fish's horse-drawn wagons over Thompson Pass. Valdez residents referred to Karstens, who "handled the ribbons [reins] of the four-horse team hauling mail supplies," as an "old sour dough." (During the first quarter of the 20th century the term "sourdough" was infrequently used. Instead, "old-timer" was used to identify a pioneer, then someone who had come North prior to, or during, the Klondike stampede.) Karstens, the "old sour dough," was just 25.[25]

After freeze-up, the partners exchanged their horses for a dog team. Maps were inaccurate and the route from the Copper River Valley to Fairbanks unknown. The partners had directions to a mine north of the Copper River but from there they were on their own. On the south side of the Alaska Range Mountains, and prior to their initial journey through it, the partners cut willow wands to mark the 30 miles of trail to the head of the Delta River. (Old-timers considered the route through the Alaska Range tougher than that over Thompson Pass which one winter recorded 975 inches of snow.)

Deep snow slowed their travel through the mountains and they were forced to break trail on snowshoes. The first night they camped in heavy willows at the head of the Gakona River and the next day broke trail to the upper Delta. By the time they reached the confluence of the Delta with the Tanana River, they were low on food with only cornmeal and tea for supper. When the ravenous dogs scented a camp they bolted. "Before we could get to them, they were in a tent, tearing things to pieces," Karstens recalled.[26]

When the tent's owners returned, they fed Karstens and McGonagall and told them of a cache of meat four or five miles downstream on the opposite bank of the Tanana River. "The river was exceedingly dangerous, as it had jammed [with ice] in the last 48 hours with lots of open stretches," Karstens recalled. "We made a ticklish crossing, we found no meat cache and had 50 miles to Salchakat . . . where an old-timer Billie Munson was building a roadhouse. We stopped a couple of days with him." In exchange for food, the two carriers helped with construction.[27]

The partners made the 45-mile run from Munson's to Fairbanks in one day. The situation in Fairbanks looked bad to Karstens. Food was scarce and the diggings unproductive. He thought that the whole stampede to the Chena River was built on false information. Later that spring when the creeks proved rich, he lamented that "mail carriers were not allowed to take time out and stake their own claims."[28]

In Fairbanks, Karstens bought another sled and team and with each partner now fully outfitted, they pushed off on the 125-mile trail to Fort Gibbon. There they flipped a coin to see who would carry the first mail east and south over their new trail to the village of Gakona on the south side of the Alaska Range. Karstens "won." McGonagall would rest a few days before starting with the second load. Karstens' 400-mile trip went well, the trail hard-packed and fast. He reached Gakona without incident just as a big storm broke.

After a day's layover, Karstens switched loads with another musher up from Valdez. Accompanied by two trailbreakers hired by Fish, Karstens started back toward the head of the Delta where he was to exchange mail loads with McGonagall.

On the trip to the divide, one of the trailbreakers, Normile, plunged through the ice, soaking one foot. He said nothing until reaching camp, where he complained that he could not wiggle his toes and his foot felt "like a club." When Karstens stripped off Normile's moccasins and socks, he found his foot frozen stiff to the instep. "We did everything we could to bring life back in the foot using slush snow and then rubbing with bacon grease," Karstens recalled. His efforts were fruitless, the damage done.[29]

The next morning, Karstens and the second trailbreaker snowshoed over to the head of the Delta to meet McGonagall. They left Normile in the tent with the stove going and a pile of wood within reach. An overnight blizzard had buried the trail concealing or scattering the willow markers. Just at dark, after a long hard day floundering in snow, the two men reached the pre-arranged rendezvous site but McGonagall was not there. Casting about in the fading light Karstens found sled tracks out on the moraine. Somehow McGonagall had missed the camp and his tracks led southeast and away from the trail.

Without firewood or bedding, the two men spent a miserable night in the unheated tent. For dinner, they mixed flour and baking powder in a can of melt water. The men wolfed down Karstens' liquid "bread."

Early the next morning, they headed back for Normile. From a prominence above the Gakona camp, they saw a black dot working its way toward them. It was a man and two dogs pulling an almost empty sled. "We hurried over to camp and we got there a little before him. It was Mac and he was a sight," Karstens said. "He had tried to make a crossing farther down the divide and got in an awful mixup."[30]

McGonagall's errant turn had led him into deep snow. Instead of the team pulling him, he ended up dragging them. The dogs gave out one by one until only two were left. By accident, and as a result of snow-blindness, he burned his snowshoes while trying to de-ice them. To save his life, he had chopped off the sled's handlebars and started a fire, which he fed with green willow branches. The smoke only worsened the pain in his eyes. To ease his agony, McGonagall brewed up tea and tied the leaves over his eyes.

The night bivouac was horrendous, the situation tenuous. McGonagall dug a hole in a snow bank and crawled in to huddle with his dogs wrapped inside his sleeping robe. When Karstens found him the next day, his sled was empty except for mail and a sleeping robe. "He was the wildest looking man I ever saw," Karstens recalled. "It was lucky I was camped there or I'm afraid Mac would have been done for."[31]

The next morning the men loaded Normile into McGonagall's sled. (Doctors eventually amputated part of Normile's frozen foot.) While McGonagall and the two trailbreakers headed south for Gakona roadhouse, Karstens headed north with a heavy load pulled by six dogs. With a fresh-packed trail, Karstens made good time. He passed the halfway camp and continued on downstream 30 or 40 miles, most of it on glare ice. By dusk the temperature had dropped to well below zero. Karstens stopped for the night and hastily pitched a tent in dense woods.

Karstens soon had the stove going. He was too tired to build an open fire and decided to cook the dog food on the stove top. He stoked the stove full, pulled off his heavy trail moccasins and socks and hung them up to dry. While waiting for the dog food to cook, the bone-tired musher dozed off. Sometime later he awoke with the tent on fire. Karstens managed to snuff out the flames but his footwear and mittens were ashes. "I should have known better [than to fall asleep] but I was too tired to care much," he explained.[32]

At about four in the morning, Karstens harnessed the dogs and headed out on the trail wearing two pairs of socks on his hands and just two pairs of socks, insoles, and light moccasins on his feet. Only rigorous work kept him warm.

DENALI NATIONAL PARK & PRESERVE MUSEUM COLLECTION, #28/0.3.

Harry Karstens freighting mail in 1904 on the Richardson trail from Valdez to Fairbanks.

"It was a hard grueling trip [of 35 to 40 miles]," he recalled. "Glare ice helped out a good deal but then I would pay for it by breaking trail and dragging the load along until it seemed I could do no more. My one hope was that someone would be camped at the mouth of the Delta."[33]

About five miles from the Tanana, Karstens picked up a hard-packed trail. The dogs scented a camp and broke into a run with Karstens barely hanging on for the final sprint. He vaguely remembered someone helping him into a tent where he fell into a deep, black sleep.

Karstens awoke many hours later to find his dogs fed and rested. He profusely thanked his savior. Later, he told a friend that he survived because he'd had "a darned good set of underwear!"[34]

In Fairbanks, Karstens re-outfitted and broke trail all the way to Fort Gibbon, where he delivered the mail.

When mail loads were light, Karstens sometimes guided travelers or hauled passengers for extra money. In the spring of 1904, Karstens led Episcopal Bishop Trimble Rowe over a new route to the village of Gulkana on the Copper River where they were to meet the northbound carrier bringing provisions. The mail carrier, however, had gotten lost for three days in a storm and had consumed all the food before being rescued. Without the re-supply, Karstens and Rowe survived on a diet of snowshoe hares. Two weeks later, when Karstens returned to Fairbanks he proclaimed Bishop Rowe "a prince. One of the finest fellows [I] ever traveled with."[35]

Passengers provided welcome income but always meant extra work and, often, grief. On one trip, Karstens broke trail or worked the geepole on his heavily-loaded sled for 300 miles and not once did his passenger offer help. When night fell, the man made no effort to help with the dogs or make camp.

"I was so hungry I could have eaten the frying pan," Karstens said. "But I cooked for my passenger first. After that fellow had stowed away about a dozen hot cakes and showed no signs of reaching a limit, I said, 'No, brother, you watch me eat! I can't stand this any longer.'"[36]

For Karstens, the winter of 1903–04 was both tough and memorable. He survived howling storms, bitter cold, treacherous overflow, deep snow, and reluctant or recalcitrant dogs. More than once, he fell through the ice or frostbit his nose and cheeks. For his efforts, Karstens was paid $100 per month. To earn it, he had to keep the schedule and turned back only in the face of the harshest conditions. Karstens ran one particularly tough section of the trail "in three days averaging over forty miles a day."[37]

With their contract completed, Karstens and McGonagall decided to go into the freighting business for themselves. In 1905, they set out for a promising new district, the Kantishna. Both thought that maybe this time they would strike it big.

Once again, Karstens and McGonagall arrived at this new strike too late to get rich, so they started a private mail and freight service. In March 1906, despite open water on the Toklat and early break-up on the Nenana, Karstens brought a passenger, Jerome Chute, to Fairbanks in a record four-day run from Glacier City.

Throughout his life of varied and storied challenges, the Seventymile Kid considered pioneer mail hauling as his most dangerous undertaking. He knew that if he could survive those perilous years, he could do anything. "Ever since the winter of 1903–04," Karstens reminisced, "Mac and I figured we were living on borrowed time . . ."[38]

Karstens quit the Kantishna District in the summer of 1906, with little regret. He saw the stampede as unremarkable, no different from the many others he had participated in. Later that summer, he would be back but this time in the company of a most remarkable man, Charles Sheldon. The almost serendipitous meeting of these two men would entwine them for life and forever alter the future of the entire region. Harry Karstens would go on to add an entirely new and unique chapter to an already noteworthy life.

4
SHELDON ON THE TOKLAT

Rumors raced through the Kantishna mining camps in the autumn of 1906. A big Canuck guide, assisted by mail carrier Karstens, was bringing some rich Eastern dandy into the hills. What is more, he supposedly was not looking for gold or mining properties to buy, nor was he another climber like that Dr. Cook who had boasted that he would climb Mt. McKinley that summer. Instead, this Easterner said he had come all this way, and spent all this money, to go *hunting!*

Some miners, suspicious of men poking around their claims and asking questions, thought the "hunting trip" was a cover to conceal the interest of some big mining outfit. A few thought the Cheechako was a government man and not at all to be trusted. Others who had heard of the nascent conservation "fad" also speculated on his motives. Those who had met him at Glacier City, however, said he seemed friendly, down-to-earth, did not put on airs, and, in short, acted just like ordinary folk. Hell, at Quigley's cabin they had even seen him do chores without being asked!

Charles Alexander Sheldon was indeed unlike anyone else to have ventured into the camps. In sharp contrast to the somewhat desperate men who had stampeded to the creeks, or the hardy few who hung on to their claims, Sheldon was not interested in mineral wealth. His focus was on wildlife, particularly the golden-horned, jewel-eyed, all-white Dall sheep. It would take a while before locals accepted the fact that Sheldon had come all the way from the East Coast to hunt an animal they killed for almost daily fare.

Chapter Four

DENALI NATIONAL PARK AND PRESERVE, MUSEUM COLLECTION, #3668

Charles Sheldon takes a break on the Toklat River in 1906. This pleasant, self-effacing man believed that by going hatless he could arrest his hair loss. "Regrettably, it seems to make no difference in my receding hairline," he lamented.

Sheldon, the oldest of six siblings, was born on October 17, 1867, into a hard-working family involved in marble quarrying and manufacturing. Sheldon, named for his grandfather, attended Andover preparatory school and graduated from Yale in 1890, the year the family business collapsed. Through family contacts, he was hired as assistant superintendent of the Lake Shore and Michigan Southern Railroad. From there, he moved to Mexico and became general manager of the Chihuahua and Pacific Railroad in 1898, the same year as the Klondike stampede. He invested in the Chihuahua and Pacific Exploration Company, developers of *Potasi*, one of the richest silver and lead mines in Mexico. In just four short years, this investment secured Sheldon's financial future and he retired at age 35.

Sheldon's conservation career began in 1904, when he contacted C. Hart Merriam and Edward W. Nelson of the U.S. Biological Survey and offered to collect specimens and make field observations. Sheldon, a life-long hunter and fisherman, pursued all manner of wildlife but North America's wild mountain sheep fascinated him most. He first hunted desert sheep in Mexico's Sierra Madre and then pursued bighorns in the Rocky Mountains. Stories of the so-called thinhorn sheep of the northern wilderness attracted his attention and in 1904, he hunted and studied Stone sheep in Canada's Yukon. His first book, *The Wilderness of the Upper Yukon*, detailed his sheep hunting exploits in the Yukon Territory in 1904 and 1905.

His love of these "noble and splendid" animals eventually led him to Alaska in search of Dall sheep, then the least known of the four species of America's wild sheep. In late June 1906, Sheldon reached Dawson City in the Yukon, where he bought five horses and tack from the White Pass Railroad.

On the advice of a friend, he hired Horace "Jack" Haydon, a dog musher, trapper, and hunting guide to be his packer and assistant. Haydon and his brother Wilbur had stampeded to the Klondike from Michigan. He later married an Athabascan woman and raised a family on the shores of Kluane Lake. The men loaded their horses and gear on a steamer and headed down the Yukon to its confluence with the Tanana River. En route up the Tanana to Fairbanks, Sheldon dropped Haydon and the horses off at the mouth of the Kantishna River to await his return.

In Fairbanks, Sheldon met with Judge Wickersham who recommended that he hire Bert Webb to guide him in the Kantishna. After meeting Webb, Sheldon declined and said, "this man…would not do [and] so I employed 'Kid' Karsteens [sic] and I like him very much." Sheldon's favorable first impression of Karstens proved accurate. "I recall no better fortune than that which befell me when Harry

SMITHSONIAN INSTITUTION ARCHIVES, RECORD UNIT 7172, IMAGE #2005-7054

Pioneer naturalists, like Charles Sheldon, collected large numbers of animals for national and private collections. At the turn of the 20th century many species were still relatively new to science which then focused on basic natural history and taxonomy.

Karstens was engaged as an assistant packer . . . He is a tall, stalwart man, well poised, frank, and strictly honorable . . . peculiarly fitted by youth and experience for explorations in little-known regions, he proved a most efficient and congenial companion."[1]

As events unfolded, Karstens' knowledge of the country near Mt. McKinley proved to be indispensable. The piles of sheep carcasses that Karstens had seen while mushing in the Kantishna and his own hunting there excited Sheldon, his destination now confirmed. Karstens, an inveterate explorer, fell easily into the role of hunting guide.

"Inquiries about the game of the neighborhood all led back to Harry Karstens," wrote one hunter. "When one tried to locate a person in this [Fairbanks], as in other towns, the answer frequently was, 'You'll find him at the *Northern*, or the *Palace*, or one of the other bars.' But not so with Karstens: 'You'll probably find him at Hall's bookstore' . . . For a congenial companion Karstens was willing, if he had leisure, to undertake a trip to the head of the Toklat River . . . although he did not make a business of acting as a guide."[2]

On July 14, 1906, Sheldon and Karstens left Fairbanks on the chartered sternwheeler *Dusty Diamond*. At the mouth of the Kantishna, they picked up Haydon and the horses and headed upstream for Roosevelt.

Sheldon immediately began taking notes on wildlife, plants, landscape, and the gold camps. "The main object of my trip was to study the life history of sheep and incidentally to gather as much information as possible about other mammals."[3]

The region's prospectors and miners impressed Sheldon and he compared them favorably to early-American pioneers. "He [the prospector] does not have to contend with hostile Indians, but he must face and conquer more serious conditions—those of a barren country, intense cold, long winter darkness, and still more, the danger of starvation and disease." Sheldon's obvious and genuine respect for the people he met alleviated their anxieties regarding this rich easterner.[4]

Within days, Sheldon made his first kill, a lactating cow caribou. He went on to kill everything from shrews to bears and even attempted to tame a grizzly cub for transfer to the Bronx Zoo. At the time of Sheldon's trip, Dall sheep had been known to American science for little more than 40 years. Rather than behavior or ecology, most early research focused on taxonomy, the classification of animals. Sheldon's work established the link between Stone and Dall sheep as a single species. Some people today view Sheldon's killing as excessive and repugnant. From a historical perspective, however, the years 1880–1930 constituted the era of on-going discovery and classification of North American fauna. Sheldon without a doubt relished the hunt but he also was an astute observer and chronicler of nature.

Karstens described Sheldon as dedicated and "very thorough," stopping at camp only long enough to care for specimens. "We collected every type of animal and bird in the area," Karstens wrote, "preserving the hides and skulls and taking measurements and stomach contents and all useful data for the Biological Survey."[5]

For nearly three months, Sheldon's party roamed the piedmont. Almost no day passed without adventure of one sort or another. On July 27, 1906, they found a camp that Judge Wickersham had used on his unsuccessful summit attempt.

Sheldon's journals are full of detailed accounts of hunting and wildlife but also landscape and topography. "Now, all the country was resplendent with fall colors," he wrote. "A rich brown spread over the mountains, the dwarf birches were carmine, the blueberry bushes deep scarlet, the willow leaves yellow, crimson, and various shades of green . . ."

He also commented on the landscape's personal effect. "Alone in an unknown wilderness hundreds of miles from civilization and high on one of the world's most imposing mountains, I was deeply moved by the stupendous mass of the great upheaval, the vast extent of the wild areas below, the chaos of the unfinished surfaces still in process of mouldering . . ."

He detailed northern magic: "Suddenly I stepped out of the enveloping mist and found myself . . . with a wonderful sight before me. The whole bar was covered with a dense low fog, reaching only to my waist, while overhead the stars were shining brilliantly. An arc of northern lights was flashing through the heavens . . . The thin layer of dense mist seemed to glow with gentle light . . . Only the white mountain tops, so dimly seen . . . brought back a sense of limitation to the apparently endless expanse . . ."

He missed little: "When walking in the woods, if I paused to listen . . . a movement in the branches . . . would catch my eye and one or more chickadees would be discovered . . . Soon one would see me and . . . it would come down within a few feet and suddenly greet me with its sweet plaintive . . . *chickadee-dee-dee.*"

Numerous entries in Sheldon's journals describe the mountain's impact. ". . . Denali in all its magnificence and imposing grandeur reared its massive snowy bulk toward the sky . . . It ever dominated the landscape, glorifying that mountain world." Also, "[t]he vision can never fade, and the ecstasies produced by such long intimacy with it will linger vividly throughout my life."[6]

Not only did Sheldon bond with the country, but with Karstens. Near the trip's end, and just before Karstens rode up Moose Creek bound for the mail trail to the Tanana, the two said goodbye. "When we shook hands before he started up the creek . . . I felt as though I were departing from a good friend."[7]

That this sophisticated, wealthy easterner bonded so closely with this tough, rugged frontiersman seems surprising at first. America's class structure in those years was often as rigid as that existing in Europe—two percent of the population controlled sixty percent of the nation's wealth. The annual average American family income was $500. Although Sheldon was considered "New Money," his social circle included the so-called American Royalty. His friends included Theodore Roosevelt, George Bird Grinnell, Gifford Pinchot, Carl Rungius, Wilfred H. Osgood, Alexander Graham Bell, and Admiral Richard Byrd.

However, even a casual examination of the Karstens–Sheldon friendship reveals common traits conducive to mutual admiration. Both were resourceful and experienced outdoorsmen who viewed the challenges of the wilderness as obstacles to overcome but not fear. Neither were complainers, braggarts, or loud talkers. Each let his accomplishments speak for themselves.

Sheldon, self-effacing to a fault, cared deeply about nature, wildlife, hunting, and family. Throughout his life he preferred to be called Sheldon, or Billie. After his service in World War I, some people referred to him as Colonel Sheldon, which embarrassed him. "Sheldon was personally a most attractive man. He possessed great sweetness of nature and was friendly, frank, and forthright," wrote George Bird Grinnell. "He was deliberate and cautious in deciding about new matters and took abundant time to make up his mind about them . . . He strove to look at things from all sides and did not take a definite stand until he had given careful consideration to the matter . . ."[8]

Friends described Sheldon as possessing physical strength and endurance beyond belief. Through rain, snow, cold, or clouds of mosquitoes, the 5'10", 170-pound Sheldon hunted wildlife with obvious glee. In Karstens, he more than met his match.

Karstens possessed one trait that made it possible for him to live and work in harmony with Sheldon—"he knew when to keep quiet and leave Sheldon to himself."[9]

Although just 28, Karstens—pronounced "*Kar-steins*" by old-timers—was famous throughout the Yukon and Alaska, his trail exploits legendary. The Seventymile Kid always kept his word and could be counted on in any circumstance. Sheldon would frequently declare that Karstens was the best outdoorsman he had ever known and certainly the best dog musher.[10]

When Sheldon returned from his 65 days in the mountains, reports of his hunting success spread quickly throughout Fairbanks and outlying mining camps. Karstens paid him the highest tribute as "one of the best men he ever roughed it with." He told his peers that Sheldon often left camp in early morning and seldom returned before 10 or 11 at night. Karstens reported that Sheldon relished "plain fare and hard travel" and always helped in setting up camp and doing chores, so much so that "it would have been hard for an outsider to figure out which of the three of us was [on] a pleasure trip."[11]

Sheldon considered his 1906 expedition satisfying but only partially successful. He wanted to collect several specimens of moose and caribou but those he encountered were still in velvet and their antlers not fully developed. This kindled his desire to return for prime specimens. More importantly, he had secured only the minimum number of rams requested by the Biological Survey. Sheldon believed that to complete a life history of Dall sheep, he needed to view them in all seasons. Even before the trip's culmination, he began plotting another expedition with a larger scope.

Although to outsiders the expedition may have appeared to be for pleasure, the results would be far grander. "The success of the New Yorker is significant to historical work in Alaska," one newspaper said, presaging the full impact of Sheldon's visit.[12]

"During the months we roamed over a good part of what is now Mount McKinley National Park gathering specimens," Karstens wrote years later, "Sheldon was so taken with the beauty of the area and the amount of game . . . that he decided to try and have this area set aside for a game refuge and park. If he got my encouragement he said he would be back the following year and stay a whole year using horses in the summer and my dog team in the winter."[13]

Late in the winter of 1907, Karstens received a wire from Sheldon: "[P]repare for a year's trip." Karstens immediately began gathering equipment and purchasing supplies. Sheldon was slightly vexed when Karstens did not respond to a planning letter. He sent Karstens a telegram: "No letter received: will you go with me?" Sheldon left home without getting a response. His was a well-placed leap of faith. He trusted his friend.[14]

Sheldon might have left for Alaska with a little more anxiety had he known that Karstens had not been heard from for several weeks. Karstens, accompanied by Charley Smith, had left Fairbanks in January 1907, on a lightly-loaded sled carrying food for 25 days. Prior to departure, they said that "they were going in [to the Toklat headwaters] for the purpose of picking up a bunch of mountain sheep . . ." Old-timers gave knowing winks when they learned that they had previously prospected in the Toklat "and found good prospects." Two and one-half months after they left town, Karstens and Smith returned to Fairbanks. Brutal storms and cold had delayed their return from their camp in the last timber at the head of the Toklat River. At

DENALI PARK AND PRESERVE, MUSEUM COLLECTION, #2802

In early 1907, and prior to Sheldon's return for his year's stay, Harry Karstens and Charley Smith hunted, trapped, and prospected the headwaters of the Toklat River. Karstens, left, poses near a cache of sheep meat. John McLeod, who teamed up with the partners, peers from the tent door.

some point in their planned six week hunting/trapping/prospecting trip they hooked up with John McLeod. Just when they had accumulated a large cache of sheep and caribou meat to bring back to town a terrible storm struck. Weathered in, they had to feed their dogs the accumulated meat. During the two week delay they shot 50 more sheep to replenish the larder. In Fairbanks the partners turned in ore samples and showed off a prized silver fox skin.[15]

Sheldon traveled by steamer from Seattle to Skagway and then by rail to Whitehorse. There he boarded a paddle-wheeler for the journey down the Yukon and up the Tanana River to Fairbanks, arriving on a hot July day.

Harry Karstens met him in town and introduced the hired help, freighter Jim Wilson and ex-Mountie Billy Merrifield. Wilson's mules would pack the assembled outfit to the upper Toklat, where the men would build a headquarters cabin. After freeze-up, Karstens would bring in his dog team. The chartered steamer *Luella* was duly loaded with passengers, pack animals, provisions, and gear and promptly got underway.

DENALI PARK & PRESERVE, CULTURAL RESOURCES COLLECTION, WILDERNESS OF DENALI

Horace "Jack" Haydon, left, and Harry Karstens, right, pose with some of Charles Sheldon's 1906 collection of Dall sheep and grizzly bear specimens.

The journey up the Kantishna River in the little paddle-wheeler to the mouth of the Bearpaw River was unremarkable. It quickly became apparent that the *Luella* was ill-equipped to navigate low water on the Bearpaw and that the captain had little inclination to proceed to Diamond City as contracted. While Sheldon and his crew pulled with tow ropes, "the Captain and the mate merely looked on as we toiled."

At four in the morning, after hours of back-breaking labor, Sheldon gave up and the men unloaded their gear into poling boats. One can only guess what the no-nonsense Karstens said to the captain that day when they parted on the Bearpaw.

It took six days of brutal labor for the men to move the supplies by horse and boat to Glacier City. From there, it took five more days to relay essential dunnage across country to the Toklat River. Wilson and Merrifield spent two additional weeks packing in the last of the gear to the cabin site.

"The preceding year I had selected [a] site for my cabin . . . on an ancient level bar on the east side of the Toklat about three miles below my camp of 1906," Sheldon wrote. Nearby was a well-preserved Indian cache that the men used to store their gear while they built the cabin. "No more ideal spot for a timberline cabin could have been found. [It had] abundant water . . . spruces large enough to afford protection from the wind, [and] the place surrounded by mountains where sheep were almost always in sight. A grove of straight dead spruce . . . providing not only abundant fuel, but [logs] to construct the cabin."[16]

While Sheldon explored, the crew worked on the cabin. On August 24, Wilson rode down the Toklat with four of his mules bound for Fairbanks and Karstens with two mules headed for Glacier City. Merrifield remained in camp with Sheldon. It took Wilson and his stock ten days to reach Fairbanks; his overland epic included swimming both the Nenana and Tanana Rivers.[17]

Karstens spent almost three weeks putting up hay at Glacier City to over-winter the remaining mules and horses. After haying, he caught the steamer *Wilbur Crimmin* to Fairbanks where, in late September, he assembled a dog team and additional provisions to support Sheldon.

While Merrifield cut and hauled firewood to the cabin, Sheldon hunted for camp meat and continued his explorations. While wandering alone, he found Alfred H. Brooks' U.S. Geological Survey camp from August 1902, the date and names of the members still legible on a peeled section of a spruce tree.

In early October, Merrifield left for Glacier with the last of the horses. Sheldon was by himself. "Alone in that remote section of the Alaskan wilderness, I had a strange feeling of complete possession of these wilds."[18]

Now alone, Sheldon studied the Dall sheep's pre-rutting behavior and hunted little. Clearly he relished the solitude. " . . . [T]he wind had ceased and complete quiet reigned; not even the sound of the river running under the ice could be heard. Only the creaking of my snowshoes broke the stillness. Denali, rising in a brilliant golden sky was before me; the north sky was banked with clouds of purest pink, deepening above to the dark blue of the ether; and later, the gold behind Denali was replaced by crimson."[19]

Sheldon's solo idyll ended in early November with the arrival of Merrifield and Rice, a miner, driving two dog teams. "The delightful solitude of the wilderness I had been enjoying was thus suddenly broken," Sheldon wrote. When the two men declared their intention to hunt sheep, they unwittingly tested Sheldon's sense of ownership of the area. Merrifield had promised a set of horns to someone in Glacier City and Rice had not eaten meat in two months. "Since I did not want my sheep above the cabin disturbed by anybody except myself, they agreed to get their sheep on the outside mountain." Always the gracious host, Sheldon cooked for the men and provided meat for their dogs. On November 6, Merrifield went down river and killed five ewe sheep, three of them lambs, mostly for dog food.[20]

On that same day, Karstens mushed a five-dog team into camp. It had taken him almost a month to make the return trip from Fairbanks. The cold summer of 1907 had turned into a warm autumn with high water. Karstens had learned in Fairbanks that Tom Lloyd and Billy Taylor had chartered the *Florence S* for a mid-October run up the Bearpaw with 25 tons of supplies and equipment needed to develop their Conwyl Mining Company's quartz claims. Seizing the opportunity, Karstens, along with U.S. Commissioner Ernest J. Foster and his family—bound for their winter quarters at Glacier City—booked passage. The steamer reached Glacier City without major incident but the unseasonable weather delayed Karstens' departure for the

Toklat. While waiting for freeze-up, Karstens trained his dog team and looked after the expedition's horses.

Karstens' skills as a dog musher deeply impressed Sheldon: "He always took the best care of his dogs, taking no end of trouble to prepare ample food, and arranging the best available spots for them to rest. He always insisted however on their strict attention to work and never permitted one to shirk. In case of failure on the part of any dog the discipline was severe." One dog, *Silas*, was so attached to Karstens, Sheldon said, that "even after my kind treatment throughout the winter" the dog refused to follow him.[21]

Later in the winter, other sheep hunters passed through camp, including Sam Means and Henry Capps, as well as Joe Quigley and his partner, Fannie McKenzie. On three occasions, Sheldon heard distant rifle fire. In 1906, Sheldon had inspected sheep and caribou carcasses hauled to Eureka Creek and Glacier City by market hunters. He had heard that since then commercial hunting had accelerated with hunters hauling the meat to the Fairbanks market. The news, and now the distant sound of gunfire, alarmed him. One of the conservation organizations that he belonged to, the Boone and Crockett Club had been established precisely to promote conservation laws and a "fair chase" hunting ethic designed to curb the damage caused by the commercial slaughter of the nation's wildlife.

While in camp in late January 1908, Sheldon and Karstens again heard a fusillade of distant rifle fire. "The winter market hunters were there," he wrote, "and the following day Karstens saw numerous tracks of ewes and lambs that had been driven across the divide."[22]

Karstens visited the market hunters' camp and found that they had killed a large number of lambs and ewes. In the afternoon of February 13, the four market hunters—identified in Sheldon's journal as "Bryce, Hess, Brown and McGlaughlin"—stopped with their dogs at Sheldon's camp. "They had killed more than twenty ewes and lambs," he wrote, "but since they had been there for some time their dogs had consumed so many that . . . they did not have the desired loads of meat to take back to Fairbanks."[23]

Although Sheldon and Karstens ate sheep meat and fed it to their dogs, they both knew the risk of unrestricted trapping and commercial hunting. Karstens himself had hunted briefly for the market. Sheldon had seen Kantishna men spreading poisoned bait to kill fur

DENALI PARK & PRESERVE, CULTURAL RESOURCES COLLECTION, WILDERNESS OF DENALI

In the timber along the Toklat River, ex-Mountie Billy Merrifield leads a packhorse over-loaded with Sheldon's specimens.

animals. He even placed a few poison baits himself—in the name of science—and killed a wolverine. Throughout the winter, he noticed an increasing scarcity of ravens and learned that two trappers working lines from Sanctuary almost to the east fork of the Toklat had killed over 200 ravens with strychnine-laced tallow balls. Only after they had nearly exterminated the birds, did these "trappers" manage to kill 60 foxes, their intended targets.

Although Sheldon never saw or heard a wolf on either Toklat trip, he did find the tracks of two wolves in the winter of 1908, which he believed "were attracted here by the killing and wounding of sheep on the outside mountain by the market hunters." The indiscriminate use of poison might have explained the scarcity of wolves.[24]

The commercial slaughter disturbed Sheldon and he pondered ways to protect the region's wildlife. In mid-January Sheldon and Karstens camped on the Muddy River near the north face of Mt. McKinley. By then, Sheldon's vision of a wildlife refuge had jelled. He envisioned a national park where wildlife roamed undisturbed in the shadow of the great mountain. "When Denali National Park shall be made easy of access," he wrote in his diary, "with accommodations and facilities for travel, including a comfortable lodge at the foot of the moraine of Peters Glacier, as it surely will be, it is not difficult to anticipate the enjoyment and inspiration visitors will receive. They will be overwhelmed by the sublime views of Nature's stupendous upheaval . . . to view Denali towering in a sky of unimagined splendor evokes a state of supreme exaltation."[25]

Sheldon and Karstens also talked of climbing Denali, which name they preferred over Mt. McKinley, and discussed several plans. ". . . [W]ith time and careful study we can do it like a charm . . . in my opinion your [sic] the man," Karstens wrote Sheldon[26]

In March 1908, Karstens loaded his dogsled with part of Sheldon's specimen collection and headed for Duke's Trading Post at the confluence of the Tanana and Nenana Rivers for later trans-shipment to Fairbanks. Their time together in the mountains was almost over. On his return journey, Karstens stopped off at Glacier City, where he left the dogs, and returned to the cabin with *Silas*, his favorite dog, and Sheldon's horse, *Toklat*. (Karstens returned from Duke's unaware that in Fairbanks he had been reported frozen to death on the trail and subsequently buried in the Kantishna. The rumor persisted until spring.)

In Karstens' absence, Sheldon once again reveled in the isolation. "Complete enjoyment of the wilderness needs periods of solitude," Sheldon wrote prior to Karstens' return, "and in the silence . . . the feeling of undisturbed freedom gave me the happiness I have always realized when thus living alone."[27]

During Sheldon's winter on the Toklat River, he had seen and accomplished many remarkable things. On two occasions he saw a lynx kill a Dall sheep; he tamed a wolverine enough to have it eat from his hand; and he had collected enough hides, skulls, skeletons, and study specimens to fill many gaps in the U.S. Biological Survey collection. Eventually, the prestigious ornithological journal *The Auk* published his list of 60 regional birds.

As the days wound down and his winter in the mountains came to a close, Sheldon treasured each day as if it were his last. "Karstens, as planned, left for Glacier City early in the morning," Charles Sheldon wrote on June 1, 1908, "and I remained to enjoy the last few days in undisturbed possession of this, my wilderness."[28]

DENALI PARK & PRESERVE, CULTURAL RESOURCES COLLECTION, WILDERNESS OF DENALI

In the spring of 1908, Harry Karstens stands at the gee pole of his sled while freighting out the gear and trophies of Charles Sheldon's winter hunt on the Toklat River.

"My wilderness"—a telling remark, for Charles Sheldon had fallen in love with the high peaks, valleys, and rivers of the Alaska Range. Finally on June 11, Sheldon reluctantly left his Toklat cabin, never to return. "No words can describe my sorrow and regret as I led the horse out of the woods from the cabin . . . and started down river. I was leaving forever this region in which I had lived and hunted with a feeling of complete possession."[29]

Sheldon's solo exit journey across the wilderness offers a tribute to his superb outdoor skills. He reached the Nenana River after negotiating miles of swamps, muskeg, and stream crossings, all under the relentless onslaught of hordes of mosquitoes. Near the end of his trip, Sheldon swam his horse, *Toklat*, across the spring torrents of the Nenana River. "I was nearly swept off two or three times—particularly once when [Toklat] almost rolled over . . . My relief at escaping the danger of this crossing was profound . . . Those who love a good horse may imagine my feelings." One slight mishap and Sheldon, along with his plans for the region, would have been lost forever.[30]

Once safely on the east side of the river, Sheldon led *Toklat* on a 12-hour hike downstream to Duke's Trading Post, near the Episcopal Mission at the mouth of the Nenana. There he spent three days packing some of his specimens for shipment. On June 20, he arrived in Fairbanks on a sternwheeler. Word spread rapidly of his exploits in the "Toklat country . . . where there is more game . . . than a person could imagine." Karstens later chimed in and called the Toklat "the choicest hunting ground of this vast Northland."[31]

While Sheldon was en route to the Tanana, the *Florence S*, with Captain Smythe at the helm, steamed up the Kantishna despite "very low water" to the Bearpaw. Twenty miles up the Bearpaw, he picked up Karstens and Merrifield, who had packed the remainder of Sheldon's collection to the river for transport to Fairbanks.

The day after Sheldon returned to Fairbanks, Karstens arrived. The *Fairbanks Daily News* reported, "H.P. Karstens, guide and hunter, came down with the boxes and furs which Sheldon, the hunter, had gathered . . . Karstens had a large number of glacier bears as trophies of the spring hunting of Sheldon."[32]

Charles Sheldon finally said goodbye to Karstens on June 24, "but not without regret at severing ties formed by long companionship in the wilderness."[33]

"It is with sorrow and regret [I] leave such a delightful life," Sheldon wrote. He had just learned that the "delightful life" had cost him dearly. Upon his return to New York, he found himself facing financial ruin. He considered a return to business because his "income had stopped for nearly a year" and he was without cash. Somehow he weathered the crisis.[34]

Although Sheldon hobnobbed with America's most powerful men, he never forgot his friends in Alaska. He corresponded for years with Joe Quigley and Fannie McKenzie who wrote to tell of their lives and neighbors. He prodded Karstens to provide updates on Alex Mitchell, Fred Hauselmann, Sam Means, and other Kantishna miners and trappers. His interest in the local people was genuine. He found Means of particular interest and described him as "one of the peculiar products of the north." They first met in 1908, at the mouth of Clearwater Creek. Means lived off the land, carrying a small quantity of flour, rice, tea, and sugar, and fed his three sled dogs everything from sheep to ptarmigan. Means was neither trapping nor prospecting when they met. Instead he was trying to photograph wildlife and landscapes in hopes of being invited to exhibit his work at the 1909 Alaska–Yukon Pacific Exposition in Seattle. Means, while a prototype of the era, also foreshadowed an activity that would one day dominate in the region. In a sense, he was the first tourist.

Sheldon left Alaska determined more than ever to see his game paradise become a wildlife sanctuary. As early as January 12, 1908, he jotted notes on setting aside the region as a park and preserve. In the years after he resolved his financial crisis he began to call on influential friends and enlist their aid in creating a Mt. McKinley National Park. It would be a long battle.

The publicity given Sheldon's successful hunts on the Toklat had the unwanted outcome of attracting both sport and market hunters. Fairbanksans Al Sutton and Joe Murrow visited Sheldon's cabin in 1913, and hunted sheep there for well over a month. Locals said that the hunters "should come back with as much game as they can bring, as the sheep are very plentiful . . ." They each "killed the limit," a tongue-in-cheek statement since no one followed the game laws.[35]

Two years later, W. F. Whitely, a Karstens associate and avid hunter, led a five-man hunting expedition to the Kantishna that "took enough ammunition to clean up one of the contending armies in Europe."[36]

During his two trips to the Alaska Range, Sheldon had come to know the local people and their lifestyles. He admired their character, learned their views and politics, and saw how much they relied on the land for basic sustenance. He knew well that the fledgling notion of conservation and wildlife protection would not be embraced here but rather seen as government infringement of Alaskans' basic rights. He was well aware that if his concept of a national park ever became reality, the implementation of park rules would be difficult. He expected strong resistance—maybe even of a violent nature—from some quarters. Sheldon knew of only one man indomitable enough to handle the rugged men of the creeks and put an end to the slaughter of his beloved white sheep, his friend, Kid Karstens.

5
Market Hunters

Harry Lucke lined up a string of cartridges atop the stone wall of the blind he crouched in and settled down for a long wait. His hiding place above the mineral lick near the confluence of Big Creek and the Teklanika River had been built in the dim past by Athabascans who had hidden here with their bows and spears for a chance to ambush Dall sheep.

At about noon, with the sun just cresting the mountaintops, 20 sheep warily approached the lick, 12 of them large rams. Lucke knelt motionless in the snow, his finger on the trigger. One by one the sheep moved into the lick and began pawing at the partially frozen mud. Lucke took aim at the largest ram and squeezed the trigger.

At the crack of the rifle the herd bolted, ran a few feet, stopped, and looked back. The biggest ram lay unmoving, dead from a bullet in the neck. Another shot downed the second largest ram and a third shot killed the next largest. With each boom of the gun, the surviving sheep jumped and milled around, but did not run off. Thunder and the crash of tumbling boulders are common sounds in the Alaska Range and the rifle fire did not alarm them. Their leaders, the ones that knew better, lay dead.

Lucke quickly re-loaded and fired again. He cursed aloud when the fifth ram fell kicking and thrashing. He had missed the neck and hit the sheep in the shoulder. Now, with blood on the wind, the band panicked into flight. Three hurried shots brought down two more rams.

Lucke stood up and stretched. He straddled the stone wall and lit a cigarette. Below him seven rams bled into the snow—a good morning's work for a market hunter.

Professional hunters like Harry Lucke supplied meat to the ravenous hordes that surged north during the various gold rushes. Everything, from swans to bears, was sold in the frontier meat markets. Caribou sold for as little as 15 cents a pound and sheep meat for 50 cents a pound. Moose meat cost from 40 cents to two dollars per pound. In times of scarcity, all prices rose dramatically. Market hunting was a necessity that often meant the difference between human life and death.

The 1903 stampede to the Chena River offers a good example of the role of market hunting during the gold rush era. When the news of Felix Pedro's gold strike in the hills near present-day Fairbanks reached Dawson City, hundreds of stampeders—some alone, some accompanied by families with small children—set out down the Yukon River. Many of them carried inadequate provisions and supplies. Others wore clothing ill suited for the intense winter cold. Several hundred people took the new Goodpaster Trail, a section of the WAMCATS line blazed by Lt. Billy Mitchell. "The stampede to a new place is a terrible thing, especially in winter," Mitchell wrote in its aftermath. ". . . [A] great many moose were being killed, and I heard they were being taken into Fairbanks by the ton, which was very lucky, as the mushers got in there without food. Had it not been for this providential circumstance, a great many would have starved to death."[1]

CANDY WAUGAMAN COLLECTION

In the heart of what eventually became Mt. McKinley National Park a market hunter's cabin is adorned with Dall sheep horns, the remnant of the slaughter.

Periodic famine was common in the boom camps. A successful hunt was neither recreation nor sport. It was the business of basic survival. Commercial hunting was just another business opportunity for some of those who failed to find gold.

Market hunters gave no thought to the sustainability of the harvest. The size of wildlife populations in Alaska and the Yukon was unknown. Despite the immensity of the region, the frigid sub-arctic supported only limited numbers of large mammals even in the best of habitats. As early as 1890, prospectors in some areas had begun to notice a scarcity of wildlife due to market hunting. In 1904, near Fairbanks, a hunter killed 62 caribou in one day. On a single day another market hunter shipped 2430 pounds of caribou meat to the town. Business was so brisk that freighters established special discount rates for meat shipped by professional hunters.

Miners working on the Wood River, just east of the Nenana River, alerted the public in 1908 to what they termed a "ruthless game extermination." They cited events in the Nenana River canyon and Healy Fork as especially horrendous. Apparently three market hunters there had been hired to kill Dall sheep for 15 cents a pound. The hunters shot 40 or more sheep but too early in the season to preserve the meat. Other than a few sheep chopped up for dog food, the rest were left to rot or to be scavenged by birds and predators.

"Finally, however, a great stock [of meat] was landed at Chena. Part of it was sold there, more in Fairbanks, and other odd lots on the creeks. The market proved to be overstocked and . . . eventually [the meat was] dumped into the Tanana River as the weather turned unexpectedly warm and the meat spoiled." In this one incident, the hunters had killed an estimated 150 Dall sheep, as well as other game.[2]

Another miner working near the Nenana River reported the killing of 75 moose within a very small area and decried the waste of "tons of moose meat." One man killed 23 moose; seventeen were sold in town, three spoiled, and three were fed to the dogs. "Indians made a killing of 16 head in the same locality. Much of this spoiled because of careless handling, and the remainder was bought by Fairbanks restaurants at 15 cents a pound," the miner said.[3]

In the face of unlimited hunting, population reductions were inevitable. The wildlife resources could not sustain this slaughter. If the gold strikes had not waned enough to stall, or even reverse, the

THOMAS GIBSON COLLECTION, #78-76-45, ARCHIVES, UNIVERSITY OF ALASKA, FAIRBANKS

Fourteen caribou killed by market hunters hang ready to be shipped to Fairbanks.

influx of gold seekers, many wildlife populations likely would have been wiped out.

Hunting in Alaska in the early 20th century was not entirely unregulated, at least on paper. The Alaska Game Law of 1902 set methods and means, seasons, and bag limits, and protected birds, nests, and eggs.

This law allowed Natives to kill wildlife for food and clothing. Miners, explorers, and travelers also could kill game when in need of food, regardless of season. Wildlife killed legally could be sold during open season and by dealers up to 15 days after the season closed. "The exception [to hunting during closed season] must be construed strictly," the law stated. "It must not be used merely as a pretext to kill game out of season for sport or for market, or to supply canneries or settlements."[4]

Many people railed against these early laws which they viewed as government interference and angrily pointed to what they saw as a loophole that benefited Eastern sportsmen. The law allowed "the collection of specimens for scientific purposes . . . [and] the export from Alaska of specimens and trophies." This very loophole was one of the things that set a few miners on edge when Charles Sheldon first ventured into the Kantishna District.[5]

Congress revised the Alaska Game Law in 1908, but in the process created several more loopholes. (Incidentally, the law removed protection for the bald eagle because these birds ate salmon.) Under the new law, non-residents were required to have a guide while hunting, the sale of game meat was prohibited in designated areas, and closed some seasons for up to two years because of over-hunting. Again Alaskans largely ignored the restrictions. In isolated mining districts like the Kantishna, enforcement was non-existent. Menus everywhere offered "hunter-style," or "hunter-steak," a euphemism for wild meat. To circumvent the law caribou meat was sometimes sold as "reindeer."

The enforcement of Alaska's first game laws fell to federal marshals, U.S. Commissioners, and a handful of game wardens. Wardens were appointed by the Territorial Governor and the positions were largely considered political plums. These wardens were neither trained nor avidly interested in enforcing the law. In March 1917, for example, Territorial Governor John F. A. Strong appointed Stephen Foster of Minchumina Lake as the first game warden in the upper Kuskokwim–Kantishna area. Within a year, Foster claimed to have eliminated market hunting in the region. He pointed to his seizure of eight Dall sheep from meat hunters as proof of his success. His claim, like a lot of his talk, had little merit. Charles Sheldon regarded Foster's claims as "absurd," and said that "he was unfit to act as game warden."[6]

When the rare case did make it to trial, juries almost never returned a guilty verdict, or if they did so, the penalty was minor. In Fairbanks, for example, George Milich received a "hefty" fine—less than $100—for possessing ten sheep and parts of a moose. For every case successfully prosecuted, however, dozens more failed to reach trial. The public just did not see commercial hunting as wrong and, in fact, market hunters were often considered local heroes. In open defiance of the law, game meat was sold publicly in Fairbanks into the early 1920s.

The delicious and tender meat of Dall sheep, which tastes nothing like mutton, was in great demand in the Kantishna and other mining camps and boomtowns. These animals, named for naturalist William H. Dall, were remarkably abundant in Alaska's mountain ranges, and particularly so in the Mt. McKinley region. Very large herds inhabited areas unused today. The Nenana River gorge and plateau area, near the present day town of Healy, was the wintering ground for large herds of sheep. The Chitsia Range was called simply "the sheep hills" and on more than one occasion Joe Dalton killed sheep on the ridges above Eureka Creek. Population estimates for the area—which in 1917 became Mt. McKinley National Park—varied from 10,000 to 25,000, with one gross exaggeration of 50,000!

The actual number of sheep living in the region at that time will never be known but there is little doubt that the animals were much more numerous than today. At the head of the Teklanika River in 1906, for instance, Charles Sheldon saw an estimated 1,000 in a single day. Former market hunter John Romanov recalled that when he hunted the area, "sheep covered the hills." Adolph Murie who studied sheep in the park in the late 1930s said, "I feel confident . . . there were at least 5,000 sheep in the park during the peak, but it is possible that there were as many as 10,000."[7]

During the 20th Century, caribou in the Kantishna oscillated from scarcity to abundance. The reasons for the fluctuations are the subject of much speculation but at least one period of abundance seems to have had a discernible cause. A succession of fires—some started by lightning and others by prospectors—in the upper Kuskokwim drainage "destroyed the [plants] on which the vast herds feed . . . causing them to migrate to the country adjacent to Mt. McKinley and the headwaters of the Nenana River."[8]

In the years following the Kantishna strike, moose, wolves, and bears were less common in the central Alaska Range than they are today. The latter two species were held in check by the widespread use of poison. Moose along the Kantishna River, an area which Wickersham had described as "magnificent moose range," were nearly wiped out within the first two years of the Kantishna strike. Hunters shot every single moose they saw—cow, calf, or bull. The more numerous sheep and caribou were the main targets of commercial hunters. The largest bulls and biggest rams were prime targets. Small cows and ewes were killed routinely for camp meat, trapping bait, and dog food, or fed to penned foxes raised for their furs.

Although market hunters worked non-stop to fill the human demand for meat many more animals were killed for dog food. Almost every miner, merchant, and prospector supported a dog team. Dozens of dogs were kept in every camp and town. Out of sheer necessity, the dogs were fed dried salmon and game meat. In summer, a few men operated dog liveries where they cared for several teams. These dog yards were always located near abundant sources of game meat or fish. On the Savage Fork, Eli "Bill the Turk," Radovich, took care of 40 to 60 dogs, all belonging to various market hunters. "The Turk would shoot a sheep and drag it down to the dogs and when that was gone, he'd get another," Frank Glaser explained. Glaser, a former market hunter himself, counted the remains of 100 big rams near the Turk's camp but "didn't count the small ones."[9]

As mining in the Kantishna declined, and the local demand for meat slackened, market hunters utilized the trails cut by freighters and stampeders to access Fairbanks, Tanana, and other distant markets. In 1908, an estimated 15 to 20 outfits hunted the McKinley area for the Fairbanks market alone. Tom Steele and Lucke hunted the Teklanika River; Big Herman and Little Herman hunted several drainages; Radovich hunted the Savage Fork; Tom Strand hunted and trapped on the Savage Fork and the Nenana River; and a group of whites and Natives hunted the Toklat. "The Nenana Canyon was a regular slaughterhouse in the winter," one hunter remarked.[10]

Despite another revision of the Alaska Game Law in 1912, which prohibited the sale of game meat, except at roadhouses, market hunting continued unabated. In 1915, Hudson Stuck met two men near Nikolai with heavily laden sleds of Dall sheep they were hauling

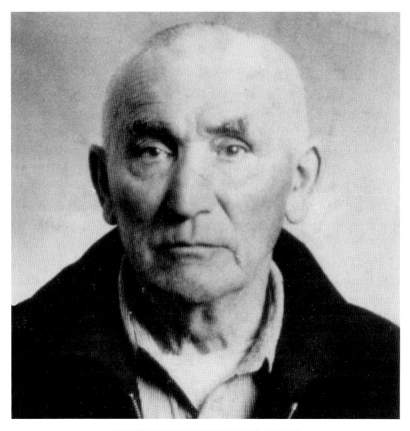

#75-209-38, ARCHIVES, UNIVERSITY OF ALASKA, FAIRBANKS

Eli Radovich, nicknamed "Billy the Turk," trapped and market hunted in the Kantishna and McKinley region from 1910–1935.

from the Alaska Range to the mining camps of Takotna and Iditarod. Kantishna trapper Slim Carlson sold sheep meat to the miners at Stony River and in one mining camp, another trapper counted 50 sheep in a single pile. Clearly the law meant nothing to most people.

Large scale market hunting occurred mostly in the winter, when the meat froze quickly and the dog trails were hard-packed. (In midsummer, hunters staged "drives" of molting waterfowl and killed large numbers of birds, mainly by clubbing.) Market hunters worked out of cabins and camps built on almost every drainage in the central Alaska Range. They shot from blinds near mineral licks or stalked sheep and caribou where they grazed. After killing a sheep or caribou, the hunters dragged the gutted and beheaded animal to a central gathering point for later shipment. They then spread strychnine-laced baits around the cache to protect the meat from carnivores like wolves and foxes. Once a sufficient quantity of meat had accumulated, the hunters loaded their freight sleds and headed to market. Within days they would return and begin hunting again. The use of strychnine by individuals, though outlawed, persisted sporadically into the 1930s. These poison baits killed everything from chickadees to grizzly bears. In 1903, Frederick Cook encountered a wolf that boldly walked right into his camp. For decades after the ban on poison such similar encounters were unknown due to the sheer scarcity of wolves.

Perhaps no one hunted the central Alaska Range harder than Steele and his partner Lucke, a former mail carrier that stampeded to the Kantishna around 1905. They used heavy freight sleds pulled by a dozen dogs to transport their loads of meat down the Toklat and over the Kantishna Trail to Fairbanks. The partners headquartered on the Teklanika River, which Athabascans called the Middle River. These two men were so closely associated with this drainage that old-timers called it the "Steele Fork." As late as 1920, Olaus Murie used "Steele Fork" as the proper name of this river.

Steele and Lucke reportedly killed hundreds of sheep, as well as moose and caribou. Steele, who in summer operated a ferry over the Chena River in Fairbanks, was said to be an extraordinary marksman. More than once he killed eight or ten rams out of a band without moving from his position. Once he killed 22 rams, all with head or neck shots, the preferred target area because it wasted none of the precious meat.

Steele eventually moved Outside, so Lucke partnered up for a time with Radovich. The two hunted moose in the forested lowlands where the Savage and Sanctuary Rivers wound out of the mountains. Lucke also hunted alone out of a crude cabin and a tent at the head of the Savage near Jenny Creek. A passerby in the early 1920s described what he saw at this cabin. "Many old sheep heads and quantities of skins lay scattered about" he wrote, "all evidences of the early-day slaughter."[11]

Lucke possessed a natural aptitude for the outdoors and adopted some Athabascan hunting tricks. Instead of calling moose in the rutting season, he lured in bulls by raking a dried moose shoulder blade through the brush to mimic the sound of antlers. In order to ambush moose he built tree stands near mineral licks or along well-used trails. He used every trick and technique he could think of to kill large numbers of animals. Judging by a telling comment that Lucke once made to a friend he was very successful. "Ya' read those stories [in sporting magazines] and those guys tell how far it was, how many bullets it took, where they hit the moose and all, but after ya' shot 400 moose, how in the hell do ya' know where ya' shot 'em?"[12]

Lucke also left a vivid published description of some of his exploits:

"From this point we went to a tributary of the Nenana River known as Middle River . . . [where] a hunter can see almost any day, large herds of caribou and sheep and it is not a matter of how many you can kill, but how many you care to kill.

". . . On this particular trip, we saw several herds of caribou, one five thousand head, and sheep in herds up to eight and nine hundred. We also saw a great many moose and bear. Of course, it is not necessary to say that we shot our limit of sheep and caribou, and killing seven more bear.

"On another hunting trip that I made in that region, I came back with a dog team bringing eight hundred pounds of sheep, but had the

COURTESY, JIM REARDEN, FRANK GLAZER COLLECTION

Market hunters used poison baits to protect their meat caches from predators. The baits killed everything from chickadees to grizzly bears. Wolves were relatively scarce in the years after the 1905 Kantishna stampede. This display of a trapper's fur catch in the 1920s is evidence of the resurgence of the region's furbearers.

misfortune to run into one
commissioner who senten
taking my meat, a further l
things come as the Alaska

Another small-time market hunter, Tom Strand, who came north during the Klondike stampede, lived in the region for decades, subsisting as a prospector, hard-rock miner, trapper, wood-cutter, and mail-carrier. His commercial hunting operation was a relatively small enterprise, never approaching the scale of Lucke's. He arrived in the Kantishna quite early, perhaps in 1904, but failed to make a big strike. Instead he labored on the claims of the lucky few. Because Strand was an excellent hunter he was often given the job of supplying meat for the camps. Strand hunted commercially for over two decades and, in just one fall, he reportedly killed 120 rams on the bluffs along the Nenana canyon.

Strand was born in Washington State on November 28, 1860, to Boedak Hicks, a Snohomish Indian, and Edward Strand, a Finn. On April 26, 1917, in Nenana Alaska, Tom Strand married Eva Henry, an Athabascan. At Ferry, on the Nenana River, the couple raised their four boys and four girls in traditional Athabascan style. Strand was a quiet, hardworking man and a stickler for the truth. He never "told stories," and believed in the power of a person's word. To him, a handshake was good as a written contract. By chance, this gold rush era Alaskan left his name on a significant regional landmark.

While laboring in the Kantishna mines, Strand had acquired an "also-known-as" name. There were several men named Tom working on one claim, and, as was customary in that era, some of them were given nicknames. Likely because of his heritage, Strand was christened "Tom Savage." He did not seem to find the nickname objectionable and sometimes even filed mining claims in that name. A few of his friends did not know him by any other name than Tom Savage. To this day, Denali National Park visitors hear many colorful stories that explain the origin of the name Savage River. Most of them are false and it is a rather ironic twist that the Denali National Park road crosses a landmark river named for the man who once market hunted there.[14]

Market hunting reached its zenith in the years just before America's involvement in World War I siphoned off Alaska's manpower. While l slaughter, anecdotal evidence [hidden] killed in the central Alaska Range near Kantishna. According to the testimony of reliable men and also evidenced by the numerous pairs of bleached horns which still remain in the vicinity of the many crude log shelters still extant along the Savage and Sanctuary Rivers, hundreds of sheep were slaughtered each year," Joseph Dixon wrote after completing the first detailed survey of the region's wildlife.[15]

While in the vicinity of Mt. McKinley, Stephen R. Capps of the U.S. Geological Survey witnessed the slaughter by three market hunters. He estimated that from 1914 through 1917, between 1,500 and 2,000 Dall sheep were killed in the "Toklat–Techlanika [sic] basins" for the Fairbanks markets.[16]

The Fairbanks warden disputed Capps, in essence saying that in the previous year no more than *twenty tons of sheep* had been sold in the area. When extrapolated from dressed weights these rebuttal figures equal 2,800 sheep in four years, with about 500 from the future park.[17]

The sheep slaughter in his "beloved" country angered and disturbed Sheldon and spurred his efforts to see the region protected. The whole idea of market hunting was anathema to his sportsman's ethic and conservation philosophy. The fledgling conservation movement he was a part of was based on a concept of wise use. Unregulated slaughter had all but extirpated the bison and bighorn sheep in the American west, and exterminated the Labrador duck, great auk, and Carolina parakeet in the east. Sheldon swore that he would not let the northern white sheep go the way of the passenger pigeon, whose flights in the millions once darkened the sky.

6

QUIGLEY OF KANTISHNA

Overnight, the thermometer had risen from -50°F to -20°F. Clouds had rolled in after dark and, by morning, a heavy snow was falling, obliterating the trail. Joe Quigley and Fannie McKenzie awoke hours before first light, grateful for the warmth of Old Marko's cabin. By 9 a.m., they were on the trail, fighting the snow and darkness. It was mid-November and, despite the recent cold snap, the Bearpaw River still had not frozen over completely. Mushing was treacherous.

Yesterday, Quigley and McKenzie had taken turns on snowshoes breaking trail for their eight-dog team. Overflow and thin ice forced many detours and delays. The partners were trail-wise and inured to hardship but the stabbing cold and hard work sapped their energy. The warm cabin and Marko's moose stew had revived them. Now Quigley was worried. It was almost balmy, compared to the cold snap just ended, but this new snow would hide thin ice, perhaps even cover a few spots of open water. A sudden dunking would freeze a hand or foot in minutes and the partners were still 15 long miles from their Glacier Creek cabin. Even if nothing went awry, the fresh snow meant that it would take two days instead of one to get home with their dogs and 900 pounds of freight.

In the darkness, Quigley broke trail cautiously, feeling for the trail with his snowshoes. He chopped off a six-foot-long sapling and where the trail curved down onto the river, he used it to probe for thin ice. Yesterday, he and McKenzie had alternated chores, but this morning, at least until first light, he would go first. McKenzie was

QUIGLEY COLLECTION, #80-46-244, ARCHIVES, UNIVERSITY OF ALASKA, FAIRBANKS

Loose sled dogs enjoy the warmth of spring breakup at Joe and Fannie's Glacier Creek cabin.

better with the dogs and he had a long stride that might distribute his weight better if he blundered onto thin ice.

As the morning slowly brightened the partners worked with heightened confidence. Once able to see most of the potential hazards ahead they picked up their pace. In mid-morning, Quigley saw the outlines of an intersecting trail under the snow and he swerved to follow it. With a hard base now underfoot, the going was a bit easier. At noon, the partners stopped and built a small fire. While Quigley boiled tea, McKenzie snacked the dogs with hunks of dried fish. In less than a half-hour, they were underway again, this time with McKenzie breaking trail.

For two hours, McKenzie broke trail through black spruce thickets and across muskeg swamps. Although slight of build and just five-foot tall, she never seemed to tire and could snowshoe as fast as her rangy partner. At one point she opened a 100-yard gap between herself and the team. When she came to a cutbank where the trail dropped back to the river, she suddenly stopped. Quigley saw her wave and pushed the dogs to catch up.

On the river ice below them was evidence of an accident that would blanch even the boldest musher. The outline of the trail they were following abruptly ended in open water. The jumbled ice at the margins of the breach, and the gear strewn across the ice on the far side, told the story. Someone had mushed onto the frozen river and broken through. It appeared that the musher had managed to extricate himself by emptying the sled so that the dogs could pull it out. The trail of the desperate musher disappeared into the timber on the far side of the oxbow. Quigley and McKenzie exchanged looks. Before today, the warmest day in the last two weeks had been -35°F, with lows to -60°F. A plunge into icy water in those temperatures meant a race with death.

Without a word, McKenzie turned left and broke a new trail along the top of the cutbank to the old trail where it left the river on the far side of the oxbow. Joe followed with the team. Just after they rejoined the trail, they stopped. In the timber was a lean-to covered with boughs. In front of it the blackened ends of spruce jutted through the snow marking where a giant fire had raged against the cold. This musher clearly had known what to do and was well prepared. Without an axe and matches the man would have died. Casting about through the woods, McKenzie found where the dogs had been unharnessed and staked out, a good sign that the musher could walk and had avoided freezing his feet and legs. Joe backtracked to view the freight strewn on the ice and was able to retrieve a few items.

The detour had cost trail time and daylight was fading fast. Unwilling to continue in the gloaming, they decided to make camp. Both were relieved that they had not found the unlucky musher frozen in the lean-to and the dogs starving. Nonetheless the find was a sobering reminder. The Kantishna in winter was clearly no place for the unwary.

In the aftermath of the Kantishna boom and bust, most of the dispirited stampeders returned to their former lives. Some of them joined the rush to the Iditarod and Flat strikes but many quit the gold fields forever. A few of the lucky ones who had found gold quit Alaska, never again to fight the isolation and bitter cold. Quigley and McKenzie, and a handful of other stampeders, settled in the Kantishna hills for good. Their lives were hard-scrabble, entailing subsistence hunting, wood gathering, mushing, fur trapping, and prospecting—always the prospecting.

Even by Alaska standards, the Kantishna District was isolated. Fairbanks, the main supply center for the entire region, was a long way away. Winter freighting was both hazardous and expensive. In summer, riverboat access was unreliable and costly. To live here required maximum resourcefulness and experience. Of all the Kantishna pioneers, Quigley and McKenzie became its best known residents, their story entwined with that of the great northern gold stampedes and the maturing of the Territory of Alaska.

Quigley arrived in Juneau by steamship in May 1891. The next year, this 22-year-old joined a party headed for the Fortymile River via the Chilkoot Pass. At Bennett Lake, his party whipsawed lumber and built crude boats for the float down the Yukon to the Fortymile.[1]

Quigley's often white-hot lust for gold took him to pioneer camps at Fortymile, Circle City, Dawson, Fairbanks, and finally the Kantishna. He was "always looking for a million-dollar mine, and never showing disappointment when we didn't find it," recalled one friend. His Quigley Gulch claim, just off the Klondike River above Dawson City, had been for him a tantalizing near-miss at great wealth.

Quigley's Kantishna strike helped lure hundreds of people into the hills, some of whom were old friends from earlier stampedes. He watched many of them leave the district broke and a few depart with heavy pokes. Although real wealth eluded him, he somehow maintained his optimism and faith in the rolling hills of the Kantishna. He would search there for decades for his own *El Dorado*.

Quigley, a superb prospector, never got his due regarding the Kantishna strike. His low-key approach to life allowed others to take the credit. Jack Horn was hailed as the "Father of the Kantishna," and Fred Hauselmann was regarded as the "Discoverer of Moose Creek gold." William Rhinehart took the credit for finding the district's incredible antimony deposits. Joe appeared uninterested in fame or notoriety, content to let others take the credit for his discoveries.

All bone and muscle, the 6'2" Quigley was well-suited to the life. This former Pennsylvanian easily could walk 30 miles a day while carrying a 30-pound pack. "Joe was a regular mountain goat in hiking," Edgar Brooker, Jr., wrote. "We went light and ate light," on a hike to the Nenana River from Kantishna. Even at age 55, Joe could walk the 80-plus miles from Kantishna to the railroad in one 24-hour day.[2]

When his placer gold claims petered out Quigley turned his full interest to quartz prospecting and mining. He enjoyed reading and

DENALI PARK AND PRESERVE, MUSEUM COLLECTION, #3511

Joe Quigley rests at the gee pole on the front of his dogsled while freighting supplies to his Kantishna mining property in mid-winter.

was always eager to learn something new. He devoured books on hard rock mining and collected books on geology, mineralogy, and mining. He purchased an assaying outfit and learned to be a scientific prospector. He mastered the chemistry of a hard rock miner, the use of cyanide and mercury to separate gold from quartz.

Area miners respected the soft-spoken Quigley for his honesty and reliability. He was generous to a fault and often went out of his way to do others a favor. Once, while hiking past a cabin on McKinley Bar and noticing that the food cache had fallen over, scattering a year's supply of food, he went right to work to salvage the goods. "Although it meant he would probably miss the mining engineers he wanted very much to see," the owner recalled, "Joe didn't hesitate but started the long job of carrying my grub into the cabin."[3]

Quigley was no recluse. He possessed a lively humor and shared with his many friends his collection of Alaskan stories and wildlife photographs. McKenzie, one of the original Kantishna stampeders, was drawn to this likeable, easy-going man.

Fannie Sedlacek was born March 18, 1871, on a homestead in Wahoo, Nebraska. She grew up speaking Czech and learned English only after she left to work her way west along the railroad. Fannie, then 27, stampeded for the Klondike over the daunting Chilkoot Pass. By the time she reached Dawson City all the creeks were staked for miles around. Likely broke and hungry, she went to work first as a dancehall girl, then housekeeper and cook.

She obtained a miner's certificate, entitling her to stake her own claims and, in early 1900, staked claim #39 Below Discovery on Clear Creek, nearly 130 miles from Dawson.

On her return to Dawson later that year, Fannie married Angus McKenzie. In 1901, the two operated McKenzie Roadhouse on Hunker Creek's claim #18 Below. Violent alcohol-fueled arguments quickly wrecked the marriage. Within the first year, Fannie had Angus arrested for assault and drunk and disorderly conduct. Angus told the court he was "drunk but not intoxicated." Fannie quit Angus for good in January 1903, when she stampeded to the new Chena River strike.[4]

Over the next few years Fannie McKenzie chased the smaller stampedes out of Fairbanks. She hauled her tent, Yukon stove, sacks of flour, bacon, and beans by boat or dog sled to the new diggings. Her simple sign—*MEALS FOR SALE*—lured in passersby hungry for both good food and the rare sight of a woman. Apparently her peripatetic ways earned her the nickname "*Fannie the Hike*," although a more ribald explanation for the nickname exists. (One old-timer said she got it by "hiking her skirts in Dawson.")

The Kantishna was her last stampede. In her cabin/restaurant on Glacier Creek—described as "Mother McKenzie's log palace"—she fed miners, laborers, and travelers but her best customer was Quigley, whom she had first met near Fairbanks. McKenzie and Quigley eventually partnered up.[5]

From 1907 to 1919, McKenzie staked over two dozen Kantishna lode and placer claims. On February 2, 1918, Quigley and McKenzie were married by Commissioner J. C. Van Orsdel at Glacier Creek. When the creek's placer ground played out that year, the Quigleys moved to a high bench overlooking Friday Creek, which locals had re-named Schaupp Creek. This new home site offered easy access to their lode claims on Quigley Ridge and was Fannie's home for the next 30 years. "Sometime this mine will be worked, and I will be a rich woman," Quigley once said. When asked what she would do then, she replied, "First, I am going to go to Fairbanks and drink all the beer I want for a whole month!"[6]

The Quigleys lived off the land. Both were excellent shots and Fannie's hunting prowess made news. One year, she shot "two big bull moose, one caribou, and a black bear, in addition to a great deal of other game . . . [she] declared that next year she will bag everything allowed by the law."[7]

Fannie's strength and ability had impressed even the indefatigable Charles Sheldon. In 1908, Joe and Fannie had hunted Dall sheep with him on Polychrome Mountain. "I went hunting with [her] and after an arduous climb, which she made as easy as any man, we came close to a band of 34 sheep," Sheldon recalled, "the [partners] came back with two ewes and a yearling ram, quite delighted with this supply of sheep meat to take to their mining cabin."[8]

Joe Quigley seldom hunted bears, probably because he had been treed by a bear in the Fortymile country. Quigley never "killed a bear for revenge, but he surely wouldn't back off from one so long as he had his trusty rifle and plenty of cartridges," an old-timer said. Fannie, however, avidly sought black bears in the autumn berry season and rendered their fat into cooking lard, an ingredient that reputedly made her piecrusts especially delicious.[9]

DENALI PARK & PRESERVE, CULTURAL RESOURCES COLLECTION, WILDERNESS OF DENALI

On a winter sheep hunting trip Joe Quigley and Fannie McKenzie visit Charles Sheldon's Toklat River cabin, 1908.

Game could be scarce. One year, after several fruitless days of hunting, the Quigleys split up and went different directions. By dark, Fannie had killed two caribou, a bear, and a moose. The next morning she tossed Joe a skirt and said, "Here, you do the housework. I'm the hunter in this family. Gimme [sic] your pants."[10]

Fannie once shot a moose from her back porch. While lugging the meat up to the cabin, she found a gold nugget worth $60. "Heck!" she said, "I seen the dern thing layin' there all the time—but I just didn't believe it. Friday Creek's been worked four times."[11]

One mythic hunt forever sealed Fannie's place in the pantheon of pioneer heroes. Late one frigid winter afternoon, Fannie shot a moose and set to work eviscerating it. Gutting a moose is tough and exhausting labor and night fell before she finished her chore. Now, bloody and sweat-soaked, she knew that she would never make it home without freezing. She looked for a bivouac site and saw nothing promising. She then focused on the steaming carcass. She pulled her parka tight about her and wriggled into the body cavity. That night the temperature plummeted but the moose's dissipating body heat kept her warm. Early the next morning, she hacked and cussed her way out of the half-frozen moose. She was cold, stiff, and reeked of moose but she had survived.[12]

During the fall grayling migration, Fannie netted and preserved fish for winter use. What food the couple did not shoot or catch, Fannie grew. Her garden on Glacier Creek had been outstanding but her garden on the slope above Friday Creek gained renown. Because the soil on the hillside was poor, she gathered dirt from Moose Creek's flood plain and hauled it home by dog team or backpack. In dry spells, she toted water up from the creek. She terraced her garden with rocks, forming a series of beds. The sun warmed the rocks during the day and at night they radiated heat, warming the soil. She grew potatoes, strawberries, rhubarb, cabbage, turnips, and ornamental plants like pansies. She pressed many of her finest flowers and used them for embroidery reference, a skill she had learned in Nebraska. "I wish that you could see the lettuce, Cauliflower and Celery," she wrote Charles Sheldon. "Ever [sic] man has a garden in the camp."[13]

Scurvy was a pioneer scourge. In some cases, men lost their teeth and sometimes their limbs turned black and useless. Some pioneers believed in the curative power of an all-meat diet, which only worsened their vitamin C deficiency. Autumn berries provided some of the needed vitamins. Fannie picked gallons of wild blueberries and cranberries, prepared them in jellies and jams, and preserved them whole. "I pickled 12 hundred pounds of berrys [sic] last summer so we have berrys [sic] last tel [sic] new year come and vegetables."[14]

Fannie stored her meat, produce, blueberry wine, and homebrew in a three-room tunnel near her cabin and in barrels sealed with tallow. Although she annually filled her cold storage with the harvest, staples had to be freighted in twice a year. On infrequent trips to town, Fannie gossiped with other women and read the latest newspapers. "I went to Fairbanks in February. That was my first trip to town in 7 years," she wrote in 1913. "I tell you I got lonesome. I have not seen an automobile yet."[15]

This indomitable woman also cut and hauled much of the firewood for the hillside cabin. She wrote her sisters that she cut all the wood for four wood stoves at the camp, just to keep fit. "Her strength seemed more an ironclad stubbornness of will than any physical attribute," wrote a biographer.[16]

For cash, Fannie ran a winter trapline. She taught others how to identify red, silver, or cross foxes by their tracks. "The red fox," she told one partner, "has a big foot; a silver, a small tight foot with very little hair around the toes; and a cross fox, being a cross between a red and silver, may have a neater foot than a red, but usually not so dainty as a full silver." She had her facts wrong—the colors are all variations of the same animal—but it did not prevent her from becoming one of the best trappers in the area.[17]

Each of her tiny trapline cabins was equipped in the same way, with a small sheet-iron Yukon stove, frying pan, a coffeepot, and mush pot. A typical trapline breakfast included rolled oats, bacon, and either sourdough hot cakes or bannocks. When leaving the cabin, she always hung a package of dry groceries from the ridgepole, with a flat tin over the top to keep squirrels and rodents out. If she could not reach a cabin, Fannie sometimes slept in her sled wrapped in her sleeping roll, even in brutal sub-zero cold.

Fannie never hesitated to kill what she caught. This became a problem when she tried to teach Lois McGarvey, a Fairbanks seamstress, all the trapping secrets: what to use for bait, where and how to set traps, tips for disguising human scent, and how to skin and stretch fur.

After introducing McGarvey to the trapping arts, Fannie sent her down one trail, while she went down another. Fannie's new partner came to a set holding a silvery lynx whose fur would bring $150. She pulled out a .22 pistol and carefully approached the lynx, which was caught by only one toe. McGarvey needed the money but could not pull the trigger. Instead "[I] reached out and got my end of the trap chain and gave a mighty jerk. Off came the lynx's toenail, and away [it] went . . . I looked nervously behind me, and there stood [Fannie] watching the lynx disappear. 'Now, that is just enough of you!' she said. 'I knew something was screwy, as I gave you the best part of the line. You can just go to h— back where you came from! You are a sissy, and better go into a sissy business!'"[18]

If nothing else, Fannie's cooking made her famous. She liked to cook and treated almost any passerby to a meal. Mining engineer Ernest Patty once spent two weeks examining the Quigleys' claims. Each morning Fannie prepared "oatmeal, a big stack of hotcakes, and stewed wild rhubarb, dried peaches or dried apricots, sometimes with a few raisins added," he recalled. Dinner would feature game meat, but Patty knew enough not to ask what kind of meat was being served. If a porcupine came along, she would kill it, clean it, and put it in a big crock, seal it with lard, and store it in one of her tunnels. "You never knew what she'd dig up," Fritz Nyberg said.[19]

"Never knew what meat you were eating," another man recalled, "and never asked." During one dinner, a female guest asked about the grouse they were eating. Fannie nodded her head politely and when no one was looking, winked at another guest as if to say, "If I tell her it's porcupine she'll probably get sick and die on me."[20]

Usually one taste of Mother Quigley's specialties quieted the wary. "For the greatest delicacy in the world, some claim caviar, others like crab meat, some claim quail, but all doubts on this score will banish after one feast of moose's nose," a newspaper account said, in reference to Fannie's favorite.[21]

A typical Christmas dinner consisted of black bear roast, gravy, mashed potatoes, fresh cabbage, hot rolls, currant jelly, cranberry sauce, and fresh blueberry shortcake, with only the flour and sugar freighted in.

Fannie had no tolerance for finicky eaters and would not tolerate waste. "I believe in folks' cleaning up their plates," McGarvey quoted her as saying. "Nothing makes me madder than to have people push this to the edge of their plates, and that to the edge of their plates, and leave it!"[22]

One person neatly trimmed off all the fat from a thick caribou chop. "I can't eat any more fat," the guest said. "Oh, that's all right," Fannie replied, "I'll just fry it over for your breakfast."²³

"If she liked you Fannie Quigley was a wonderful cook," Denise Abbey recalled. "If she didn't like you, heaven help you. I can't tell you what a bad cook she was. Often she had very bad food which she made worse." A few people avoided her cooking completely. "Nobody would eat her cooking," Pete Bagoy added, "enough to gag you. It was awful."²⁴

Every guest got a meal, drink, and a story. "You eat it all," she told a visitor, "or you get the same plate next meal with the grub still on it." Fannie then pointed to a cross on the skyline near the cabin and said, "See that . . . That guy starved to death trying to mine [Eureka] creek." When the visitor expressed disbelief, she replied: "He had a weak stomach; couldn't eat my cooking."²⁵

Joe was a good cook, his sourdough bread and hot cakes a specialty. When Fannie was laid up with a broken leg, Joe did all the cooking and suffered few complaints from his partner.

You never had to strain to hear Fannie talk and she could be heard "two miles away." In the 1930s a surveyor remarked on her vocal ability. "We called her 'Foghorn Annie,'" he said, "because you could hear her half-way to park headquarters." Joe Burns operated a movie house in Nenana in the 1920s. On her annual trips to town, Fannie would attend the "flickers." "Fannie, with a dress on top of her overalls would, in a loud voice, explain what the movie was all about and what was going to happen next. No one had the nerve to ask her to keep quiet," one person remembered.²⁶

When Fannie broke her leg and had to go into Fairbanks for treatment, she was happy to return home where she did not "need to lower her high, ringing voice to conversational tones . . ."²⁷

Years of toil inured Fannie to hardship. "There was something about her that . . . resembled well-cured sinew," McGarvey said. "Her skin was brown and lined, and the muscles of her arms showed through her sleeves."²⁸

"She lived the wild life as the men did, and was as much at home in the open as a city woman is on a city avenue," wrote climber Belmore Browne in 1913, "and she could not only follow and hunt successfully the wild game of the region but she could do a man's share in packing the meat to camp. From a physical standpoint she was a living example of what nature had intended a woman to be . . ."[29]

Alcohol was a life-long problem, however. With a, "Here, Jack, have a drink," Fannie served guests homebrew or grain alcohol. An itinerant preacher once offered to send Fannie a case of chocolate in repayment for her hospitality. "What's your favorite brand?" he asked her. "Schlitz," she replied.[30]

"Both Fannie and Joe liked their booze . . . Fannie at great cost and trouble had acquired enough beer bottles, caps, malt and other ingredients to brew up home made beer . . . Joe was not in favor of her making and getting boozed up on beer, but somehow just before Joe would return home from hunting or prospecting, Fannie would hide the beer—except for one occasion when he had been away about a week and returned from Fairbanks," one visitor recalled. "The stock of beer was out in plain view. Fannie was plastered. Joe broke all of the bottles, a real calamity. At 100 miles from civilization, beer bottles are priceless."[31]

Fannie's compassionate heart was camouflaged by her gruff facade—the greater the emergency, the crustier her language. "It's a good thing that her dogs could not understand English," Abbey commented, "because she would curse them unmercifully, even while playfully scratching their ears! Whenever she went out to hitch up her team, my dad told us to come home."[32]

One winter, a Fairbanks teacher asked Fannie to visit the school and talk to the students. Because "she had so many swear words" they only let her speak to one class. Despite her vexing language, Fannie was genuine and sincere, a truly great personality. "I [carried] the conviction that I had never known a more indomitable soul than Fannie Quigley," said Patty, a mining engineer and personal friend. "She had enough energy, courage, and intelligence to supply a dozen women."[33]

"Her vocabulary made all of us blush," wrote one visitor. "Yet she was highly respected and by many dearly loved for her integrity, kindness of heart and general goodness."[34]

Over the decades, Fannie's reputation grew to mythic proportions, but a letter written to her sister Mary Katherine McClean in Washington State reveals a touching humanity:

Glacier Creek, July 23, 1909.

My Dear Sister Marry,

 I recived your letter some time ago and was sorry to hear that you lost your little Girl you didnt say what happn to her and whatsh one you lost. I have not been very good this summer I have been having teeth ack and there is no one to fixt them here. I hope that you are geting long better then I am. I think that I have to come out and get me home some ware in Wash or Oregon I get lonesome sometime I dont see any woman there is only one here and she lives 12 miles from here. I cant leave my place so long to go to see her She was over last May. I got only 8 [boarders] this summer I dont know how my claim is going to turn out I didnt get much last fall I am bicy fruiting up berrys now and I got big garden. And 5 dogs to cook for and 8 men so it keeps me going all day. if there was little more Money there I would like to have you come out here for year or so. you would have to learn how to Shout Rifle and 22 so you could get your onew meat, last fall I got 2 bid moose and 12 sheep I never got to kill Bear.

 will I must close for this time write soon so i could get letter this fall you see we get only one mail this spring that 25 Aperl my Best wishes to you all, your sister

Fannie McKenzie
Chena Alaska[35]

Decades later, however, she told a would-be prospector she did not have the time to get lonesome. "The first time I saw the Kantishna I knew that was where I belonged. I'll die here Jack. There's not a hill . . . I haven't had my boots on . . ."[36]

With her callused hands, weathered brow, and salty language, Fannie became a legend in her own time. In her latter years, some people referred to her as "the little witch of Denali." "Yet she neither looked nor acted like a witch," Patty said. "During the day Fannie worked with a bandanna wrapped around her hair, a man's woolen shirt, and overalls tucked into rubber shoe-pacs," he continued, "but in the evenings her hair would be nicely combed and she would always wear an immaculate housedress. But if you glanced down, you would see the shoe-pacs sticking out below the hem of her skirt."[37]

Kantishna mining transactions were rather incestuous. The Quigleys bought from Dalton; Dalton sold to Stiles; Lloyd bought from Taylor; Taylor and Lloyd dealt with McGonagall. Properties switched hands from one old-timer to another, each thought they would be the one to find the mother lode. The focus of activity shifted from Moose Creek, and the Eureka camp, to Glen Creek.

Whenever either of the Quigleys staked a claim, or conducted a transaction, they hiked over to the recorder's office on Glen Creek. William Robert Lloyd, the *ex officio* recorder, enjoyed the trust of everyone. Billy, an Englishman, came north in 1888 to the Fortymile. He followed strike after strike—the Fortymile, Circle, Fairbanks, and then Kantishna.

Lloyd wrote the miners' ditty, *Are You Rockin' Every Day?* which was sung in saloons from the Klondike to Nome. It became the anthem of the Order of Pioneers of the Yukon and the Order of Alaska Pioneers. This ode to the "rocker," a basic stampeder's mining implement, contained the refrain:

> What do you do with your gold dust?
> What do you do with your pay?
> Tell me, are you rocking,
> Rocking every day?[38]

On one trip, Joe and Fannie found Billy Lloyd suffering from "stomach trouble." Fannie, known locally for her nursing skills, did what she could with her home remedies but Billy died in B. Taylor's cabin on June 14, 1914.

Old-timers remembered Lloyd, who had owned a saloon in Circle City, as generous and sweet-tempered. "His memory will live long in every camp in the far North, for he was known and respected in all of them . . . No more will Billy Lloyd sing the old song . . . which

STR. MINNEAPOLIS

WILL SAIL FOR

KANTISHNA RIVER POINTS

*Including McKinley City
and Bear Paw*

THURSDAY, SEPT. 14TH 1906
7 pm

THIS IS ONE OF THE BEST STEAMERS ON THE TANANA RIVER, PLENTY OF ROOM FOR FREIGHT AND PASSENGERS. THE SEASON IS NEARLY OVER FOR STEAMBOATING AND THOSE DESIRING TO GET INTO THE NEW CAMP SHOULD TAKE ADVANTAGE OF THE PRESENT MODERATE RATES.

CALDERHEAD & HALL, AGENTS

The year following the gold stampede, the FAIRBANKS DAILY TIMES *ran this advertisement for river transport to the Kantishna District. Exorbitant freight costs coupled with unreliable service greatly hindered mineral development in the remote Kantishna Mining District.*

he sang from the Klondike to Fairbanks, to the delight of every old sourdough who heard it. His heart went out in that song . . . visions of the golden days in the diggings and the music of running sluices and creaking rockers moved those around him . . ."[39]

Only a handful of people, among them Joe and Fannie Quigley, attended Billy Lloyd's burial. They had seen friends die from exposure, freezing, drowning, mining accidents, and violence. Some had simply disappeared into the sullen silence of the north. Now it was their beloved Billy, just another man, buried somewhere in the Kantishna hills, the grave unmarked and soon unremembered.

7
COMMUNITY IN ISOLATION

ALBERT MAURICE lay in his bunk dying. Paroxysms of coughing left him weak and gasping for breath. He huddled under his fouled and filthy woolen blankets and caribou robes praying for the rescue that would never come. It was mid-winter; the snow was deep, and the cold brutal, well below -40°F. After the last fire in the wood stove went out his cabin cooled to a point barely above the outside temperature.

Maurice, a Swiss immigrant, came to North America during the rush of 1898 and had never returned home. Like so many others, he followed the series of stampedes. He was trapping on the Kantishna River when his health failed. His illness—perhaps tuberculosis—attacked remorselessly and left him helpless. His final notes convey his desperation:

> February 4th
>
> All in. Can not get to wood pile.
> So I either have got to freeze, or shoot myself.
>
> Albert Maurice
>
> 5th
>
> have postponed hoping that some one would come
> but no one did. Can't go any further
> all the wood in cabin is gone.
>
> A.M.

> it is rather a joke to have a bunch of wood
> within 10 [feet] of the door and can't get it
> I cannot go three steps but my wind give out
> and I drop any place for fifteen or twenty
> minutes before I am able to go on a step
> further.
>   A.M.¹

Within hours after the last scrawled note, Maurice shot himself. His body was not found until weeks later. Fear of the terrible agony of frozen limbs—common injuries for men of the trail—drove him to suicide. He had witnessed what the frost could do to human flesh: missing toes, fingers, parts of ears, and blackened and scarred noses and cheeks. The cold maimed for life. Joseph Brochu, who had lost both feet to the frost, was only alive because of the help of friends.

STEPHEN FOSTER COLLECTION, #69-92-276, ARCHIVES, UNIVERSITY OF ALASKA, FAIRBANKS

Early Kantishna mining partners, Fred Hauselmann and Alois Keim persevered on Little Moose Creek for almost two decades. Isolation exacted a terrible toll. In 1922, Keim died alone in his small cabin after a long, agonizing bout with stomach cancer. That same year the sweet-natured Hauselmann, a Swiss, was judged "insane" and shipped to Oregon's Morningside Hospital for treatment. When he returned to the Kantishna a year later he discovered his claims and property in the possession of another miner. Keim's death coupled with his erroneous belief that another friend, Rudolph Lambert, had been murdered, apparently triggered Hauselmann's temporary mental illness.

Maurice took his own life to avoid the same—or worse—fate as his friend Brochu. Although he died by his own hand, Maurice was equally a part of winter's grim harvest.

Before World War I, less than 3,000 white men wandered the Alaskan wilderness. Many of these men went to town for supplies once a year; otherwise they lived in isolation. Even the most independent and boldest men recognized that a minor accident in the wilderness could result in gruesome death or dismemberment. As a result, many trappers and prospectors worked in pairs, a partnership borne of necessity rather than friendship. Because of tales of abandonment and treachery, partners often wrote contracts that required each man to care for the other in case of illness or injury, and share in any expenses incurred. Maurice lived alone; his rescue would have been Providential.

The reasons why so many people stayed in the unforgiving northern wilderness varied from person to person. A few people could never return home, fearing either the law, or the retribution of a family tragically left in the lurch by the rush for gold. Wanderlust gripped others with the thrill of discovery and exploration. Others, their quest for wealth turned to ashes, simply never accumulated enough money to leave. Apart from the lure of gold, an elusive chimera at best, the territory offered an opportunity to succeed on a very basic level. Back in the States many stampeders would have had minimal prospects for ever escaping the bonds of poverty. In Alaska, however, with hard work a person could have a simple home, food on the table, and an un-fettered freedom. Here an individual could chase dreams without the hobbling laws and regulations even then viewed as sapping the country's pioneer spirit. An independent life, or a life in self-imposed exile, required a daily joust with nature's implacable forces.

Not everyone who stayed in the Kantishna led lives as rewarding or good as that of the Quigleys. Many led hardscrabble lives. Table fare might have been solely "rapid-fire, smokeless strawberries," a common term for beans, and porcupine, but at least there was food. After the initial rush of 1905 subsided, the Kantishna community evolved into a widely scattered collection of cabins and camps without a centralized town. The boom settlements were ghost towns and only a few claims, such as those at Friday and Eureka Creeks, boasted more than one or two inhabitants. For two decades, the total area population seldom topped three dozen people. Neighbors often lived miles apart with gatherings a rarity. There were no restaurants, saloons, or social halls to entwine people; instead a sense of community was forged through travail. These pioneers were a disparate lot, of varied nationalities and opinions, with their only common trait a shared lifestyle. Some of these men were close friends, others bitter rivals and often openly antagonistic. Nonetheless, Kantishnans came to depend on one another in time of emergency and need. These resourceful and hardy people were not immune to illness and accident. Without a doctor or clinic, Kantishnans doctored themselves or relied on distant neighbors for help. Nursing was a community effort and medicine a pooled resource. Mother McKenzie, as Fannie Quigley was known before her marriage, alleviated the suffering of many of her neighbors with concoctions she made or bought with donations. Anyone going to Fairbanks would post a sign asking for $5 pledges to buy communal bandages, unguents, and painkillers.

Until after the end of World War I, a cluster of cabins at Glen Creek was the only semblance of a "town" in the district. This swift and narrow south-flowing tributary of Moose Creek was mined by several area pioneers, notably Charles McGonagall, William Taylor, Tom Lloyd, and Pete Anderson. Other miners and trappers built cabins in the thin spruce along the creek and near its confluence with Moose Creek. Here, in time, was the U.S. Commissioner and recorder's office, and post office, all in one cabin. Letters to residents were addressed, Glen, Alaska.

Placer deposits first lured prospectors to the creek. Here they worked shallow gravel up to three feet deep with pay streaks that ranged from 30 to 150 feet wide. The stream seemed to have great potential and a bright future. Intrigued by the possibilities, in 1910 Judge Wickersham bought four claims near Discovery. To his disappointment, however, the richest placer claims were quickly exhausted. Lode claims on the slopes of Glacier Peak at the head of the bifurcated creek raised hopes of finding the elusive mother lode. Lloyd and Taylor's 1906 Glen Prospect was the first exciting find on the peak. John Stendahl developed a promising gold- and silver-bearing quartz vein on his nearby Humboldt Prospect. McGonagall also staked a claim on the slopes. In the end, the mother lode never materialized to the extent everyone had hoped.

Community in Isolation 101

DAWSON CITY MUSEUM

In this portrait of a meeting of the Yukon Order of Pioneers, taken in Fortymile in 1895, are several notable pioneers, including trading legends Al Mayo, top right, and L.M. "Jack" McQuesten, seated front row middle. Saloonkeeper "Grizzly" Bill McPhee, who one day would be considered for the position of Mt. McKinley National Park's first superintendent, is seated second from left. Because he allegedly encouraged men to drink into insolvency he was not universally admired. At least two others in this picture stampeded to the Kantishna in 1905. On the far left is trader Gordon Bettles. The man standing third from the right is William "Billy" Lloyd who died and was buried at Glen Creek.

For most residents life in the hills was often lonely. A year after the stampede the Kantishna was a community of men with only three women in the entire district. A dozen years after the big strike the situation had not changed. Knute Lind no doubt expressed the sentiment of many when he wrote his brother: "I would advise you to bring your girl friend, because we have hardly any women here and the ones that's [sic] here are very ugly looking . . ."[2]

Some prospectors were by nature reclusive and the day-to-day hardships and isolation turned others that way. A few notable exceptions were gregarious and nonstop talkers with any excuse good enough for a gabfest. John Bowman's story was typical of the era. He had once made a small fortune in the Klondike but had lost it all. In a single night in a Dawson saloon, he had blown "one or two thousand dollars" in gold. From Dawson, he went to the Koyukuk and from there to the Kantishna, but never struck it rich again. The loquacious Bowman was often the target of practical jokes. On one of his birthdays, a crony on Slate Creek frosted a wooden cake. After a few glasses of homebrew and repeated attempts to cut the cake, Bowman declared, "It musht be froshen."[3]

Except for the reclusive hard cases most everyone was anxious for news and visitors. Alex Mitchell, a Scot, operated a still and sold homebrew from his Moose Creek cabin. In the timber behind the cabin, he tended a small garden. He welcomed visitors like prodigal sons. Charles Sheldon and Harry Karstens visited Mitchell who served them his wine and a superb blueberry pie. Years later they exchanged stories of the "Pie Man."

Mitchell's hospitality was widely known. Travelers all got a bunk, meal, and a pie but had to listen to Mitchell's lengthy recitations of Robert Burns' poetry, which earned him the nickname "the Bard of the Kantishna." As the "hootch" flowed, the poetry gathered passion and volume. (The infamous and ubiquitous pioneer homebrew, called "hootch" was made with molasses, dried fruit or berries, fermented with sourdough.)

Mitchell's tiny cabin was neat and spotless. He lighted his cabin with candles and a kerosene lamp. He loved to read things he could sink his teeth into, as he liked to say, and enjoyed the Atlantic, Harper's Monthly, Scribner's, North American, and Century magazines, all of which he read over and over. "It's a long wolf howl from Nenana to the lake and trash is not worth hauling," he told a visitor in his latter years. Mitchell said that his sister in Ontario had once mailed him a cake, which he received ten months later. Perhaps to rectify such unreliable service, Mitchell sporadically contracted to haul the district's mail.

As much as he loved to read, Mitchell suffered from poor eyesight and a doctor told him not to read after 9:00 p.m. His solution was to set his clock back three hours. Each day he arose for breakfast at 3:00 a.m. and went to bed promptly at 9:00 p.m., which was actually midnight by everyone else's time.

The Bard worked claims on Moose, Granite, and Glen Creek, and, in winter trapped out of a line cabin in Big Timber on the McKinley River. Each spring before the snow melted, Mitchell sledded in his supplies from Duke's Trading Post or Fairbanks, traveling the long way around through the Thorofare divide. One year, he began freighting in March and made three round trips before the end of April, the temperatures between -30°F and -50°F the entire time. His life of subsistence hunting, trapping, and mining was typical.

Famine was common in isolated mining camps, especially at freeze-up and break-up when travel was difficult or impossible. Surviving a winter in the wilderness required planning and the proper gathering and storing of food supplies. Unanticipated events could lead to catastrophe. In the winter of 1914, a distemper outbreak decimated the area's dog teams. Miners combined surviving dogs and pieced together teams to haul freight. Athabascans camped at the head of the Kantishna River lost almost all of their dogs to distemper. They faced starvation because they had no way to move their large village or haul in substantial amounts of meat and supplies. Twenty children were at risk. Area miners provided what assistance they could but had little to spare. Prospector Tom Savage loaned villagers his three dogs so that they could haul in a man with a broken leg. On the return journey two of Savage's dog died of distemper but the injured man made it safely back to camp.

Inevitably the region's isolation and privation led to feuds and petty squabbles. Partnerships broke up over the simplest tasks. Heated quarrels in mid-winter destroyed friendships, which led to division of property. By necessity, some partners continued to share their tiny one-room log cabin but divided it down the middle by an imaginary line. Weeks went by without a shared word. Petty arguments sometimes led to violence and tragedy.

In late April 1909, a breathless William Kuhn rushed into Fred Brelle's cabin at Eureka Creek and cried out that he had been in a "scuffle" with Billy Rhinehart. Kuhn said that Rhinehart had threatened him with a knife. Kuhn said he broke free, then rushed to his "sleigh" and pulled out his rifle. "[I] . . . seen Rhinehart standing in the door with his gun so [I] fired . . . Rhinehart said [now] 'you did it' and then [I] fired again and ran, thinking Rhinehart after me . . ." Kuhn pleaded with Brelle for help. Several miners rushed to Rhinehart's cabin at the mouth of Eldorado Creek. They found Kuhn's cap and dogteam outside the front door and Rhinehart dead in a pool of blood on the cabin floor. They also found Rinehart's rifle hanging in the rack over his bed.[4]

Daniel Koch took Kuhn to Commissioner Foster at Glacier Creek. Foster held an inquest but could secure only three jurors and three witnesses, "as all of the other miners had gone to the hills hunting or prospecting to avoid serving on the case." Foster's mini-jury found that Rhinehart had died of two gun shot wounds from ". . . a .30-40 Winchester rifle in the hands of William Kuhn." It took two men three days to dig Rhinehart's grave in the frozen ground near the mouth of Eldorado Creek.[5]

At his trial in Fairbanks, Kuhn claimed self-defense. Critical testimony focused on the rifle found hanging on the wall. Despite this contradiction to Kuhn's earlier statement that Rhinehart had threatened him with the rifle, the jury found him not guilty.

The dark and brutal winter, coupled with isolation, drove many men mad, at least temporarily. (The widespread use of liquid mercury for extracting gold may explain in part the almost epidemic level of insanity rampant in Alaska in that era.) Without regular mail service, social gathering places, radio, or the diversions of town life, it was no surprise that suicides occurred with alarming frequency. It will never be known what drove Albert Morris to kill himself in 1913—he left no note of explanation. No one knows why John Evan shot himself on Birch Creek. Cabin fever is an easy, but convenient, explanation. Haljmar "Slim" Carlson, an even-keeled man, explained that "lots of men" went crazy, or "got bushed," but "I never felt lonely by myself. Once in awhile, there'd be a blue spell, but I'd get over that." Carlson explained that the secret was to possess a good disposition and never worry about tomorrow, but live fully in the present. He went on to say that he talked to himself on occasion but did not answer. "When a man starts to answer himself, that's the time to make a move real quick—that's the time a man gets bushed."[6]

One key to sound mental health was activity. The hibernators—men who simply waited out the winter—were the ones who ended up "shaking hands with the willows," as the pioneers said. To avoid madness or boredom, a few residents immersed themselves in intense labor, no matter the darkness and outside temperature. Bowman one winter cut firewood until he had a pile bigger than his cabin and kept right on cutting and hauling until spring breakup. With little else to do in winter, almost everyone set at least a few traps or snares. In marginal mining camps like the Kantishna, the fur trade eventually became both a common occupation and an economic mainstay.

Trapping was—and is—a tough life: a battle with cold, darkness, and weather extremes. Miles of trails had to be cut and packed on foot or by dogteam, cabins built and maintained, animals skinned, furs prepared and dried. On an hourly basis, most trappers made pennies. A winter's outfit for a full time trapper cost anywhere from $1600 to $2000, and for many trappers a good catch meant a few hundred dollars profit to buy badly needed goods. As a financial incentive to trap wolves, which were thought to be exterminating large prey species, the territorial legislature in 1915 initiated bounty payments.

Over the years, fur prices increased to the point where a trapper could make a living catching foxes, whose "stylish" fur went for exceptional prices. In 1912, Mitchell sold a matched pair of highly-prized silver fox skins for $1000, a small fortune in that era. That same year, and before shipping their pelts to a London fur auction, two Kantishna trappers displayed in Fairbanks an exceptional "black-gray" fox, described as the finest such fox seen in "many a day." Another district trapper "came out . . . with $4,000 worth of furs."[7]

Trapline trails were a gauntlet hung with hundreds of leg-hold traps, snares, and cunning deadfalls. In the 1920s, for example, Frank Giles regularly set 380 traps over 140 miles of trail. Carlson once set 900 traps—a phenomenal 100 per day—over 200 miles of trail. Foxes were highly sought after but trappers also targeted lynx, ermine, beaver, and the easily-trapped and abundant marten. One year, Carlson caught 250 marten, the next 175. Fish, meat, bones, and scent-concoctions lured animals to their tortured death.

As fur prices rose newcomers set up camp in the region joining old-timers like Old Marko, Clarence Beauchamp, and Fannie Quigley. Deserted cabins were appropriated and repaired for use as trapline camps.

Beauchamp, another veteran of the Klondike stampede, went by the name Clarence "Boatman," a name he had picked up years before when he had enlisted in the U.S. Army in Miles City, Montana. After his stint in the Klondike, Beauchamp rushed to the Fairbanks strike but quickly tired of mining. In 1906, he poled a boat up the Kantishna River to Lake Minchumina, and from there up the Foraker River. Near White Creek he built a cabin and cleared trails, becoming one of the district's first full-time trappers. After six years trapping along the glacial Foraker, Beauchamp moved to the mouth of the Kantishna.

He used both steel traps and "deadfalls"—weighted logs that crushed any animal that touched the baited trigger under it.[8]

The region's prolonged frigid winters were ideal for raising animals with dense, luxurious pelts. Some Kantishnans saw fur farming as the road to riches. Trapping was hard, dangerous work with often-negligible profit. Why not raise fur, these people reasoned—it was cheaper, easier, and far more lucrative. In 1914, Charles Ingersoll said that "a number of old-timers have deserted the mining game to take up the business of raising fur-bearing animals." Ingersoll, who truly loved the Kantishna and called it an ideal place to live, "with many pretty places with beautiful gardens, and even flower beds, in the wilderness," primarily raised silver foxes but also tried breeding lynx and marten.[9]

Rising fur prices in the two decades after the gold strike lured many unscrupulous people into the wilderness. Pelts were currency and these men meant to cash in no matter what it took. Not only did these men lack even the rudimentary knowledge of trapping; they knew and cared nothing about the animals they sought. Poison was their tool. They spread poison baits along trails and laced animal carcasses with deadly substances. Later these "trappers" returned to their bait stations and followed tracks in the snow to the dead animals. Loss and waste was enormous. According to Archdeacon Hudson Stuck, the aftermath of the gold stampedes brought "wholesale destruction of game, and trapping of fur."[10]

"Promiscuous Distribution of Poison Has Devastated the Entire Country," howled one news account of the slaughter. The story described legitimate trappers returning empty-handed and of the circle of death wrought by "persons too lazy or unskillful to trap . . . whose vandalism has desolated the entire country." The Kantishna district was especially hard hit and legitimate trappers were outraged. "One man [an honest trapper] in fact who had spent the winter on the Kantishna did not have a skin to his credit . . . So far two silver fox skins have come into town; these from the McKinley district, and where in previous years hundred of foxes wrote their records on the snow, not a track was to be seen last winter, the work of the poisoner having been of sweeping effectiveness."[11]

The use of poison in the Kantishna hills peaked in the year following the stampede and declined somewhat after that. During his 1913 expedition to Mt. McKinley, Stuck reported the resurgence of

U.S. GEOLOGICAL SURVEY, P.S. SMITH COLLECTION, #1404

A resurgence of interest in the Kantishna's mineral wealth began shortly after the end of World War I. Hydraulic mining on previously worked gravels near the mouth of Eureka Creek re-invigorated the old mining camp. The future site of the modern-day Kantishna Roadhouse is just above the cluster of tents and cabins on the left bank of Moose Creek.

foxes and other fur-bearers but recalled witnessing the past use of poison there in the "most reckless and unscrupulous way."[12]

The resurgence noted by Stuck materialized slowly. In 1915, Athabascans near Minchumina complained to the Archdeacon that a white man, Stephen Foster, had been wiping out foxes. After hearing the rumor that Foster had been murdered by the Indians for his use of poison, Stuck investigated. He found Foster alive and well but short of money. "He frankly admitted the poisoning," Stuck said, "telling me that he had never trapped before, and *had* to get some skins."[13]

It took almost three decades for the fur-bearer populations to recover from the poisoning campaigns. In the Kantishna, "fur bearing animals had become practically extinct by poisoning and excessive trapping," a newspaper later reported.[14]

Real trappers shunned poison and the men who used it. At least one poisoner was driven from the Kantishna at gunpoint after a freighter's dogs died from eating poisoned tallow. In such a small community, nothing was a secret and identifying the culprit was easy.

Trapping was a perilous existence, even for the most experienced men. Dan Keeler, a Dawson man, was no stranger to the Kantishna. He and his family had arrived on the steamer *White Seal* during the peak of the stampede and had established a roadhouse at the mouth of the Bearpaw. Later, he mined Eureka and Glen Creeks. One winter when

```
C. HERBERT WILSON                DEPARTMENT OF JUSTICE
  COMMISSIONER                         FOURTH DIVISION
                                     TERRITORY OF ALASKA

                          OFFICE OF U. S. COMMISSIONER
                                   KANTISHNA PRECINCT

                                      GLEN, ALASKA
```

US COMMISSIONERS, KANTISHNA PRECINCT

LEE VAN SLYKE, 1905–06, OFFICE AT ROOSEVELT

E.M. CARR, INTERIM, AUGUST 1905

ERNEST J. FOSTER, 1907–1911, GLACIER CITY

WILLIAM R. LLOYD, 1911–14, GLACIER CITY & GLEN

WILLIAM TAYLOR, 1917, GLEN

JOSEPH C. VAN ORSDEL, 1917–1919, GLACIER CITY

CHARLES HERBERT WILSON, 1919–1921, GLEN & EUREKA, 1919

EDGAR BROOKER, SR., APPOINTED DECEMBER 23, 1921, EUREKA

CHARLES TRUNDY, APPOINTED MARCH 19, 1924, EUREKA

An important difference between the Klondike and the Kantishna mining districts was the enforcement of the rule of law. The Northwest Mounted Police kept the peace in the Yukon while in Alaska remote mining districts were administered by appointed Commissioners without the assistance of a local police force.

checking traps with the temperature at rock bottom, he plunged through thin ice on Birch Creek and froze his feet. A passerby loaded him in a sled and took him to Rodman's Roadhouse in Roosevelt. Despite his serious condition, Keeler refused treatment but his friends took him to town where his blackened and shriveled toes were amputated.

Ironically, the isolation that drove some men from their cabins and onto the trapline lured them deeper into the sullen solitude. In critical situations, feuds were quickly forgotten and help energetically offered. Every one in the district knew the dangers of the trail and their frozen world and counted on their neighbors for succor should misfortune occur. In crises the miners pulled together.

On rare occasions a Cheechako—like Sheldon —would venture into the hills and arouse both suspicion and concern. A few odd balls even showed up in winter, inexplicably risking life and limb for sport instead of gold or fur. When the "mysterious musher of the Northland" passed through the Kantishna, his travels ignited fevered speculation.

The mystery man, Deming Wheeler, spent summers in the lower 48 states and winters in Alaska, a schedule that of itself piqued Alaskans' interest. Over the course of several winters, Wheeler mushed throughout Interior and as far west as Nome. Wheeler later claimed to be the first person to circle Mt. McKinley by dogteam. He was on his way to the Iditarod gold fields when he passed through the Kantishna. The very fact that he was not going there to stake claims or run a trapline perplexed old-timers.

Wheeler was perhaps Alaska's first recreational /adventure dog musher. On his honeymoon, he mushed his new bride into the wilderness, carrying her in the basket of his sled. Over the years, he studied and observed sled dogs and worked to develop sturdier and stronger dogs better suited for the harsh northern climate. (During the series of stampedes any big, furry dog—regardless of suitability — was put in harness.) He bought wolf pups when offered and, on one trip, he announced his plan to own and drive a team of pure wolves.[15]

Wheeler came from a prominent and wealthy East Coast family. To most Alaskans he was just another wealthy dilettante like the Easterners who came north on hunting or climbing expeditions. More than a few Alaskans derided these Easterners, no matter how capable, because their exploits challenged their pioneer pride. As more and more Cheechakos came into the northern wilderness, a few introspective Alaskans saw them as ominous harbingers of change. Most of these class-conscious, proud miners, however, loathed the independent rich and viewed their "expeditions" as nothing more than publicity stunts. Alaska was no playground; it was a battleground where only "real" men survived. In 1910, a group of Glen Creek miners vowed to show up the Easterners at one of their own games, mountain climbing.

8

The Glen Creek Boys

"Drinks for the house!" shouted "Grizzly Bill" McPhee and his *Washington Saloon* exploded in cheers and a rush for the bar. Some men jostled to slap Tom Lloyd on the back, while others bee-lined for the free drinks.

"Hooray for the Glen Creek boys! Hooray for the Kantishna! Here's one for Tom Lloyd!" Revelers hoisted toast after toast in honor of Lloyd and his fellow miners who had been first to the summit of Mt. McKinley.

Where all those others from Outside had failed, ordinary miners using everyday equipment had scaled the peak and planted an American flag. Lloyd's exploit brought great pride to the men of the creeks. His accomplishment showed up "Professor Parker of New York and a Bunch of Be-spectacled Highbrows," then in Seattle and bound for Alaska and an assault on the roof of the continent.[1]

Many Alaskans viewed the summit attempts prior to Lloyd's 1910 triumph with both amusement and disdain. While most of these pioneers grubbed the ground for a few flakes of gold to support a hardscrabble life, rich easterners wasted the entire summer in frivolous endeavors. These tough, proud, self-made men tended to look askance at the Cheechakos who came north to engage in what these pioneers considered play.

The shared attitude of come-uppance engendered by Lloyd's success was displayed in a headline and story on the front page of a Fairbanks paper. "Stampede to McKinley Now On. The Streets of Seattle Are Being All Cluttered Up with Cheechako Mountain

112 CHAPTER EIGHT

VF ADD-EXPEDITIONS, #80-84-113, ARCHIVES, UNIVERSITY OF ALASKA, FAIRBANKS

An expedition often called the "Sourdough Expedition," composed solely of Glen Creek miners, reached the north summit of Mt. McKinley in 1910. In this formal portrait, standing from left to right, are Charles McGonagall, Pete Anderson, and William Taylor. Seated is the climb organizer, Thomas Lloyd.

Climbers, Who Reach That City, Tied Together with Ropes, in Assorted Sizes and Colors . . . Each expedition daily sends back telegraph reports of the . . . hairbreadth escapes they have in reaching [Seattle] and they will keep the wireless apparatus on the steamer they travel on very busy until they [disembark.]"[2]

Local antipathy towards the sport climbers had festered for years. In 1906, Dr Frederick A. Cook, a New York physician, accompanied only by blacksmith Ed Barrill, made a short trip and soon telegraphed the news: "We have reached the summit of Mt. McKinley."[3]

Cook's alleged conquest of McKinley was openly challenged by his former expedition members. Prospectors who had worked the south side of the Alaska Range called the story an outright lie. The claim infuriated old-timers like Grizzly Bill who thought most explorers were nothing more than rich dandies that earned headlines for trips that the average pioneer would consider commonplace.

The all-Alaskan climb of Mt. McKinley resulted from a barroom boast. One night in December 1909, Glen Creek miner Tom Lloyd, who was in Fairbanks to buy mining supplies, visited the *Washington* and bragged to McPhee and others that he knew for a fact that McKinley could be climbed. "[I] consider it an easier matter to make the climb to McKinley's summit than it would be to fake a story of the climb," he said.[4]

McPhee sputtered that no living man could do it, especially Lloyd, now 50. Lloyd was too old and too fat to even try, McPhee said. The saloonkeeper knew Lloyd all too well. He and associates David Petree and Gust Nelson owned claims in the Kantishna, some in partnership with Lloyd. Lloyd countered that his "boys" could do it and that for two cents he would do it himself, just to prove that it could be done. Grizzly Bill offered $500 for expenses if Lloyd would make the trip and disprove Cook's claims. Another businessman, E. W. Griffin, of Chena, also pledged $500 for expenses. The Order of Alaska Pioneers voted to underwrite the expedition but Lloyd turned them all down. With a handshake, he accepted McPhee's challenge.[5]

Lloyd claimed that he "didn't care" if the climb made news or not. He wanted to prove he was as "husky" as ever and had the "desire to give the Cheechakos 'the laugh' by proving that what the Easterner brags about . . . the sourdough does as a part of a day's work."[6]

In early December, Lloyd's employee, Pete Anderson, left town with a load of mining and climbing supplies. At one in the afternoon on the winter solstice of 1909, Tom Lloyd, William R. Taylor, Charles McGonagall, Robert Horn, Charles A. Davidson, and William Lloyd posed for photographs in front of the Pioneer Hotel. The crowd roared when Petree bet McPhee $5,000 that one of the Lloyd party would reach the summit of Mt. McKinley before July 4, 1910. The expedition set off to wild cheers.[7]

"The departure of the expedition yesterday was a thrilling sight, indeed. Robert Horn . . . took the lead with a sturdy team of dogs. Following him was Mr. Taylor with a double-ender sled and horse. Next came Tom Lloyd, [and] Mr. Davidson, a civil engineer, with a horse and double-ender outfit. After them rode Charles McGonigle [sic], widely known as a musher and mail carrier, with horse and double-ender. The rear was brought up by William "Billy" Lloyd . . . with double-ender and mule."[8]

It took the men nearly the entire brutally cold month of January to relay their supplies to the Kantishna. All but two of the expedition members lived at the community of Glen, on Glen Creek. Partners Tom Lloyd and Billy Taylor employed McGonagall and Anderson, both of whom also owned claims there. Lloyd originally hired Horn and Davidson to survey his quartz property but later invited them along on the climb. Billy Lloyd, 59, would keep base camp while the others made the climb. Only Taylor, 27, and Davidson, 36, were under 40.

Glen Creek provided ideal views of the mountain. "From the crest of the high ridge behind Lloyd's cabin extended a magnificent unobstructed view, reaching along the Alaska Range east and west of Denali," wrote Charles Sheldon. "While standing there with Tom Lloyd I told him of the double ridge summit and the great icefall descending easterly . . . and asserted my belief that if no technical difficulties should be found below the upper areas, the great mountain could be climbed from the ridge bordering the north side of the glacier."[9]

The Glen Creek boys had several advantages over the Outside climbers, local experience being foremost. Once, while prospecting a fork of Cache Creek at the base of the mountain, McGonagall emerged at a little pass overlooking the vast Muldrow Glacier, unaware at the time that he had discovered the door to the summit. He found no gold, "just a lot of snow and ice and rotten granite." Pete Anderson pioneered a short cut through the range from Broad Pass to the Kantishna. In 1908, Tom Lloyd and the ex-Mountie Billie Merrifield left Glen Creek and followed Anderson's route through the mountains and in three days reached the Chulitna River. Later, Anderson guided McGonagall and Taylor through the pass that would one day bear his name. In all, Anderson crossed the range 11 times. Importantly, these men were accustomed to cold, snow, and daily hardship. Finally, unlike other expeditions that began in unstable late spring and summer weather, the Glen Creek boys left Fairbanks in mid-winter. Lloyd's party was the first with a realistic promise of success.[10]

The climbers outfitted themselves with their everyday trail clothes: bib overalls, long underwear, wool shirts, duck-canvas "parkees," mittens, fur or wool hats, and gumboots with felt insoles. At very cold temperatures, they would swap their boots for knee-high moccasins made of moose-hide and caribou skin. For bedding, they took caribou hides, wolf-fur robes, Dall sheepskin sleeping bags, and down sleeping bags. The only specialized equipment they possessed were homemade crampons and "long poles with double [steel] hooks on one end . . . and a steel point on the other." Blacksmith Jim Johnson of Fairbanks' Samson Hardware had forged the crampons and hooks from McGonagall's design.[11]

Most importantly, the miners would rely on their snowshoes. Later, they agreed that the climb would have been impossible without them. "There are glaciers there that [Cook] . . . at that time of year [he claimed to have made his climb] neither he nor any other man could pass over them; nor at any time of the year can any man pass over them without using snowshoes and Dr. Cook mentions no snowshoes."[12]

At Glen Creek, Billy Lloyd helped the men prepare their usual trail rations: bacon, beans, donuts, and bread. They made stews and cut steaks to cook over a coal oil, or wood stove. They packed butter, coffee, chocolate, sugar, and dried fruit. Tom Lloyd anointed himself both leader and expedition cook.

In mid-February, the men set up a relay camp in the last timber on the McKinley River, near where Alfred H. Brooks had camped in 1902. By the end of the month, the expedition had established the climb's base camp, dubbed "Willows Camp," above timberline near the mouth of Cache Creek. Taylor hauled spruce poles to the camp by dogteam and the men hewed them into hundreds of trail markers. Taylor also gathered longer poles to use for bridging crevasses.

On March 1, Anderson and McGonagall hiked ten miles up Cache Creek and through what they called "McPhee Pass" (now McGonagall Pass), and out onto an ascending glacier they called the "Wall Street

Glacier" (the Muldrow). This river of ice would be their highway to the ridges leading to the summit.

Progressing up the heavily-crevassed glacier, the climbers went un-roped, a dangerous practice. Each carried a spruce pole to stop a fall into a hidden crevasse. Many years later, an interviewer asked Taylor why they went un-roped. "Didn't need 'em," he replied. "We took our chances independently."[13]

"Going across the glacier toward McKinley for the first four or five miles there are no crevasses in sight, as they have been blown full of snow," Lloyd wrote, "but the next eight miles are terrible for crevasses. You can look down in them for distances stretching from 100 feet to Hades or China. Look down one of them, and you will never forget it. Some of them you can see the bottom of, but most of them appear to be bottomless . . . Over the upper eight miles of that glacier you cannot move a foot in safety unless you have snowshoes on . . ."[14]

Charles Davidson, hobbled by a bad knee that had plagued him through much of February, decided to quit the climb at Willows Camp. The temperature was -32°F. According to one story, Lloyd and Davidson got into an angry row, which degenerated into a fistfight. For whatever reason, both Davidson and Horn quit the party on the second day of the climb.

The loss of Davidson, a photographer and an experienced surveyor, and later surveyor-general of Alaska, was a serious blow to the expedition. The withdrawal of the man designated "to map the route and keep track of elevations," reduced the climb to a "sporting" ascent. To complicate matters, two days after the men separated, Tom Lloyd lost the aneroid barometer lent him by Davidson.[15]

On the day the surveyors quit, Taylor hitched his dogteam and headed for Glacier City, 35 miles away, to retrieve a load of dried fish for dog food. In Taylor's absence, Anderson, Lloyd, and McGonagall marked a route to a second camp, "Pothole Camp," in a depression on the glacier about four or five miles above the pass. Everyone relied on Anderson's knowledge and nerve. An avalanche "seemed to be taking the glacier under the tent away," Lloyd wrote, "and startled by the sound, like a great gun . . . I jumped up . . . the Swede, who had crossed many glaciers, paid no attention at all. He simply looked at me and smiled and said: 'It's just rippling a little below; it is safe here.'"[16]

The weather turned warm and blustery with low clouds and occasional snow. While waiting for the weather to change, the men did chores and read. "We had one magazine in the party—all the reading matter we had—and we read it from one end to the other . . . I don't remember the name of the magazine, but in our estimation it was the best magazine published in the world."[17]

When the weather moderated, Anderson and McGonagall, trailed by the flabby Lloyd, pushed ahead marking the trail. Taylor, who had rejoined the party, ferried wood and supplies up from Willows Camp. The use of dogs to support the climbers was a labor-saving innovation that would be copied by others in the years to come. Some of Taylor's dogs were taken to almost 11,000 feet.

The men quickly came to the conclusion that warm summer weather would turn their route into a death trap of unbridgeable crevasses and thundering avalanches. Even in winter, countless hidden crevasses laced the glacier, threatening the men and their dogs. "In many places we had to put long poles across them, as they were too wide to jump over," Lloyd said. The men then shoveled snow onto the poles to form a bridge. After the snow hardened, they snowshoed across. "This was the theory upon which we attempted to climb Mount McKinley at the time we did . . ."[18]

Moving up the glacier, each man escaped close calls. Taylor slipped on an incline and shot downhill "with the speed of an express train." Taylor used his hooked pole to arrest his fall at the very edge of a precipice. "One day, in coming down, McGonagall, who is quick as a cat on his feet, thought he would escape the full climb down by taking a cutoff," Lloyd recalled, ". . . and when he stepped on what appeared to be solid footing he went right down through, in a crevasse . . . He had his pole, of course, and it fell across the walls . . . and held him suspended there, in snow up to his waist, with limitless space below him. He [pulled] himself out . . ."[19]

The climbers coped well with their constant foe—the cold—but nonetheless suffered injury. Anderson froze one of his toes, which "bled something fierce every night," Lloyd said, "but he never complained."[20]

On March 18, the men established their last camp on the Muldrow in a tent in a snow cave just below a ridge leading toward the summit. Although Tom Lloyd estimated this "Tunnel Camp" at not less than 15,000 feet, it actually was 11,000 feet and the highest elevation he reached.

The waning days of March ushered in snow and fluctuating temperatures. Taylor, who was attempting to move gear up from Willows Camp, was on his own for five days because of storms. "In this trip we were always praying for the thermometer to drop, so that it couldn't snow any more and the trail could not soften," Lloyd wrote. "We didn't want any weather above zero."[21]

In the last week of the month, Anderson and McGonagall used a coal shovel to cut steps in the ice up to the top of the 14,600 foot ridge. After each passing storm, the climbers cleared away fresh snow. Lloyd, possibly suffering altitude sickness, took the dogs down to Willows Camp.

On the first day of April, Anderson, McGonagall, and Taylor headed for the summit but turned back when a storm hit. On April 3, they tried again, leaving Tunnel Camp at three a.m. They wore their crampons and carried their ice poles and a 14-foot spruce pole to use as a summit marker. For food, they took two thermoses of hot chocolate and six donuts.

Anderson led the route up the long ridge, the only practical way to bypass the icefall at the head of the Muldrow. Step by slow step, they ascended the ridge to a gentle snow-filled basin. They then crossed the Grand Basin, as it was later named, to the base of the north peak. Un-roped, they climbed a steep, icy, 2,200 foot couloir—later named Sourdough Gully—to the summit ridge. McGonagall waited a few hundred feet below the north peak, while Taylor and Anderson continued on to the 19,470 foot summit. For two and one-half hours, in temperatures to -30°F, the climbers soaked in the breath-taking views of the surrounding lowlands. "I know it was colder than hell," Taylor would remark later. "Mitts and everything was all ice."[22]

On the descent, in the last exposed rocks near where McGonagall had quit, Anderson and Taylor planted their spruce pole. "We dug down in the ice with a little axe we had and built a pyramid of [rock] 15 inches high and we dug down in the ice so we had a support of about 30 inches." They then guyed the pole with four cotton ropes.[23]

From the pole, they unfurled their 6'×12' American flag, which bore the supplier's name, E.W. Griffin. At the base of the pole, they left a piece of board torn from a candle box inscribed with the date, climbers' names, and those of Petersen, McPhee, and the Pioneers of Alaska.[24]

They later said they chose this location, rather than the south

Charles McGonagall, left, and Tom Lloyd, right, rest on the slopes of Mt. McKinley during their 1910 climb.

summit of the mountain, because they believed that with a strong telescope it could be seen from Fairbanks, 150 miles away, proof that McKinley had been conquered.

Taylor and Anderson soon reunited with McGonagall and the trio descended, reaching Tunnel Camp just after ten p.m. Taylor still had three of his half-dozen donuts left. Anderson and Taylor had climbed 8,000 vertical feet and returned in an astounding 18-hour round-trip. "We made it all in one day, by God!"[25]

Years later, when asked why they did not climb the south peak—the true summit at 20,320 feet, Taylor replied that "We set out to climb the North Peak. That's the toughest peak to climb—the North."[26]

A day or two later, the climbers rejoined Lloyd at Willow's Camp and he heartily toasted Anderson and Taylor's triumph. At the very least, their success set Lloyd's imagination to work.

The party returned to Glen Creek on the evening of April 6 and tucked into a "big feed" of fresh meat and bread. Two days later,

Tom Lloyd left "for Fairbanks alone with a team of four dogs, while the other boys returned to our claim to work."[27]

On April 11, Lloyd received a tumultuous welcome in Fairbanks. He claimed that *all four men* had reached both the north *and* south summits. He fabricated a story of the transit from the south peak to the north peak over an immense glacier, calling it the toughest part of the climb. Lloyd, always the prospector, said he brought back rocks from the summit for analysis by Alfred Hulse Brooks and the Smithsonian.

He also reported finding no evidence that Cook had been anywhere near the summit, but Lloyd's account of his part of the climb was almost as fanciful as Cook's. His bragging would forever tarnish the expedition's triumph.

Lloyd could not stop his bragging. He offered to take scientists to the summit for $5,000 and boasted that for $50,000 he would build a permanent trail to the summit, complete with lumber bridges across the crevasses and "fifteen or sixteen miles of handrails!"[28]

On April 12, under the banner headlines "M'Kinley [sic] Conquered," the story of the "Stars and Stripes Placed on Top of the Continent" made world news. President Taft sent a congratulatory telegram and James Wickersham, now Alaska Delegate to Congress, declared that at the end of the legislative season "he will personally make the ascent . . ." The Order of the Alaska Pioneers, Igloo #4 in Fairbanks, honored the Glen Creek boys with a lifetime membership in their fraternal order.[29]

In one detail, Tom Lloyd was wholly honest: "I wish to state emphatically that I, personally, could never have got any place if it hadn't been for Pete Anderson, Charley McGonagall, and Bill Taylor . . . they were far superior to me in ability at any stage of the climb . . ."[30]

Lloyd could not praise Anderson enough: "Mount McKinley must be 21,000 feet high, but that Swede is a wonder. If it was twice as high as it is I believe the Swede could go to the top of it."[31]

Many Fairbanksans could not stifle their delight with the news. "Alaska will this summer be the Mecca of all the he and she mountain climbers of the world, who will come here keen to climb the blazed trail of the Lloyd party and eat their noonday luncheon of predigested sawdust upon the summit . . . When these Cheechakos, dressed up like horses, with enough harness on them to keep from climbing the Ester hill, are forced to sit down near the foot of the mountain [they will] gaze upward at the flag of the Pioneers waving above them in a saucy manner . . ."[32]

Not everyone believed Lloyd's story. Perhaps in a subtle caution, one headline described Lloyd's story as a "Proud Boast."[33]

When Lloyd's wife, living in Seattle, heard the news, she believed "implicitly that her husband made the ascent . . . as he always was a truthful man." Alone, she had raised Lloyd's three sons and a 10-year-old daughter who did not remember him because "he has been north the past nine years."[34]

Even those who were willing to overlook Lloyd's previous tall tales thought him physically unable to make such a climb. When word of Lloyd's embellishments reached Glen Creek, his partners erupted in outrage. In public, they kept silent either out of loyalty, financial concerns, or tacit complicity.

On the East Coast, Charles Sheldon, cautioned the press "not to encourage full credibility in the reports . . . until all the facts and details are authoritatively published. Only Tom Lloyd apparently brought out the report, the other members of the party having remained in the Kantishna District 150 miles away; so we haven't had their corroborative evidence."[35]

Sheldon continued to express his skepticism. "Charles Sheldon … [who] for years has known Tom Lloyd, Charles MeGonnigle [sic], W. R. Taylor, three of the four men who claimed to have climbed McKinley on April 3, 1910, declared last night that the public could well afford to await a fuller report of the details of the ascent before complete acceptance of the claim . . . The press reports contain so many assertions that are not in accordance with the facts that little reliance can be placed on them."[36]

In private, Sheldon was more direct and unusually curt. "Lloyd is a windbag and cannot climb. If he climbed Mt. McKinley (He is over sixty and fat and full of whisky pickled in it) any 15 year old boy can do it," he wrote.[37]

Even though McGonagall and Lloyd were Sheldon's "personal friends" and "courageous and capable," he cautioned that "it is ridiculous to suggest that a trail was established to the top of the mountain, it is ridiculous to say that snowshoes were used most of the way up the mountain."[38]

Opinions varied. Barrill, the blacksmith who had recently gained infamy by recanting his story of Cook's climb, declared flatly that

Lloyd's party did not make the summit. E. T. Barnette, Griffin, McPhee, and others countered with a bet of $100,000 that Lloyd's story was true. New Yorker John Bradley, one of Cook's former millionaire backers, believed Lloyd and publicly stated that Cook lied.[39]

But where was the proof? Although Kantishna miner Phil Ott looked for the flagpole from his Kantishna diggings and did not see it, he believed his colleagues. "I did not look very closely. I am sure the flag is there."[40]

Lloyd's delay in providing a full account of the climb sparked considerable scorn. He falsely claimed that "the climb was made at the expense of the Pioneers" and would not give out the story until they were reimbursed, "and his men obtain a grubstake as a result of their trip . . ."[41]

As time passed, most people demanded physical evidence. On clear days, Fairbanksans used binoculars and a small telescope to look for the flagpole but saw nothing. The pictures Lloyd took on the climb were worthless and he had no aneroid barometer readings to corroborate his claims.

Under the pressure of the national controversy that he had engendered, Lloyd asked his partners to retrace their steps to the summit. Anderson, Taylor, and McGonagall set out in May with a borrowed camera to take pictures of the summit and flagpole. Despite spring conditions and soft snow they reached the 18,200 feet pass at the head of the Grand Basin but deteriorating weather beat them back.

In June, newspapers reported the astounding news that on May 17, the miners had again climbed to the North peak. "Lloyd had asked the boys to get as near the summit as necessary to get a good picture and as they figured they could not get any nearer to the summit than the top, they just kept on climbing until there was no more mountain left to climb." Lloyd just could not leave well enough alone and thus robbed the men of the acclaim due for a second remarkable success.[42]

Tom Lloyd's full account of the climb, including his embellishments, appeared under headlines in London and New York in early June. On June 11, perhaps to mitigate the damage, Anderson, McGonagall, and Taylor each signed a notarized statement that "a party of four in number known as the Lloyd party" in fact had attained the North summit. Perhaps the men signed the statement backing Lloyd to garner some credibility for their achievement, or maybe the simple pressures of their business ventures influenced them. "He [Lloyd] was fine in his way, but he was lookin' for too much fame," Taylor recalled years later. "He conflicted his stories by telling his intimate friends that he didn't climb it and told others he was at the top."[43]

Lloyd's contradictions eventually discredited the entire expedition. "[Lloyd] was the head of the party and we never dreamed he wouldn't give a straight story . . . I wish to God we hadda [sic] been [in Fairbanks] . . . We didn't get out till June and they didn't believe any of us had climbed it," Taylor said. "I had implicit confidence in Lloyd so I never kept no data on it at all."[44]

The controversy simmered until early 1912 when twin blows fell. First, an all-Fairbanks expedition led by Ralph Cairns, a newspaper telegrapher, failed to secure proof of Lloyd's claim. (In a little known story, a lone trapper Slim Carlson, found the pass and reportedly reached 16,000 feet on Muldrow before turning back.) Next, an expedition led by Herschel Parker and Belmore Browne, reached 20,100 feet on the south summit before being beaten back by a roaring wind and whiteout.

"On our journey up the glacier from below we had begun to study [with binoculars] the North Peak," Browne wrote. "We not only saw no sign of the flagpole, but it is our concerted opinion that the northern peak is more inaccessible than its southern sister."[45]

And with that, the Sourdough Expedition, as it became known, seemed just one more "Windy Bill." Even to this day, some people believe that the one-day climb was humanly impossible but, by contemporary accounts, all of these men—with the exception of Lloyd—possessed unparalleled strength, stamina, and the nerve to pull off the feat.

Certainly Harry Karstens never doubted his old partner McGonagall. Though diminutive, McGonagall—age 40 at the time of the climb—was tough and resilient, possessing the ability to work as hard as bigger men. Karstens described Taylor and McGonagall "as strong, well trained men and Anderson as a man with an exceptional ability to travel long distances without becoming tired."[46]

Hudson Stuck described Anderson and Taylor "as two of the strongest men, physically, in all the North," and said they worked well as a team. Taylor described Anderson as "A Big husky Swede. Hell of a good fellow on the trail. Him and I would go along and never have no trouble at all. He was a husky sonofagun. We done all the work but we never got credit for nothin'."[47]

Years later, Fritz Nyberg met Taylor at Kantishna. "Bill Taylor was built like a packhorse," he said, "one of the toughest of them all." Nyberg vividly described Taylor's ability to backpack 150-pound loads up a hill that fellow miner John Stendahl could barely manage with 50 pounds.[48]

The key to the climb, McGonagall said, was that the men were "hardened to travel with dogs and that experience stood them in good stead when they came to grips with the mountain." Lloyd concurred, saying "the entire trip was simply a matter of endurance—work day after day."[49]

Except for the notarized statement, McGonagall never publicly claimed to have made the summit but always said he stopped at 18,700 feet, and turned back after a rest. Years later when asked why, he replied: "My job was to haul the pole and that was as far as it would go. Why go farther?"[50]

McGonagall's friend Grant Pearson offered a different reason: "At 16,000 feet the altitude got Charlie McGonagall. Taylor and Anderson went on with their flagpole, hauling it to 19,000 feet, then returning to help McGonagall back to the [Tunnel Camp]."[51]

McGonagall was known for his truthfulness, but so was Taylor, whose nickname was "Honest Bill." To his dying day, Tom Lloyd had nothing but praise for his partner. "Taylor and I have been partners for years," he said, "and, I don't claim that is because of any good qualities of mine, I have never had words with him. He is beyond question one of the finest men you ever met."[52]

For his part, Anderson rarely spoke of the climb. In his latter years he would tell anyone that asked to forget climbing and go mining instead. For him, the "Sourdough Climb," was something in the past, an interruption in the search for gold.

Even though the Glen Creek boys did not surmount Mt. McKinley's true summit, their climb was a tremendous achievement and testament to the fortitude and courage of the northern pioneers. Unfortunately, instead of glory, the climbers' reputations were sullied by the lies of a blowhard. Lloyd's exaggerations dogged these stalwarts for three long years before another group of pioneer climbers reported the dramatic truth. Meanwhile they watched an array of climbers—both the admirable and the absurd—attack the mountain. Each attempt rekindled the controversy and the dark mutterings of fraud and deception.

9
Frontier Justice

John McLeod ran for his life. At any moment he expected the whoops of his pursuers or shots fired from ambush. Thoughts of his murdered brothers flashed through his mind. The long trip from Kantishna to Fairbanks was nightmarish.

After McLeod's arrival in Fairbanks in December 1910, he reported an Indian uprising in the Kantishna and described his own narrow escape from scalping and death. A subsequent headline screamed "Kantishna Man Reports Reds Bloodthirsty." The story quickly took on a life of its own. In Dawson City, the paper reported "Alaskan Indians Now on Warpath" and the robbery and murder of "six white men."[1]

McLeod, who had been trapping in the Kantishna since his part in the Wickersham climb, said that he had been camped at Van Chobin twenty miles from the Bearpaw River when a lone Indian used a fur-trading ploy to lure him to a river encampment. McLeod knew most of the Athabascans in camp and initially felt at ease. While resting in one of the tents, McLeod became alarmed by the sudden singing of what he called a "war chant." Fearing for his life, McLeod grabbed his rifle, ducked under the tent, and escaped half-dressed into the woods. McLeod claimed that the Indians had chased him to Glacier City, twenty miles away. Once safely in the mining camp, McLeod told his story to Commissioner Ernest Foster and swore out a warrant for "assault with intent to kill." Foster deputized Pete Anderson, "to make an investigation of the unusual evidence of hostility."[2]

CHARLES SHELDON COLLECTION, BOX 5, FILE 3, ARCHIVES, UNIVERSITY OF ALASKA, FAIRBANKS

In late 1910, John McLeod carried to Fairbanks alarming tales of murder and an "Indian uprising" in the Kantishna. McLeod, who accompanied James Wickersham on his 1903 expedition to Mt. McKinley, was once described as the "Strangest Alaskan."

McLeod waited three days in Glacier City for Anderson's report and when the deputy failed to return, McLeod high-tailed it to Fairbanks. There he told authorities that he believed the Indians had killed six others. As his only evidence of foul play, McLeod reported that the Indians had supplies of flour, hardtack, sugar, and "such articles not often seen in an Indian's outfit." He also said that it was likely that by now Foster and Anderson had been murdered.[3]

Even in a region filled with eccentrics, McLeod's behavior was of special comment. An era newspaper story entitled the "Strange Life of the Strangest Alaskan" described his preference for the solitary existence of life in the Bush. McLeod lived off the land; his diet strictly meat and fish. By all accounts, he excelled as a trapper and regularly brought in large, well-handled catches of fur. Apparently, McLeod tried to avoid even small towns and any bigger than Fairbanks. In the bush, he often avoided contact with people. In a pinch, he relied on himself for succor. Judge James A. Wickersham always spoke kindly of his former guide and often praised McLeod's way of living off the land. Perhaps McLeod's loyalty on the return journey from the mountain in 1903 explains why the Judge glossed over the man's shortcomings.

For some reason, McLeod erroneously believed that Indians had killed his father. In early 1909, after he received word of the alleged murder of his brothers in the Finlay River region of British Columbia, he canoed to Fairbanks for more news. There he told reporters that he knew Indians were responsible and he planned to leave Interior "and go into the Finlay to shoot Indians for a while."[4]

In the half-dozen years since his journey with Wickersham, McLeod's behavior—always a little strange—became even more erratic, in turn friendly then suspicious and withdrawn. His mental instability became even more apparent after McLeod convinced himself that Indians had murdered his brothers. His beliefs were totally unfounded. Murdock McLeod, John's father, left the north because of failing eyesight and, in 1899, moved to Edmonton, where he died. Brothers Frank and Willie McLeod disappeared in 1908, while searching for gold on the Nahanni River in the Northwest Territories. A year later, searchers found their headless skeletons at an old campsite along the river. Rumors circulated that their missing partner—not Indians—had murdered them for gold. A more recent interpretation suggests the men died of starvation or exposure, their bodies dismembered by animals. Both Deadmen's Valley and Headless Creek along the Nahanni are named for this incident.

Many who heard McLeod's tale of an uprising deemed it bizarre and unbelievable. One man bluntly termed it a "Windy Bill." Hostility by Athabascans was almost unheard of in Interior Alaska. Old-timers knew that these Indians eked out a tenuous existence and spent most of their time foraging for food. In the lowlands, they trapped or speared fish in the lakes and streams; in the foothills and mountains, they hunted caribou, moose, black bear, and Dall sheep. Bands, usually extended family groups, moved camps with the seasons, pack dogs carrying loads of up to 40 pounds each. Through the course of a year, a band might range across a territory, ranging in size from 2,700 to 5,700 square miles, just to achieve a subsistence lifestyle. The influx of whites in Interior Alaska brought diseases, such as measles, influenza, and diphtheria, which decimated entire Native villages. Market hunters and trappers using poison devastated many prime subsistence hunting areas. Despite such provocations and their precarious existence, the generosity of Athabascans was often remarkable. Rather than a threat, these Native Alaskans, some still animists rather than Christians, rescued lost or starving prospectors and explorers. Consequently, even the Fairbanks papers, prone to sensationalize any story, expressed skepticism about McLeod's tale.

In mid-December, Anderson returned from visiting the suspect Indian camp where he found three men, two women, and two children, and "nothing to justify any assumption that there had been an attempt to rob or murder anyone." It appeared that McLeod had been the victim of a practical joke. Anderson described two of the men as friendly locals. The third man, a "mission Indian" from Fort Gibbon, was fluent in English and admitted that he had concocted the practical joke on McLeod "who is known to be timid with regard to the natives."[5]

The ill-advised joke could have had tragic results. In Glacier City, McLeod told Foster that out of fear he "would have shot anyone that he met on the way." Kantishna miners were not surprised and reported that McLeod was known to be "slightly unbalanced" regarding Indians. Two years earlier, McLeod had complained that his cache had been robbed by Indians and that he had been threatened. People speculated that McLeod had gone "round the bend" from years of solitude and poor diet. He apparently believed that he was a marked man doomed to die by Indian hands.[6]

Until Anderson reported the truth, McLeod's tall tale provoked concerns for travelers and isolated trappers and miners. Fairbanksans also began to inquire about Emil Maurer, alleged to be a German count, and his young wife, who had come to Alaska to hunt and climb Mt. McKinley on an adventurous honeymoon. Nothing had been heard of the couple since they had left Fairbanks for the mountain in the spring of 1910. In response to specific inquiries, word came back from the Kantishna that no one had seen the missing couple.

The Maurers arrived in Fairbanks by steamer in the autumn of

1909, but were stranded in town by an early freeze-up, postponing their expedition to the Kantishna. Locals described the husband as "eccentric" and said that during the winter of 1909–10, he "studiously avoided strangers." He also loathed newspaper reporters and only grudgingly outlined his plans. Maurer claimed to be the son of the German consul in Chicago, although German archives indicate that no one by that name ever worked there. The Maurers' only friends in Fairbanks were artist Max Kollm and his wife. (Kollm came to Skagway in 1902, and spent 25 years in Alaska. He eventually went blind but after two years a "miracle" restored his vision.) That winter, the Maurers witnessed the departure of the Glen Creek boys and the excitement over their expedition to the mountain. How all of the uproar influenced the Maurers' plans is unknown.[7]

In the winter of 1909–10, Maurer, obviously a man of means, solicited guide services and received several proposals. He ultimately rejected the quoted fees as exorbitant, or the guides unfit, and instead paid $700 for a top-notch dog team and sled. Maurer next set about making what locals called "elaborate" preparations for his expedition. He bought the finest food and equipment and enlisted a local musher to teach him how to drive dogs. In the spring, with the weather moderating, the Maurers left town bound for the Kantishna and the mountain. Upon departure, Maurer told Kollm that he planned to return to Fairbanks by autumn's first snow.

What happened next is open to speculation. Either the Maurers missed the well-used Kantishna trail, or they purposefully took a more difficult trail to Mt. McKinley. Apparently a miner had told them that a good route to the mountain would be from Duke's Trading Post up the Nenana River to Broad Pass, which was actually on the opposite side of the Alaska Range from the Kantishna. Perhaps the Maurers simply changed their plans and intentionally headed up the frozen Nenana River and away from Kantishna.

There is no evidence that the Maurers ever attempted to climb Mt. McKinley or any other peak. In fact, the young Mrs. Maurer was now pregnant, which may have limited her endurance and capabilities.

The couple ended up in snowy, windy Broad Pass. An early spring break-up forced them into camp not far from present-day Cantwell, which at that time had no settlement of any kind. With their limited provisions nearly exhausted, they were forced to wait until early winter, when they again could continue by dogteam. To survive they would have to fish, hunt, and subsist off the land.

Ensuing events indicate that the Maurers were clearly out of their element in the wilderness. That summer, the Count hunted but without much success. Starving, the couple resorted to killing and eating their dogs. In August, Mrs. Maurer gathered ripening berries but otherwise gathered little else to eat. Maurer later blamed his failure to kill game on Indians who would not allow him to hunt, but that seems more an excuse than reality. If Maurer and McLeod shared any trait, it was an obvious disdain for Indians, a rather easy target to blame for any of their own shortcomings.

With the return of frost and darkness in autumn, the couple set off for Fairbanks, their progress hampered by Mrs. Maurer's advanced pregnancy. They edged north along the banks of the Nenana River, making a series of camps as they went. On their downstream journey, the couple took shelter in a cabin—possibly at Panorama Mountain.

In late autumn, Maurer left his pregnant wife alone and went hunting. Several days passed before Maurer finally killed a moose five miles down river near what miners called Una Creek, perhaps today's Carlo Creek. While Maurer was away from the cabin, his wife, without assistance, gave birth to a son. For thirty-six hours, mother and newborn son lay in the un-heated cabin awaiting the return of the Count.

When the exhausted Maurer finally stumbled into the cabin, he was without food. In his weakened state, he had been unable to bring back any meat. The Maurers were still in camp when a Healy Fork prospector wandered by and found them eating dog meat. He noticed right away that neither the mother nor baby had proper clothing or food. The prospector offered help but Maurer told him "that he could get along very well if other people would mind their own business." Judging by this comment, the prospector was not the first to encounter the two in their perilous condition.[8]

When his son was just five days old, Maurer took his family to where he had cached his moose. Apparently, they planned to camp on site and "eat it up."[9]

In November, with the weather turning colder and the rivers beginning to freeze, miners T.J. Knight and Richard Berry left their Valdez Creek claims in the Susitna district, where they had been working for eight months, and set out for Fairbanks. Near the head of the Nenana River, the two men encountered a distraught Indian woman. The men immediately recognized the elaborate sled she was using as Maurer's. When the woman calmed down enough to be questioned, all she could say in English was "Nagita. Cabin. White man." Clearly, something terrible had happened but the miners did not know what. A few days later, they found a traditional Athabascan grave house and opened it. In it was the body of an Indian who had been shot twice.[10]

Fifteen to twenty miles to the north, Knight and Berry found the Maurer family huddled in a crude cabin. For three months, the now-filthy, ill-clothed couple had subsisted almost wholly on dog and moose meat. They were just eating the last of their dogs. The two prospectors immediately asked about the dead Indian. Maurer told them he had shot a moose and had moved camp to Una Creek. When they then returned upstream to their cabin, he said, they found it stripped of most everything of value, including their sled, clothing, and $1200 in currency. He said a poke of $5 and $10 gold pieces had been over-looked. Only Mrs. Maurer's size 10 hobnailed climbing boots remained under the bed.

Maurer next told the miners that just after their return to the cabin on or about November 10, a Native named Nagita had arrived with his wife and three children. "Maurer ordered the native to hold up his hands. Nagita disregarded the order and began fumbling with the lashes of his sled, the one [Maurer said was] stolen from the cabin. Again Maurer said, 'Hold up your hands' . . . Thinking the native was trying to draw out a rifle, Maurer fired when Nagita disregarded a third order . . ." With the second shot, Nagita fell dead. Maurer watched as the wailing "squaw" and her children took her husband's body away in the sled.[11]

Appalled by the story, and the Maurers' current plight, the two miners back-tracked several miles to a spot where they had found cached moose meat and brought it back to the cabin. (What had become of the moose that Maurer had killed at Una Creek is unknown.) They spent the next three days hunting for the Maurers who otherwise once again faced starvation.

Knight and Berry failed to convince the Maurers to return to Fairbanks with them. They gave the Maurers a Yukon sled and exacted a pledge that they would come in when conditions improved. Despite sub-zero weather, and detours around the open water and thin ice in the Nenana Canyon, Knight and Berry reached Fairbanks ten days later. Maurer had instructed them not to say a word to anyone, as he had a "dislike for newspapers." Knight and Berry felt that, in light of the facts, they could not comply. Upon arrival in town they relayed the Maurers' "harrowing story." When asked if the dead Indian was the same one who had menaced John McLeod—the facts of that case then still in question—the miners said that it was impossible because "McLeod's Indians inhabited an entirely different country, fully sixty miles from where Maurer had his trouble."[12]

The next day, both Fairbanks papers headlined stories of Maurer's ill-fated escapades. "Eccentric German Shoots An Indian," proclaimed one headline, while another read, "German Count Lives On Dog." Knight and Berry told their friends that something about the story did not add up.[13]

Public response was swift and blunt. Some called the shooting murder. In a territory largely populated by European immigrants, many of whom either disliked or despised royalty, Emil Maurer no doubt was the object of much gossip. Many saw him as just another well-heeled Cheechako out to make a name for himself. Others condemned the so-called count for the needless, shameful treatment of his wife and infant son. "In a country well supplied with game and in a district only a few days travel from Fairbanks, there was no occasion for suffering," stated one reporter.[14]

Unaware of the furor, the Maurers started for Fairbanks in early-December, apparently on foot. What became of the sled that Berry and Knight had given the Maurers was never explained. Not surprisingly Mrs. Maurer, carrying her baby on her back, lagged far behind her husband. Inadequately dressed and wearing her over-sized, uninsulated, hobnailed boots, the emaciated woman gamely trudged on despite sub-zero conditions. At one point, Maurer again left his wife and went on alone. Eventually, he blundered into Charles Zielke's claim on Moose Creek near present-day Ferry. Zielke hurried back with his dogteam and picked up Maurer's wife and child and brought them to his camp. After a respite, Zielke then took the Maurers to Duke's Trading Post and from there they went on to Fairbanks.

Several long months after their departure, the Maurers finally returned to Fairbanks and the Nordale Hotel, where they retrieved their stored possessions. A doctor looked in on the haggard and malnourished woman and her baby.

On December 22, 1910, Maurer spoke at great length with District Attorney Crossley. Unwilling to accept Maurer's word, Crossley demanded a thorough investigation. Two days later, C. H. Calhoun, a local athlete, was appointed special deputy and sent south with two dogteams to bring in Nagita's body, his widow, three children, and an unrelated Native witness.

When word got out that Maurer had left his wife behind and had gone on alone, some miners were quick to believe that the ersatz count had abandoned his wife in order to save himself. Maurer had few supporters, and fewer friends, in Fairbanks, but a number of people accepted his story of self-defense. Many people routinely disbelieved and distrusted Indians. A few said that Nagita had a "bad reputation with the other natives of the region because of his thieving propensities . . . an habitual cache robber." Other miners stepped forward to express support for Nagita, who was recognized as a Chief. Nagita and his family had been based out of the now-vanished village of Beyadatenna, somewhere in the vicinity of Carlo Creek, and enjoyed good relations with Natives and whites alike. Clearly more evidence was needed before a judgment could be rendered.[15]

After a month afield the redoubtable Calhoun returned with the corpse and surviving family members. When examined by the Coroner, Nagita's body was still clad in two pairs of Maurer's underwear. In mid-January 1911, U.S. Commissioner John Dillon certified that "the deceased came to his death . . . at Broad Pass, Alaska, from two gunshot wounds inflicted by a rifle in the hands of one Emil Maurer." According to Dillon, either wound would have proven fatal. The victim's remains were interred in the Clay Street cemetery.[16]

An inquest into the shooting convened on January 12, 1911. Berry and Knight testified first and retold their story under oath. Both Maurers then testified on their own behalf, establishing their case of self-defense. Next the jurors heard from the widow and two of her children—daughter Sophia, 14, and son William, 10. A younger daughter, who was present at the shooting, did not testify. Through interpreters, the family testified to their version of events and stated that Nagita was neither armed nor did he have a gun in his sled. The last witness was one of the interpreters, Titus Bettis, who testified to Nagita's good reputation. The verdict, as signed by four of the six-member jury, read: "That the deceased was named Nagita; that he was a native of Alaska; that he came to his death on or about the 10th day of November, A.D. 1910, at Broad Pass, in the Fairbanks precinct, by two gunshot wounds from a rifle in the hands of Emil Maurer; and that Emil Maurer is responsible therefor; and that said Emil Maurer was justified in the said killing."[17]

The two dissenting inquest jurors flatly rejected Maurer's version of events. Likely they were swayed by the testimony of both the eyewitnesses and their own knowledge of local practices. The mere fact that Nagita was wearing underwear that had belonged to Maurer was not evidence of wrongdoing. Miners commonly abandoned cabins and kit. After the recent stampedes up the Nenana River to Valdez Creek, perhaps Nagita had thought that Maurer's cabin was abandoned, like so many others, and took what he found. Furthermore, Nagita's family had testified that the clothing had been a gift to Nagita for his help with the Maurers' sled dogs. Like the dissenting jurors, Berry and Knight, as well as some others in the community, did not believe Maurer's story of self-defense.

The day after the inquest, C.H. Calhoun took Nagita's widow and children to Nenana for care at Saint Mark's Mission, far from home and extended family.

Berry seemed incensed at what appeared to be a miscarriage of justice. In the succeeding weeks, Berry used his own funds to file court papers and lobby to keep the case open. On April 4, the U.S. Commissioner's Court, at the request of the Fairbanks District Attorney, filed an arrest warrant for Maurer. The next day, John Brown, Assistant U.S. Attorney, appeared before the court seeking dismissal due to insufficient evidence. The Commissioner concurred, closing the case on the grounds that the evidence obtainable was insufficient to warrant prosecution.

In all the long history of the Kantishna region, the killing of Nagita remains one of the more puzzling mysteries. Violence by Athabascans towards whites was rare but the reverse not uncommon. In an era when justice was not equally applied to Alaska Natives, the very fact that an inquest even took place is remarkable. A contemporary review of the court record, along with published accounts and allegations, leads only to more questions.

From the time of the very first gold rush, stampeders flooding north ran rough shod over Alaska Natives, ignoring their rights and destroying their land. The law clearly did not treat whites and Natives equally. The enquiry into the shooting of Nagita was, in some ways, a watershed event. At least it sent a signal that justice would apply to all, and that the days of vigilantism, like the lynching that Gordon Bettles had witnessed on the Hogatza River, were coming to a close.

In the days and weeks after the Glen Creek boys scaled Mt. McKinley's north peak, and while Maurer was blundering deeper into crisis, another group of climbers slogged toward the summit from the south side of the Alaska Range.

10

Mountain Men

GALE FORCE WINDS pounded Belmore Browne and his climbing partners, Herschel Parker and Merl LaVoy. In sub-zero, whiteout conditions, they staggered upward toward the summit of Mt. McKinley, now just a few hundred vertical feet away. They battled to keep their climbing ropes taut; the blizzard so intense that the last man on the rope could not see the first. Survival hinged on trust and teamwork.

Each step, each breath was torture. Several times the men paused to pound life and warmth back into their frigid feet and hands. They dared not stop for long, even to dig through their rucksacks for dry mittens. Exposed skin would freeze in seconds. They had to keep moving. Above 20,000 feet, the cold and the blasting wind exacted a terrible mental and physical toll. Here the diminutive, bear-tough Browne took the lead. He saw the worry and fatigue etched on his partners' faces and knew they were near their end, but he determined to press on to the last possible moment. Perhaps a lull would allow them to reach the summit.

They battled on, one agonizing step at a time. Just below the mountaintop, they moved out of the lee of a low ridge and into the tempest. "I was struck by the full fury of the storm. The breath was driven from my body and I held to my ax with stooped shoulders to stand against the gale; I couldn't go ahead," Browne recalled. "As I brushed the frost from my glasses and squinted upward through the stinging snow I saw a sight that will haunt me to my dying day—*The slope above me was no longer steep!*"[1]

Chapter Ten

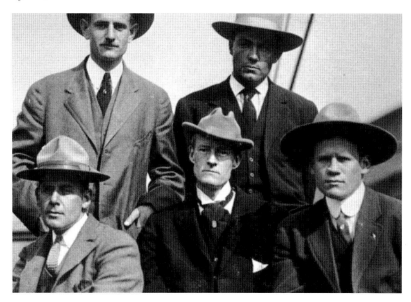

DENALI PARK AND PRESERVE, MUSEUM COLLECTION, #7070

This group of climbers, which era Alaskans denigrated as the "Egghead Expedition" was at that time the most scientific and capable group ever assembled to attack Mt. McKinley. A main goal of the 1910 expedition was to investigate Dr. Frederick A. Cook's controversial claim to have reached the summit in 1906. Seated at left is Belmore Browne, next to him is Herschel Parker with Merl LaVoy standing at right. The three would challenge the mountain again in 1912.

On his hands and knees, Browne plowed forward a few short feet toward the summit, then quit. At victory's door, the game was up. To continue was suicide. The climbers used their ice axes to chop out a hollow depression to rest in. Despite huddling together, they began to freeze. Browne yelled above the tumult that they had to go down. Parker wanted to press on but LaVoy pointed to their back trail vanishing in the drifts. Without the trail to follow to camp, they would die. Just 125 feet below the summit elevation, an easy 200-yard walk in good weather, the defeated climbers began their perilous descent.

Late that evening, the half-frozen men staggered to safety at their high camp. Although Browne and Parker would make one more attempt, their six-year-long struggle to reach the summit of Mt. McKinley was over.

The icy slopes of the tallest peak in North America were a long way from home for Belmore Browne. He was born on New York's Staten Island on June 9, 1880, and as a small boy lived in Europe. His family eventually settled near Tacoma, Washington. As a youth, Belmore spent summers in the west, hunting, climbing, and riding, and winters in the east attending school. He studied art in Paris and New York and developed into an exceptional wildlife and landscape painter, his twin passions of hunting and exploration informing his work.

Belmore Browne first visited Alaska in 1888, when just 8 years old. In 1902, he came north again as a hunter and artist for an American Museum of Natural History expedition to northern British Columbia. Afterward, he accompanied expedition leader Andrew Jackson Stone, at that time the leading explorer-naturalist of western Canada and Alaska, in an exploration of Southeast Alaska.

A year later, again on behalf of the museum, Browne hunted brown bears on the Alaska Peninsula. That same summer, he spent six weeks alone cutting a horse trail from Kachemak Bay into the Kenai Mountains so that Stone could collect Dall sheep specimens. From a mountaintop Browne saw Mt. McKinley for the first time, "two hundred long miles to the northward, rolled up like a white cloud above the horizon."[2]

Over the next two years, his career as artist and author rapidly accelerated, with numerous articles on hunting and climbing appearing in national magazines. A chance encounter on a westbound Canadian Pacific train in 1905 transformed his life. In the smoking parlor, Browne saw a lone man, "whose physical and facial characteristics were so unusual that I was instantly drawn to him." Despite the man's rather austere demeanor, Browne introduced himself and struck up a conversation. His new friend, Parker, was a Columbia University physics professor and Swiss-trained technical climber. The men bonded quickly and talked at length of their fanatical zeal for climbing and exploration, starting a friendship that lasted 40 years. Parker explained that the next year he would attempt to climb Mt. McKinley as a member of the Cook expedition and toward the end of their conversation invited Browne to enlist. ". . . when I left the smoking car I had cast my lot with his," Browne said.[3]

The expedition leader, Dr. Frederick A Cook, had distinguished himself as a member of several arctic and Antarctic expeditions. After an unsuccessful expedition to the South Pole, famed explorer

DENALI PARK AND PRESERVE, MUSEUM COLLECTION, #7070

Belmore Browne called the north side of the Alaska Range in the shadow of Mt. McKinley, the "happy hunting grounds." The Dall sheep he killed fed and restored his climbing partners after their arduous 1912 winter cross-country trip to the mountain.

Roald Amundsen had praised Cook's "unfaltering courage." Despite his polar adventures Cook had absolutely no climbing experience other than what he had obtained on a failed 1903 expedition to McKinley. Prior to setting out on that expedition he told his companions that once they reached McKinley's base they would ascend the mountain "at a rate of 5,000 feet a day," a ridiculous goal. Cook had followed the tortured route to the mountain blazed by Alfred Hulse Brooks a year earlier. Two months after Wickersham's retreat from Mt. McKinley, Cook made his attempt, also from the northwest side. He too failed on the avalanching slopes and steep terrain above the Hannah (now Peters) Glacier. In retreat, starving, feuding, and desperate, he and his companions forged a new route eastward and re-crossed the Alaska Range through a difficult pass. Cook's party returned to tide water via the Susitna drainage, completing an incredible 750-mile circumnavigation of the mountain.[4]

The remarkable 1903 circumnavigation failed to appease Cook. His life's goal was clearly to reach the North Pole and he apparently believed that a conquest of Mt. McKinley would help finance his own expedition. His first McKinley expedition received enough attention to finance a second attempt.

Cook's 1906 expedition—sponsored by *Harper's Monthly*, businessman Henry Disston, and the wealthy Parker—would be the first to challenge the southern approaches to the mountain. The overland journey from Cook Inlet to the mountain turned into an epic wilderness struggle. ". . . the problem of *reaching* the mountain offered as many difficulties as climbing the mountain, and it was this perplexing problem that we determined to solve," Browne explained. "Geographically Mount McKinley seems to have been placed in the most inaccessible position obtainable. It lies just north of 'sixty-three' [in the] geographical center of the great wilderness . . ."[5]

After weeks of hazardous trekking, the expedition reached the outer summits of the Alaska Range. An initial exploration of the peaks revealed the enormity of their task. "At the head of the Tokositna River . . . Cook, Professor Parker, and I climbed a high mountain west of the glacier that gave us an unobstructed view of the southern and western faces of Mount McKinley. At the first glance we all saw that the scaling of the peak was a hopeless undertaking," Browne wrote.[6]

After over two months and an exploration of 3,000 square miles of wilderness, the expedition returned to the coast. Since a second attempt on Mt. McKinley that season was out of the question, Parker, the expedition's technical climbing expert, left for home. Cook's plans for the autumn suddenly changed when expedition sponsor Disston cancelled out of a hunting expedition he had scheduled with Cook.

With winter rapidly approaching, Cook decided to devote the rest of the season to exploration rather than climbing. "As a final task of our season's work," Cook explained, "I now determined to explore the river systems and glaciers to the east of Mt. McKinley . . . for a route to the top of the mountain for a future ascent." The choice seemed strange to Browne because Cook had already explored a significant portion of that drainage. Cook rejected Browne's request to go along, and instead asked Browne to go east to secure zoological specimens for Disston. Browne assented. In late August, Cook left the coast with just two men, horse wrangler Edward Barrill and a prospector. Neither of Cook's companions had climbing experience. Just before he left, Cook contradicted his earlier statements to Browne by sending out a telegram that read, "Am preparing for a last, desperate attack on Mount McKinley." A few weeks later Cook returned with the astonishing news that on September 16, he had climbed Mt. McKinley.[7]

Browne was incredulous. A thirteen-day round-trip from the Alder Creek camp to the summit? Impossible! "I knew the country that guarded the southern face of the mountain . . . and knew that the time Dr. Cook had been absent was too short to allow his even reaching the mountain," he explained.[8]

At the first opportunity, Browne took Barrill aside. The two had become friends and Browne expected Barrill to tell him the truth. In private, he asked Barrill for corroboration. "I can tell you all about the big peaks just south of the mountain, but if you want to know about Mount McKinley go and ask Cook," Barrill replied. Browne interpreted the comment as an admission of fraud. In the face of Browne's prodding, Cook said that he had not planned to climb the mountain at all, but once he discovered a way to reach the summit he changed his mind. He offered no satisfactory explanation for his earlier contradictory telegram. "I found myself in an embarrassing position," Browne explained, "I knew that Dr. Cook had not climbed Mount McKinley . . ."[9]

Back in New York both Browne and Parker rejected Cook's claim. They knew beyond doubt that two men without climbing experience could not have climbed the mountain in less than two weeks. In private, they stated their views to the American Geographical Society but encountered strong support for Cook. In public, they muted their comments, believing it unseemly for them to challenge Cook, one of the founders of the American Alpine Club, and member of the Explorers Club. "[Our] knowledge however did not constitute proof," Browne wrote, "and I knew that before I could make the public believe the truth I should have to collect some facts . . . we were willing to give Doctor Cook every chance to clear himself."[10]

The American public hailed Frederick Cook as a hero. His book, *To the Top of the Continent*, received wide acclaim in 1908. As proof of his climb, Cook published pictures of Barrill holding a flag atop what he described as the summit of Mt. McKinley. After publication, Browne wrote that he and Parker found "misstatements that we knew to be downright falsehoods." And saw them as "irrefutable proof of the deception." Again they muted their skepticism. Both were fair men who wanted to give Cook every chance despite the fact that one photo contained a damning flaw. In one view of the so-called summit, a distant and *higher* peak was visible.[11]

Cook's book for the most part is a rich and detailed description of the 1906 expedition, but turns vague in describing the summit route and details of the alleged climb. Why Cook lied and concocted his scheme is unknown. Experts have speculated that he was swept up in his desire to pass this stepping stone on his way to his real goal, a polar triumph. If Cook had merely rested on the laurels of his 1903 circumnavigation and 1906 expedition, he would have been amply honored. Instead, he perpetrated an astounding hoax, risking everything he had previously achieved.

If not for another and greater controversy that Cook created, his claim of climbing Mt. McKinley may eventually have been accepted. In 1909 he astounded the world by claiming to have reached the North Pole. A week after his announcement, Admiral Richard Peary returned from his own polar challenge and sent news that he had made the pole and that Cook had been nowhere near it. The controversy generated headlines worldwide. In Alaska, miners quickly hailed Peary as a hero and assailed Cook as a liar. "Ever since Dr. Cook described his ascent of Mount McKinley, Alaskans have been suspicious of the accuracy of this explorer," one editorial stated. Judge James A. Wickersham bluntly offered his own opinion. "All of us who know anything about Mount McKinley know that Cook's story of his successful ascent of that mountain is a deliberate falsehood," he wrote. "His story was so fraudulent, that one does not have time to talk about it."[12]

The Peary-Cook polar controversy ignited an international uproar and renewed interest in Cook's Mt. McKinley story. When questioned about the details of his climb, Cook claimed that the hardships of "his long polar night" had affected his memory and that he could not answer any questions without his diary. In October 1909, Cook's climbing companion, Barrill, recanted his story and was paid $5000 to release his faked diary. Barrill's inflammatory affidavit detailing the fake climb enabled Browne and Parker to finance a new expedition to the mountain to gather irrefutable proof of Cook's deception.

Browne and Parker now found themselves in the middle of the polar controversy. Public opinion favored Cook but proving he had not been to the pole was impossible. An increasing number of people believed that if Cook had lied about Mt. McKinley, he had lied about the pole, too. Public opinion now teetered on Browne and Parker's case against Cook. Proof, one way or another, would have sweeping consequences. Up until Barrill recanted, Cook had threatened Browne and Parker with a slander suit if they spoke out against him. "Originally our claims against [Cook] were really more or less private and personal," Browne explained. The announcement of their new expedition and public reports of their skepticism placed them directly in the line of fire. "Looking back on that remarkable controversy, I am still astonished at the incredible amount of vindictive and personal spite that was shown by the partisans of Dr. Cook," Browne wrote. ". . . scarcely a day went by when we did not receive abusive anonymous letters."[13]

Backed by the American Geographical Society and Explorers

Club, Browne and Parker assembled a superlative team of scientists and experienced climbers to explore and attack the south side of the mountain. The 1910 Parker Expedition had three main goals: To reach the summit; produce the first reliable map of the region; and primarily to ". . . duplicat[e] Dr. Cook's photographs and settling once and for all time his [summit and] Polar claim."[14]

When the news broke that Tom Lloyd's group of miners had reached the north summit, Parker, preparing for his departure to Alaska, expressed open skepticism. He said that the climb neither disproved nor proved Cook's claims as Lloyd had attacked from the north not the south side. Alaskans, gloating over Lloyd's success, poked fun at what they called the Egghead Expedition then heading for Alaska.

The Parker expedition left Seattle in May 1910, unaware of yet another expedition heading for the mountain. On the shores of Cook Inlet they crossed paths with a rival four-man expedition led by Claude Rusk. The members of the Mazama Mountaineering Club of Portland, Oregon, vocal supporters of Cook, were bent on climbing the mountain to prove Cook's claim. Despite their divergent goals, the two groups hit it off and from the initial meeting enjoyed a friendly competition.

To avoid the cross-country ordeal of the previous horse-powered expedition, Browne selected a powerboat that could push heavy loads up the rushing rivers leading to the mountain. Browne successfully steered his remarkable boat up the Chulitna River, almost to the terminus of the Ruth Glacier. From a base camp near the terminus, the climbing team slogged up the glacier searching for Cook's false summit. For reference, the men carried Cook's published description and pictures of his route and peak. "Our mountain detective work was based on the fact that no man can lie topographically," Browne wrote. "In all the mountain ranges of the world there are not two hillocks exactly alike."[15]

The central Alaska Range is a wilderness of innumerable peaks and finding one otherwise unremarkable pinnacle seemed an impossible task. Incredibly, in late June the explorers found the Fake Peak, in reality a mere 5836-foot-tall minor outcrop almost twenty miles southeast of McKinley's true summit. Herman Tucker posed for photographs on the summit holding an American flag, duplicating the pose that Cook had offered the world. "After this discovery we no longer expected to find that the Doctor had actually climbed a high peak," Browne wrote, "climbing with printer's ink was far easier." Browne proclaimed the discovery of the Fake Peak as "the end of the polar controversy," unaware that the battle over Cook's summit and polar claims would persist to this day.[16]

After this stunning success, the expedition now turned in search of a route to McKinley's summit. While Browne and Parker were reconnoitering, Rusk floundered into one of their lower camps to report his expedition had run out of food and was quitting the mountain. Even though Rusk had failed to find the Fake Peak, "his sympathies were no longer with the Brooklyn explorer…" He also had found that Cook's map bore no resemblance to the actual terrain. Rusk "realized how utterly impossible and absurd was the story of this man who, carrying a single pack, claims to have . . . stood on the highest point of McKinley," Browne said.[17]

The expedition began its final push toward the summit on June 2, almost two months to the day after Anderson and Taylor had scaled the mountain's north peak. In late July, Parker, Browne, and Tucker made it to the very head of the west fork of the Ruth Glacier before yawning crevasses and thunderous avalanches at 10,300 feet ended their quest. "This is the end! Our farthest North," Browne wrote. "10,000 feet does not seem much in the abstract . . . we have given all of our best efforts, we have actually won every foot of our way . . . proud in a small way of our work, for we have proved Mount McKinley unclimbable from the south side." Even with 50 days more of food, Browne said, the expedition could not have reached the summit, another blow to Cook's claim since he had been only lightly provisioned.[18]

The success of the Parker Expedition neither silenced Cook's defenders nor satisfied Browne and Parker. "Immediately after our second failure to climb Mount McKinley Professor Parker and I began to plan a third attempt," Browne wrote. "We were through with the southern approach—and our next attempt would be made from the northern side of the Alaska Range." Browne had deduced from the written accounts and conversations with Brooks, Cook, Lloyd, and Wickersham, and a photograph shown him by Charles Sheldon that the best route to the summit would lie to the east of Wickersham's ice wall. The planned 1911 trek was postponed when Browne and

Parker suddenly came down with gold fever and stampeded to new strikes in Prince William Sound looking for the cure.[19]

Wiser but no richer, Browne and Parker left Seward by dogteam on February 1, 1912, bound for the north side of the Alaska Range. Two weeks later at the town of Knik, just west of present-day Anchorage, they teamed up with Arthur Aten and LaVoy, both veterans of the 1910 expedition. These two stalwarts had just returned from sledging the expedition's supplies up the Chulitna River. From that supply cache, the men planned to forge north and find a way to cross the Alaska Range. The entire success of the endeavor hinged on finding a pass through the mountains.

In a mining camp, Browne heard rumors of a pass through the Alaska Range discovered by a nameless prospector. Weeks of hard sledding brought the men to Broad Pass, where they then veered north up an unnamed creek in search of the pass. The creek ended in a jumble of 6,000 foot peaks and ridges. By luck, they located a high gap in the range, lowered their dogs and sleds down the other side, and found themselves a few short miles below the mythic pass, actually Anderson Pass.

A modern-day Mt. McKinley climbing guide who has been to the exact gap in the mountains that Browne and Parker crossed was amazed by the difficulty of the route and the ability of these pioneers to piece their way through without maps.

On April 12, the expedition set up camp on the Muldrow Glacier on the north side of the range, in view of the summit. Two and one-half months of hard travel had taken its toll on the men and they needed rest. Less than a week later, bolstered by fresh Dall sheep meat, the men descended the glacier to timberline. They established the twenty-fifth camp of their journey on the McKinley Fork of the Kantishna River. By chance, they had found Tom Lloyd's old climbing camp—a wall tent equipped with a wood stove and various odds and ends. Inside, they found evidence of recent habitation and a bundle of newspapers. Unbeknownst to them, the tent had just been vacated by Ralph Cairns, the leader of a Fairbanks Daily Times-sponsored expedition that had attempted to verify Tom Lloyd's story. Cairns explored far to the west and gave up without ever finding McGonagall Pass. (Cairns, George Lewis, and Martin Nash attempted to climb Pioneer Ridge but were stymied by a sharp pinnacle at 9240 feet.)

While Parker and Aten mushed to Moose Creek in the Kantishna to buy supplies, Browne went in search of a route to the mountain. He soon found Charlie McGonagall's pass, the key to the upper Muldrow Glacier. "I was overjoyed, as in one day's travel from [camp] I had actually prospected a route to an altitude of 12,000 feet on the big mountain," he said. "With a light heart I started down from the pass, which was 6000 feet in altitude . . ." In a little over fourteen hours, Browne had hiked 35 miles and climbed 6,000 feet.[20]

Modern climbing guides do not believe that Browne meant to say that he had actually ascended to 12,000 feet. Rather, they think he identified the route from McGonagall Pass that lead upward to about that level.

While waiting for Parker's return, Browne prowled what he later called "The Happy Hunting Grounds." The month of April on the north side of the Alaska Range is often the most delightful of the year. The nights are still crisp, but the long days are warm enough to melt snow and sprout early wildflowers. The first birds return from the south and bears stagger forth from hibernation. Hard-frozen rivers begin to thaw and gurgle with melt water and the earth smells rich and clean. "I spent all my time wandering through the mountains with my gun and camera," he wrote. "The mountain country at the base of Mount McKinley is the most beautiful stretch of wilderness that I have ever seen, and I will never forget those wonderful days when I followed up the velvety valleys or clambered among the high rocky peaks as my fancy led me."[21]

Meanwhile over in the Kantishna, Parker purchased supplies and met with Charles McGonagall. What they discussed remains a tantalizing mystery. Did McGonagall describe or sketch the route to the pass? Or detail his route up the mountain? Offer other insights that Parker found to be helpful or accurate? Later, Parker said that McGonagall had told him that his partners had left a snow shovel to mark the actual summit. What else they might have discussed is lost to time.

Soon after Parker's return to base camp, the men used their dog teams to relay their equipment and provisions up the Muldrow Glacier via the route pioneered by the Glen Creek boys. The advent of warmer weather brought snow squalls and countless avalanches. Crevasses were a constant danger. In early May, LaVoy and Browne mushed their teams to about 11,000 feet and cached a total of 300 pounds of food, fuel, and equipment.

With their supplies now in place, the men were in no hurry to begin the actual climb. Browne and Parker freely admitted that they had greatly underestimated the distances and difficulties of their journey and needed time to recover their strength for the actual climb. The sojourn lasted three bucolic weeks. It can be argued that by taking such a long break, Browne and Parker missed a lengthy period of stable weather, which might have offered innumerable summit opportunities. Finally on June 5, over four months after their start from the tidewater, Browne, Parker, and LaVoy began their final assault on the mountain. Aten stayed behind to care for the dogs.

The three climbers moved rapidly up the glacier to their high cache. Next they climbed to the crest of what Browne called the "central north-eastern ridge" and established a camp in the col, near the site of the Glen Creek boys' Tunnel Camp. In the following days, they fought storms and mild symptoms of altitude sickness to relay heavy loads to a higher camp on the ridge. A bad knee hobbled the powerful LaVoy but they all suffered in some way. By the time they reached the lofty basin between the twin summits, "we were awful objects to look at," Browne said. "LaVoy and I were always more or less snow-blind . . . our eyes were swollen to slits and ran constantly; we were all almost black, unshaven, with our lips and noses swollen, cracked, and bleeding, our hands, too, were swollen cracked and bloodstained."[22]

The climbers relayed loads upward for several days and established their ultimate camp at 16,600 feet. Here conditions fluctuated rapidly. Frequent and violent storms pulsed over the summit and plunged temperatures far below zero. The altitude sapped their strength and they slept fitfully. No previous McKinley expedition had established a camp as high or as well provisioned as this one. Everything seemed ideal for a final assault on the summit but the men had made a terrible mistake. For food, they had brought only canned pemmican—a pressed cake of dried meat, fat, oats, and fruits, an almost indigestible concoction at high altitude. Their diet tormented and weakened them. Early on June 29, 1912, the three climbers, miserable with fatigue and indigestion—but confident of success—launched their attack. LaVoy and Browne

148   CHAPTER TEN

DENALI PARK AND PRESERVE, MUSEUM COLLECTION, #7070

Members of the 1912 climb rest en route to their defeat just below the summit of Mt. McKinley. The crystalline, calm weather turned rapidly into a raging, dangerous storm that turned them back just a few feet from the top.

traded the lead, chopping steps only where necessary, conserving their strength for the toil ahead. At 18,500 feet, they paused to celebrate setting what they believed to be the official American altitude record. (Anderson and Taylor went to 19,470 feet.) Overhead and to the north, the cloudless sky seemed to stretch forever. To the south, ominous waves of clouds enveloped the peaks and a light breeze began to stir. Pushing beyond 19,000 feet, the climbers surmounted a rise and saw the summit in sharp relief. "It rose as innocently as a tilted snow-covered tennis-court and as we looked it over we grinned with relief—we *knew* the peak was ours."[23]

The weather rapidly deteriorated and turned into the gale-powered blizzard that soon battered them into submission near the summit. That afternoon, the beaten men moved blindly down hill. A false turn or lost trail meant death. "We reached camp at 7:35pm after as cruel and heart-breaking a day as I trust we will ever experience," Browne wrote.[24]

The climbers shivered through a frigid, restless night but by dawn the weather was again clear and calm. Dead with fatigue, they could not try again. Instead, they tended their frozen clothing and treated their snow-singed eyes. A day later, operating on will alone for they had not eaten or slept, they mounted a second attack. Again, a sudden blizzard broke over the mountain. For an hour Browne lead upward into the waxing storm but finally stopped, the futility obvious. With barely a word, the climbers turned and lurched back down, reaching camp at three in the afternoon. After hot tea and a brief council, they decided to head down. Three hours later they stumbled into their camp at 15,000 feet.

The retreat down the mountain to base camp signaled the end of Browne and Parker's McKinley quest. The defeat pushed Browne into depression—what he later called one of the darkest periods of his life. "The last period of our climb on Mount McKinley is like the memory of an evil dream," he recalled.[25]

Aten greeted the climbers' return to base camp with tears of joy. The planned two-week climb had taken a month and Aten had all but given up hope. The relief was mutual. Browne had tortured himself with visions of the terrible accidents that could have befallen Aten. "Those weeks of suspense must have been a trying ordeal," Browne wrote, "but [Aten] stuck to his post and determined to wait until the snow had come or his food was gone . . ."[26]

On July 6, a tremendous roar from the peaks roused the men from their tent. The earth trembled and the men fought to keep their footing. Trees whipped back and forth and their gear caches toppled to the ground. Fissures opened in the earth and filled with mud. A nearby lake boiled as if heated. "I can only compare the sound to thunder, but it had a deep hollow quality," Browne wrote, "a sinister suggestion of overwhelming power that was terrifying. I remember that as I looked, the Alaskan Range melted into the mist and that the mountains were bellowing . . ."[27]

Minutes after the earth settled, Aten looked up and yelled, "Good God! Look at Brooks!" The other men bolted from the tent to stare toward the peak they had just named. ". . . the whole extent of the mountain wall that formed its buttress was avalanching," Browne wrote. "The avalanche seemed to stretch along the range for a distance of

Climbing expert Herschel Parker, left, and photographer Merl LaVoy, in camp at McGonagall Pass in 1912.

several miles . . ." He watched as a white cloud of avalanche debris obscured the entire range and pushed thousands of feet into the air. As the blast advanced toward them at a mile a minute, they frantically braced the tent's guy ropes and rolled boulders onto the tent pegs. After the shock wave passed, the men emerged from the tent and found the tundra around camp spotted with ice and snow from an avalanche ten miles away.[28]

Far to the south, the cataclysmic eruption of Mt. Katmai on the Alaska Peninsula, and the attendant earthquake swarm, had triggered the massive avalanche. The climbers had escaped certain death by just a few scant days, or so they believed.*

Now began the arduous cross-country trek north to the Yukon River and the eventual boat journey home. In Kantishna, miners welcomed the climbers with typical hospitality. Joe Dalton turned his cabin over to the men and several miners provided food. The months-long struggle had exacted an obvious toll. At the outset of the expedition, the 5'6" Browne had weighed 145 pounds but now

---

*Modern science does not support a connection between the earthquake/avalanche and the eruption.

barely registered 125. His waist had shriveled from 30 to 23 inches. The others were equally emaciated, especially the lanky Parker. Fannie McKenzie stuffed them with what Browne called "the most delicious meal that I have ever eaten."[29]

As they lingered on the claims, they met the Glen Creek boys. Parker introduced Browne to McGonagall. Pete Anderson hosted the men at his cabin in Glacier City. En route down river, they met Billy Taylor. During these friendly encounters, Browne and Parker must have formed some opinion of these men. Anderson's impressive size and strength was obvious. Surely they heard of Taylor's reputation for honesty. They must have compared their own experiences on the mountain with what they heard and made some judgment. During their climb they had looked for the spruce pole. "We saw no sign of a flagpole but it is our concerted opinion that the Northern Peak is more inaccessible than its higher southern sister," Browne later wrote. His only public comment on these electrifying personal encounters was circumspect. ". . . the lack of photographic evidence, added to the contradictory statements made concerning this climb, make it a difficult matter for an outsider to tell much about it."[30]

Even though the expedition of 1912 failed to reach the summit, it goes down as one of the grandest achievements in North American climbing history. The seven-month long expedition is still the only one to cross overland from sea level to summit.

During the attempt, Browne, Parker, and LaVoy set the North American altitude record and pioneered a practical route to the true summit. And finally, the expedition proved beyond doubt—at least to reasonable people—that Cook had lied. The real summit looked nothing at all like his summit photos. "If Mount McKinley is ever climbed to the final dome the men who climb it will follow the very trail we pioneered, until, weather permitting, they walk the short distance to the . . . highest point on the continent," Browne wrote.[31]

For their singular achievement, all four men deserved the highest respect. Instead, Alaskan newspapers brayed their derisive commentary. Of course, Browne and Parker did not make the summit; they were Easterners! The disdain with which many Alaskans viewed the Egghead Expedition was in sharp contrast to the way Browne viewed them. "The more you see of the Alaskan prospector, the more you admire his breed, for these men pay a thousand-fold more in toil and suffering than the treasures that they win are worth," Browne said. He could have applied the same comment to himself and his three companions.[32]

Browne returned home to pursue his artistic career and marry the girl of his dreams. Although he never again attempted to climb the mountain he remained active in the region's issues and politics for decades to come.

11

The Deacon and the Sourdough

In a small log cabin on the banks of the Yukon River near Tanana, Hudson Stuck sat by the wood stove reading a days-old newspaper. His eyes fairly glittered as he read the thrilling news—Belmore Browne and Herschel Parker had failed to reach the summit of Mt. McKinley. The Archdeacon bore no personal malice toward Browne or Parker, but climbing the mountain was a cherished dream. Even though he often had said that he was "concerned much more with men than mountains," reaching the summit first was important to him both personally and professionally.[1]

Stuck lowered the paper and looked at the young Athabascan man who sat reading at the table. Quietly he told Walter Harper that he was going to make the climb and asked Harper to join him in what he viewed as God's work.

Harper smiled back. The two had discussed the possibility of a climb numerous times but the demands of Stuck's ministry always took precedence. Through experience and dashed hopes, the Archdeacon knew he had but one chance left to make the summit. His young, powerful assistant would be key to his own chances for success.

In 1912, Hudson Stuck often referred to as "Archdeacon of the Yukon" because of his lengthy journeys by dogteam and boat throughout Interior Alaska, had wanted to publicize the Episcopal Church 25th Alaska anniversary in a spectacular way. He thought an ascent of the mountain he called *Denali* would draw both attention and funding to the church's work on behalf of Alaska Natives. He said he viewed a successful climb only in terms of what it could do for the

HISTORICAL PHOTOGRAPH COLLECTION-VF, #73-66-223N, ARCHIVES, UNIVERSITY OF ALASKA, FAIRBANKS

The Episcopal Church's Hudson Stuck, "ARCHDEACON OF THE YUKON," *organized the first successful climb of Mt. McKinley in 1913. Without his climb leader Harry Karstens, and his protégé, Walter Harper, Stuck would not have made the summit.*

native people of Alaska, whom he saw as a gentle and kindly race, threatened with extermination.

The controversy generated by the claims of previous Mt. McKinley climbers guaranteed maximum publicity and money for anyone who reached the summit. Stuck had long resented the fame and money that Dr. Frederick Cook accrued for his disputed climb. Cook's publisher had paid $28,000 for his story, and a single speaking engagement at Carnegie Hall netted $3000. In the fall of '09 Cook may have received up to $69,000, a huge sum when compared to the budget of the perpetually cash-strapped Alaska missions. After considerable debate, Bishop Peter Trimble Rowe gave Stuck permission to plan the 1912 climb but warned him that he would have to finance the climb himself and use his vacation time for the effort. The Bishop's sudden and serious illness in the winter of 1912, however, resulted in the cancellation of the Anniversary Climb. Stuck asked Rowe and everyone involved to keep the postponed expedition secret from the "hungry stupid little Fairbanks papers."[2]

Throughout the spring of 1912, Stuck kept a worried eye on the Browne-Parker expedition then assaulting the mountain. News of their tragic defeat just a few hundred feet from the summit spurred Stuck into renewed action. He re-doubled his efforts to raise the $1,000 needed for supplies and to order necessary equipment. His attack on the mountain would begin in the spring of 1913.

At first glance the Alaskan frontier seemed an odd place to find a person like Stuck. He was born on the outskirts of London on November 11, 1863. After his graduation from King's College, the 22-year-old set out to see the world. A coin toss led him to America, and on to Texas. After three years of odd jobs, Stuck signed on as acting principal of San Angelo's public schools. There an acquaintance described Stuck as an "obvious Britisher" and a "brilliant, refined gentleman," a novelty in Texas cow towns. He began his church career as a lay reader in the local Episcopal Church and from the pulpit railed against child labor. In Texas, as elsewhere, children as young as eight worked in factories and farms 10 hours a day, six days a week, an abomination that Stuck fought with typical dogged determination.[3]

In 1889, Stuck entered the Theological Department of the University of the South, at tiny Sewanee, Tennessee, where he was ordained four years later. He returned to Texas and soon became Dean of St. Matthew's Cathedral in Dallas. In 1904, he resigned from this influential and wealthy parish to assist Bishop Rowe, the first Episcopal missionary bishop of Alaska.[4]

When asked many years later why he left a comfortable position in Texas to work in the Alaska wilderness, Stuck said, "When . . . [I] realize[d] how long they [Alaska Natives] have inhabited this land in which God has planted them, a great wave of indignation [swept] over me that they should now be threatened with a wanton and senseless extermination."[5]

On September 1, 1904, Rowe, who had spent eight difficult years in Interior Alaska, turned his quarter-million-square-mile parish over to Stuck and transferred to Southeast Alaska. Stuck's first winter trek by dogteam looped through Circle City, Ft. Yukon, Eagle, Bettles, Coldfoot, Rampart, and then back to Fairbanks. In all, he and his Native assistants covered 1,480 miles in 62 days in temperatures averaging -32°F, an auspicious start for a Cheechako minister.

The Archdeacon applied enormous energy to his work. During his first posting in Fairbanks, he started a hospital, school, and library. By early 1907, *Ginkhii Choo*, "the big preacher," had visited every mining community and Native village in Interior. At Allakaket on the Koyukuk, he built the region's first church, St. John's in the Wilderness. In 1908, he moved to Ft. Yukon to be nearer his chosen congregation.

Although charged with the spiritual and physical welfare of both whites and Natives, Stuck felt that Natives, "threatened by the steamroller of civilization," needed his help the most. He wanted to create a "viable, Christian Native people, living in a traditional way, free of white influence." He thought it nonsense to encourage Natives to abandon all tribal and cultural traditions. He fought bitterly against liquor sales, which he viewed as "unscrupulous greed." He waged "fearful battles against the 'hooch-peddlers' and the degenerate riff-raff," and sought a territorial-wide ban on liquor. The passage of the so-called Bone-Dry Law of 1918, which outlawed all liquor sales throughout Alaska, was partly the result of his efforts. His support of prohibition made Stuck many enemies.[6]

He also opposed the concept of Indian reservations because he believed it limited Natives the necessary freedom of movement for a subsistence life. Not only did he fight for aboriginal land rights, he fought for government control of commercial salmon fishing then dominated by powerful Outside interests. He believed that unrestricted salmon fishing on the coast in 1909 had caused widespread starvation in the Koyukuk District.

His vociferous attacks on the establishment made him enemies in high places. Government policy was then fixated on economic expansion and resource extraction without regard to Native concerns. In response to Stuck's out-spoken attacks, all religious schools in the territory were temporarily threatened with closure.

Often sarcastic and proud, the authoritarian Stuck demanded a lot from those around him. Plagued by insomnia, he was sharp-tongued, easily angered, and quick to the attack. "Impulsiveness seems to be his nature," sighed Bishop Rowe after one outburst. Stuck was "a very difficult, temperamental, exasperating, somewhat egocentric man," his biographer wrote. "Not always right and certainly not always likable, he affects the course of his times by his resolute opposition to social evils."[7]

Stuck confronted anything and everything that aroused his indignation. What he called "the openness of sinners" in Fairbanks immediately roused his ire. Gambling, prostitution, drunkenness, and muggings were commonplace. The commonality of violence there awed him. He staunchly championed prohibition but realized that outlawing prostitution would never work. By backing a proposal to establish and police a red light district, he made further enemies. A crowd at a rally burned him in effigy.

Due to the Church's perpetual poverty, Stuck's work relied largely on Outside funding and in the winter of 1907–08 he went on the first of what he called "begging trips" through the States. On it, he secured enough money to pay for the construction of a four-ton gas-powered launch.

Stuck used *The Pelican*, named for its Louisiana benefactors, to bring his ministry, mail, food, supplies, and medical care to the isolated people living along Interior rivers. When smallpox cut a terrible swath through villages on the Porcupine River, the *Pelican* proved invaluable in limiting the catastrophe. "In one summer, we have managed to vaccinate almost every native in the Interior of Alaska from Eagle down to Holy Cross, and on all the tributary rivers," Stuck exulted.[8]

The Archdeacon was an amateur but eager mountain climber. As a youth, he had climbed in Scotland and Wales, and in America, the Rockies and Cascades. He devoured climbing literature and journals of Alaskan explorations. After barely three months in Alaska, Stuck wrote of Mt. McKinley and his desire to climb it. "I'd rather climb this mountain than discover the richest gold mine in Alaska," he said.[9]

Sheer stubbornness had carried Hudson Stuck a long way in life, but to climb Mt. McKinley, he knew he needed help. For his plan to succeed, he needed a stalwart guide of unquestioned expertise. Harry Karstens, a fellow Episcopalian, with his "full vigor of maturity" and "accumulated experience and self-reliance," seemed the ideal partner.[10]

Harry Karstens had long desired to climb the mountain with Charles Sheldon. On May 12, 1909, Sheldon married Louisa Walter Gulliver, a former New York horse-carriage driver. When Karstens heard news of the wedding, he saw his dream evaporate. "[Sheldon] was very much taken with [the mountain] observing it from all angles and from what I knew later he picked the only way to make the climb, before leaving he asked me if I would join him if he decided to make the climb," Karstens later recalled. "I told him I would take a chance with him, but he spoiled it by getting married."[11]

Stuck knew of Karstens' interest in Mt. McKinley. "Mr. Karstens and I discussed the proposed ascent as long ago as [1906 or '07] and I should never have attempted it without his co-operation," he said later. They first talked in-depth about the actual climb in the spring of 1911. "I didn't feel I could afford to do it," Karstens explained, "I had to make a living." Stuck promised a full share in the profits. In December, Stuck pressured Karstens for a commitment and chafed at the delayed response. Karstens had gone Outside to visit family in Chicago and then Charles Sheldon in New York. "My heart is set on this attempt and having you with me," Stuck pleaded. "I don't think there is anyone who can take your place." Finally, in late March 1912, Karstens returned to Fairbanks and the men reached an understanding. Stuck agreed to finance the venture, keep the records, and conduct scientific observations. Karstens was to furnish nothing more than the critically needed experience.[12]

Karstens based his decision on several factors. Foremost was a genuine desire to climb the mountain. Next, he wanted to vindicate Charley McGonagall and prove that the Glen Creek boys had told the truth. And, finally, despite knowing of Stuck's checkered reputation, he was swayed by Stuck's self-promotions and promises. He fully expected to make a little money, maybe even a handsome profit, for his toil and sacrifice.

Karstens was not rolling in cash. In the six years since Charles Sheldon's first trip to the Kantishna, Karstens had been involved in several business enterprises, most involving transportation. Typically, these pursuits entailed hard work and personal risk. One year he and E.S. Bunch started a dogteam express service from Fairbanks to a new strike on Tenderfoot Creek, 12 miles downstream from the confluence of the Delta and Tanana Rivers. On one trip, with the temperature at -40°F, severe tonsillitis incapacitated Bunch, so Karstens loaded him in his sled and raced for Fairbanks. While breaking trail ahead of the dogs, Karstens suddenly plunged through thin ice into a deep channel on the Tanana River. Somehow he managed to extricate himself. Now soaking wet, Karstens lashed the dogs into a run for a cabin a few miles ahead. Karstens, his clothing stiff with ice and his skin beginning to freeze, drove the dogs hard and reached the safety of the cabin in record time. After drying out, Karstens took off again, running the 63 trail miles to Fairbanks in sixteen hours. Only after Karstens delivered his partner to the doctor did he seek treatment for his frozen nose and face.

Such exploits added luster—but little wealth—to the *Seventymile Kid's* solid reputation for honesty, courage, and indomitable dependability. Judge Wickersham held Karstens in such high regard that in 1908, he offered Karstens the position of Deputy U.S. Marshall. Karstens declined.

More than once, Karstens had attempted to capitalize on his knowledge of the country and mining. In the spring of 1909, W.F. Whitely and Richard C. Wood, known as "the dean of banking in the Tanana," opened the R.C. Wood, Company, with Harry Karstens as treasurer. The new partners had first worked together in 1905, when Wood and Whitely had staked claims in the Kantishna and used Karstens' express freight service. Wood was a genuine Fairbanks pioneer. He started the Tanana Restaurant in 1903, and had worked as chief clerk for the First National Bank. A year after opening the new company, Wood turned it over to the management of Whitely and Karstens, "both of [whom] are well and favorably known here."[13]

The Whitely-Karstens Company dealt in real estate, with an emphasis on mining properties, loans, collections, and accounting. The partners brought different but complimentary skills to the business. Whitely traded in claims throughout Interior and Karstens had the ability to oversee field operations.

The distant Iditarod district piqued the new company's interest. In December 1910, Karstens mushed seven dogs from the Yukon River to Iditarod, carrying 600-pounds of freight and two passengers, the *Kantishna King* James Chronister, and his wife. Karstens then inspected claims throughout the district and transported bulging pokes of gold. On one 33-day trip, he carried $10,000 in gold from Iditarod to Kaltag, on the lower Yukon. Even though bandits sometimes waylaid gold freighters, Karstens—his reputation well established—was never bothered.

During summer months, Karstens used his 30-horsepower launch, *Snoqualmie*, to haul freight and passengers to the mining camps. He hired his old friend Mason "Mace" Farrar to help out. In 1911, the two took the launch and a barge load of supplies up the Koyukuk to the foothills of the Brooks Range.

Karstens spent the winter of 1911–12, in Chicago and returned to Alaska the following spring. After he and Stuck reached their agreement, Karstens returned to the diggings. When the ice went out, he moved to Goldstream valley to oversee the cleanup on Mrs. Walter Aubert's rich claims. (Mrs. Aubert often rode Karstens' horse *Toklat* in Fairbanks races.) With Karstens keeping a hard and watchful eye on the laborers, the cleanup went without a hitch. No stray nuggets found their way into pants pockets.

Harry Karstens was arguably the best man that Stuck could have chosen as the expedition's field leader. Not only was Karstens trail-hardened and indefatigable, he at times seemed immune to the extremes of cold and storm. What he lacked in climbing experience, he made up for with good sense, toughness, and determination. How the two men would function as part of a team was still unknown. A few people who knew both of them predicted trouble.

Stuck, who an acquaintance then described as "energetic but frail," chose his trail assistant and protégé, Walter Harper, as his climbing partner. Stuck seemed to understand that his only chance for the summit relied on a blend of Harper's strength and patience and

Karstens' wilderness savvy. Stuck's belief in his protégé proved accurate. After the climb he wrote that Harper "ran Karstens close in strength, pluck, and endurance . . . his kindness and invincible amiability endeared him to every member of the party."[14]

Walter had notable parents. His father, Arthur Harper, had been hailed as the "father" of the Klondike strike, and his mother was a respected Koyukon woman, *Seyn-dahn*, or Jennie Albert. Together they had seven children. After Arthur Harper died of tuberculosis in 1897, Jennie raised Walter in traditional Athabascan fashion. Harper was a teenager when he first attended school. When he arrived at St. Mark's Episcopal Mission in Nenana, he spoke little English and could neither read nor write. In his first year he made swift and remarkable progress. Stuck first met Harper, then 16, at the mission school in 1909.

Stuck employed several Native boys in his traveling ministry and in Walter he saw the perfect combination of interpreter, guide, dogteam driver, and operator/mechanic for the *Pelican*. Stuck clearly respected Harper's self-reliance and ingenuity, an obvious by-product of his traditional Native up-bringing. "He was adept in all wilderness arts . . . axe, a rifle, a flaying knife, a skin needle with its sinew thread—with all these he was at home; he could construct a sled or a pair of snow-shoes . . . and could pitch camp with all the native comforts and amenities as quickly as anybody I ever saw," Stuck wrote.[15]

Constant travel, almost 2,000 miles a winter by dogteam, kept Walter away from school for weeks at a time, but his education proceeded apace. Stuck taught him mathematics, literature, history, and writing. They read aloud everything from Treasure Island to Hamlet. In the diary that Harper kept on the McKinley climb, there are lists of Presidents and States, the books of the Old Testament, and the names of the week from Norse and Latin mythology. Harper was one of the first Native Alaskans to be schooled for service in the Episcopal Church.

Stuck praised Harper's character. "The lad [possessed] a modesty, a courtesy, a deference, that marked him a gentleman in any company and a sweetness of temper and an amiability that attracted people to him."[16]

Walter was not perfect and he sometimes angered his mentor. On one river trip, Stuck recorded a galling incident. ". . . I heard shot after shot, shot after shot, fired from the roof of the launch. I craned my neck out of the pilot-window and caught a glimpse of something brown moving in the brush which I thought at first was a bear; it was a moose! . . . the boy had killed it. It was a senseless and useless slaughter. We had no use for the meat and could not take care of it. Moreover it was against the law; doubly against the law, for we were in the closed season for moose and the shooting of females is forbidden at all times . . . it is hard to realize the excitement that seizes a Native boy, trained all his life in the reckless hunting of the Indian, at the sight of big game. His hand goes to his gun instinctively and he is shooting before he has time to think whether or not he has need of the meat."[17]

By the spring of 1913, Stuck and Harper had been together for three years. By all accounts, Stuck genuinely loved his young apprentice and offered the best education available. Their complex father-son, teacher-student, employer-employee relationship would last nine years.

To support the expedition, Stuck also chose two other students at St. Mark's Mission, John Fredson and Esaias George. Stuck picked them for their exceptional dog handling and mushing skills.

Other than that he hailed from Stevens Village, little is recorded of the life of Esaias George. Fredson's life, however, is well-known and respected. He was the ninth child of "Louise" and "Fred," nomadic Natsit Gwich'in Athabascans. He was born about 1895 near the Sheenjek River in northeastern Alaska. His Native name was *Zhoh Gwatsan*, "Wolf Smeller."

Louise died giving birth to her tenth child. Unable to care for all of his children, Fred took his youngest to the boomtown of Circle City in 1902, and turned them over to the Episcopal Church. Stuck met young Fredson there in 1905. When he turned 14 Fredson was sent to St. Mark's in Nenana, a step toward advanced education Outside. One teacher described him as "the most capable and reliable of all the boys." Another called him a "prize student . . . very much of a gentleman."[18]

Stuck had high hopes for Fredson. "We hope to make him a clergyman. He is a very intelligent boy . . . But better than that, he is a true-hearted loyal youth. His word I would take absolutely, about anything." The Archdeacon's high opinion was well placed. Later in his life Fredson would wage a successful battle to preserve and protect his traditional lands, and as a result be regarded as the "George Washington" of his people.[19]

The final member of the climbing team was Robert G. Tatum, a theology student at the University of the South and younger brother of a Signal Corps Lieutenant then serving in Alaska. Stuck had initially dragooned another Athabascan youth, Arthur Wright, as a member of the team but when Wright went Outside for medical treatment and high school, Stuck cast about for a replacement. The Church's 1912 Anniversary brought several young seminarians to Alaska, Tatum among them. Although inexperienced, Tatum possessed strength, enthusiasm, and commitment. During his first winter at St. Mark's Mission, he distinguished himself on a dogteam supply run to an isolated mission on the upper Tanana River. Tatum jumped at the invitation to replace Wright as camp cook. As part of his pre-expedition duties, he supervised the storage and collection of the climbing supplies at St. Mark's. After the climb, Karstens described Tatum as a "good worker but slow and green at trail work."[20]

For the expedition of 1913 to come off as planned, most of the supplies had to be transported and cached in the Kantishna the preceding autumn. Stuck had planned to use the *Pelican* to transport the supplies "as far up the Kantishna as she can get," but in August she stripped gears. With time running out, Stuck telegraphed Karstens in Fairbanks and directed him to purchase additional equipment in Fairbanks and use his gasoline launch to take their 4,500 pounds of gear to the Kantishna.

Karstens reached the cache at Diamond, beating freeze-up by only a few days. "I do very greatly appreciate your faithfulness and resourcefulness and kindness," a relieved Stuck wrote. "Please let me know if there is any expense you have had to bear."[21]

All was now set for the assault. The team was chosen and the supplies in place. When compared to the members of the Parker Expedition of 1910 and the Browne-Parker Expedition of 1912, Stuck's crew looked almost laughable. Two were teenagers, one a green Cheechako, and the leader a skinny, rather frail, 50-year-old. Only Harper and the sinew-tough Karstens appeared to have the physical strength necessary to make the summit, but even they had no real climbing experience. This was clearly an amateur expedition. Like the Glen Creek boys, however, they held trump cards. All of them, save Tatum, were absolutely at home in the wilderness and used to the rigors and extremes of winter travel. Karstens probably viewed climbing the mountain as just another challenge to defeat with hard-work and perseverance. In the end, it was Karstens' never-turn-back, never-back-down style that would secure the ultimate prize.

12

The Summit at Last

Day after day men and dogs toiled mightily to relay hundreds of pounds of gear up the Muldrow Glacier from McGonagall Pass to the high cirque below the Great Icefall. Hudson Stuck's "highway of desire," rose gently in its first four miles, but where it turned south, the glacier inclined steeply between towering, slab-sided ridges. Here countless crevasses entwined and it took days for Harry Karstens to unravel and mark a route around and over them. Some of the crevasses could be stepped over, others yawned wide and bottomless. In places, the men built snow bridges to get the dogs and sleds across.

For the push upward to the high camp at 10,800 feet, Karstens had split the team of six dogs into two teams each drawing a small Yukon sled. One roped climber led the dogs while another followed the dogs on the sled's gee pole, a braking and steering device. Dogs and men pulled for all their worth, inching ever upward, through alternating days of storm and blistering sun and wind. Only with the help of the dogs could the expedition's mountain of gear and firewood be ferried to high camp.

On the first day of May, the climbers awoke to find their hard won trail buried overnight by heavy snow. They had only two loads left to ferry to the head of the Muldrow, but now the trail had to be broken and packed yet again. Late that day the exhausted trail breakers set up a makeshift camp at the midway cache between the first and last glacier camps. The next day, Karstens, Stuck, Walter Harper, Robert Tatum, and Johnny Fredson completed the relay from the midway cache and deposited another load at the site selected for their last glacier camp. Before heading down for yet more supplies, the men took a break. Several hours later as they again approached the high cache, they saw a tendril of smoke. Stuck stared in disbelief. "Had some mysterious climber come over from the other side of the mountain?" he wondered. "Had he discovered our wood and our grub, and perhaps starving, kindled a fire . . . *smoke* must mean *man*." Alarmed, the climbers pressed forward to an intervening serac and from there saw their cache in flames. In shock, they dashed forward to douse the mystery blaze. "A sack containing woolen socks and many pairs of gloves and mittens and fur garments was burned . . . another sack with thirty spools of film for my camera had been exposed to the heat . . . every one of them was spoiled," Stuck lamented. Three silk tents for high altitude work went up in flames and Karstens lost his fur parka.[1]

Shovels, an axe, dog food, and invaluable rations were also destroyed. "All the sugar was gone, all our powdered milk and our baking powder; a case of pilot bread, our dried apples, our dried fruit and all sorts of other supplies were burned," Stuck recounted. "[Afterward] we were without sugar for a month and without bread for a couple of weeks." By pure chance the pemmican, sausage, milk chocolate, and other essentials reserved for the higher elevations were still down glacier.[2]

Sifting through the embers, the men concluded that a careless match dropped by either Stuck or Karstens when they lit their pipes during the earlier visit, had ignited the silk tents spread over the gear. Stuck thought he saw his dream of conquering the mountain wafting away in the smoke.

The next day, under a skin-scorching sun, the climbers completed their laborious move to their final glacier camp at 10,800 feet, the highest point accessible by dogteam. Quickly they dug a pit for their tent and surrounded it with blocks of ice. When the sun dropped behind a high ridge, the temperature plunged to -26°F. In the tent that night, elation for their advance vied with despair as the men took stock of their losses. Six weeks into the expedition, the fire was the first setback in the otherwise routine and fluid movement toward the ultimate prize. The work of the next few days would determine if they could continue or be forced to turn back.

The Summit at Last 167

DENALI PARK AND PRESERVE, MUSEUM COLLECTION, #10728

Robert Tatum, Esaias George, Harry Karstens, John Fredson, and Walter Harper pose at base camp during preparations for the 1913 climb. Walter Harper, right, was the first man to summit Mt. McKinley.

Without all the hoopla that had attended Tom Lloyd's departure from Fairbanks in 1910, Karstens and Stuck had left Fairbanks quietly in mid-March 1913. Stuck's original plan was to leave Fairbanks by dogteam on March 1 and by mid-month reach the supplies that Karstens had cached at Diamond on the Bearpaw River. Two weeks behind schedule, the dogteams pulled out from Nenana on St. Patrick's Day and by following the old Kantishna trail reached Moose Creek without incident.

The climbing plan was simple and straightforward: Start from Nenana, the nearest logistical center. Begin while the trails were still frozen enough to support heavily laden sleds. Forge across country to the supply cache at Diamond. Relay the gear to a base camp at Cache Creek. At the base camp hunt and prepare trail rations. Start upward well before the spring thaw. Follow the route up the Muldrow Glacier pioneered in 1910 and re-used in 1912. Retrace Browne and Parker's steps up the summit ridge.

On Good Friday, the expedition reached Eureka Creek and shortly after Easter began hauling their ton and a half of supplies from Diamond to the base of the mountain, fifty miles away. While in the Kantishna, Karstens and Stuck spoke with Anderson, Taylor, and McGonagall, gleaning all pertinent information. Afterward neither Karstens nor Stuck equivocated—they knew the route ahead of time. "There has been no need [for us] to make reconnaissance for routes," Stuck explained, "since these pioneers blazed the way; there is no other practicable route." Prior to leaving Fairbanks, the men had poured over Browne's newly published account of his 1912 summit attempt. They compared it with a letter Browne had sent Stuck in which he had answered questions and provided a sketch map of his route to the top. The wisdom to learn from others came as second nature to these trail-seasoned men.[3]

In mid-April, the climbers established camp in the last timber in Cache Creek, a few miles below McGonagall Pass. Here they hunted for meat and hauled firewood for transport to the higher camps. Stuck blamed the failure of Browne and Parker in part on their choice of high-altitude rations. "Why should anyone haul canned pemmican hundreds of miles into the greatest game country in the world?" Stuck asked. "We made our own pemmican of the choice parts of this tender, juicy meat and we never lost appetite for it or failed to enjoy and assimilate it."[4]

Karstens directed the pemmican making. In a big pot he boiled fresh caribou meat, fat and marrow, butter, salt, and pepper. After the mixture cooked, the men rolled the delicious mincemeat into 200 baseball-sized orbs and froze them. During the climb, their mainstay was a stew of pemmican, rice, and erbswurst, a sausage of compressed split pea soup.

On April 15, Esaias George, his work of relaying supplies to base camp completed, bid farewell and set out alone with the mission dogteam for the 100-mile return trip over the melting trail to Nenana. The assault on the mountain began at once. Karstens, Stuck, and Tatum prospected on snowshoes for a route up the Muldrow, marking with willow wands a switch-backed trail from McGonagall Pass through dangerous crevasses to a cache at 8,000 feet. While the three men were breaking trail, Harper and Fredson used the remaining six dogs to transfer the expedition's supplies to McGonagall Pass. Once the packed and marked trail hardened, the two young men followed with loaded sleds, the first of numerous and tedious relays. For these men, the move from Cache Creek to the high glacier camp was little more than typical winter freighting, and, except for the fire at the head of the glacier, relatively uneventful.

The cache fire at 10,500 feet had consumed vital gear and food. Perhaps another group of climbers would have given up. Karstens, however, was no quitter. The man who once improvised a sled out of a raw cowhide and survived a sub-zero tent blaze was not easily dissuaded. He immediately set everyone to work turning blankets into socks and improvising two tents out of ragged sled covers. The lost rations, though missed, would not be a major problem. All of them had traveled in the wilderness on minimal grub before.

During the enforced delay, the climbers tended their various maladies, chiefly intense sunburn. Karstens doctored his frost-nipped, "horrible" face. Stuck rubbed a homemade unguent into his sun-burnt skin. Tatum doctored his swollen tonsils. Unlike Browne, Parker, and LaVoy, however, none of them suffered from snow-blindness. Again they had learned from others and they all wore special amber-colored snow glasses, which gave total protection from the stinging glare.

On May 8, Karstens led Fredson and Harper on the initial assault up Browne's "central north-eastern ridge." Each carried heavy packs, intent on establishing a cache atop the col. Instead of the easy snow slope that both Browne and McGonagall had described in great detail, they found a debris field of ice and rock. To move through the jumble, they set their packs aside and began chopping steps upward.

The next day, while exploration of the slope continued, Tatum and Stuck roped together to escort Fredson and the dogteam down the glacier. The dogs could not stay in high camp; they had to go down before their food ran out. Once below the most dangerous crevasse-field, Stuck bid the amiable, hard-working lad farewell and told him to expect their return to base camp in two weeks.

The ridge that Belmore Browne had described as "steep but practical" proved now to be a dangerous, jumbled maze, a sobering remnant of a gargantuan avalanche. ". . . there is no doubt in my mind that the shakeup of last year has broken up the snow slopes and left the ridge in the condition it is," Karstens wrote. "Great blocks of ice stand on top of the ridge . . . other places honeycombed blocks stand over one another, which look as if they would tumble over by whispering at them." The fractured ridge was certain proof that Browne,

Parker, and LaVoy would have perished the year before had they been on the mountain during the earthquake.[5]

What otherwise would have been a simple ascent of a known route turned into days of extreme labor. "The difficulty of our task was greatly increased," Stuck wrote. "This ridge, that the pioneer climbers of 1910 went up at one march with climbing irons strapped beneath their moccasins, and carrying nothing but their flagpole, that the Parker-Browne party surmounted in a few days . . . was to occupy us for three weeks."[6]

Led by Karstens, the climbers eventually surmounted the fractured slope to the ridge crest. Here their spirits sank anew. ". . . ahead of us [stretched] miles and miles of ice-blocks heaved in confusion, resting at insecure angles, poised, some on their points, some on their edges, rising in this way some 3,000 feet," Stuck said. Ascending the ridge would be a Herculean task, much more difficult and dangerous than that faced by their predecessors. Passing storms would hinder and complicate their onerous chore.[7]

In the dangerous ascent of the shattered ridge, Harper quickly proved his mettle. Karstens described him as "strong, fearless and as fine and lovable disposition as I ever saw in a man. He was my main stand by . . . he would have gone anywhere I told him, I never saw him hesitate only once." The Karstens-Harper tandem led the entire way up the ridge, digging steps as they went.[8]

Periodic storms slowed the work and kept the team inside their cramped 9'×11' tent for days at a time. "We did not dare venture upon the ridge for fear of avalanches," Harper noted. Stuck had mentally prepared himself for the difficult and hazardous ascent but later said he had no idea "it would be so terribly tedious and laborious." Karstens laconically adding, "shoveling out steps is becoming monotonous."[9]

In forced confinement, the climbers looked for anything to break the tedium. They packed and re-packed equipment numerous times. They read package labeling or rehashed old stories. While tent-bound, the Archdeacon drilled Harper from Shakespeare. Karstens worked on a boat design.

Personality clashes, the norm of any extended climbing expedition, were inevitable. Stuck, impulsive and temperamental, was never easy to get along with and his manner clearly grated on the plainspoken

Karstens. Karstens was a man of action, chafing at the confinement that tested his legendary temper. The first bouts of altitude sickness exacerbated things. Headaches plagued them all, especially Stuck. Even the best of friends get irritable in such circumstances. Karstens and Stuck were never the best of friends.

The Archdeacon's manner and curt comments grated on everyone. "The kindest thing the Deacon's friends could do to him was not to pay too much attention to what he said," his biographer later explained.[10]

The co-leaders, with their widely divergent personalities and styles, had already clashed. Stuck had agreed to participate in camp chores but as was his custom on other trips he instead passed them off to Harper and Tatum. It galled Karstens to see Stuck "lying in the tent" while the others worked. Karstens, the freight-hauler and wilderness guide, loathed freeloading, do-nothing passengers, or parasites, as he sometimes called them. Less than two weeks into the climb, Karstens had had enough. "No work out of the deacon yet, continuing at sanctimonious whine his bacon wasn't cooked right his tea was wrong . . . Tatum would break his neck trying to do things for him and cook savory foods . . . the best he would get was a snappy answer . . . He would sit around and make them wait on him he tried me one time and never again, I was sick of him by this time," Karstens later reported to Charles Sheldon.[11]

At high camp Karstens finally exploded. "I got his goat he was angry I shamed him to it as I never wish to shame another man, he got out that morning and worked like a good one . . . talked to him straight just how I felt on the matter to quit his whining and get in and help his self . . ."[12]

Conflict was nothing new to the acerbic, thick-skinned Archdeacon but he desperately needed Karstens' cooperation if the climb was to succeed. "I am so dependent upon [Karstens] in this expedition that I have to put up with any bad temper he may show," he said. Stuck seemed to like his partner, despite what he described as "his limitations."[13]

Work continued on the route between storms. While Karstens and Harper cut steps, Stuck and Tatum packed gear to a higher cache on the ridge. Finally on May 30, the weather broke and after six exhausting relays, the climbers established a new camp at 14,600 feet, beneath a point on the ridge now known as Browne Tower. For the first time in over a month, the climbers again could see their prize, the glittering dome of the south summit.

Forever afterward, Stuck rejected any credit for conquering the ridge and unequivocally extolled Karstens' superior judgment and daring for the feat, which he described as "a brilliant piece of mountaineering." He proposed an appropriate honor. "[I] would like to name that ridge Karstens Ridge, in honor of the man who, with Walter's help, cut that staircase three miles long amid the perilous complexities of its chaotic ice-blocks."[14]

The climbers now moved into one of their small, improvised tents, just big enough to sit in but not stand up. At night, to roll over, the four men had to move in unison. Another enforced confinement in that tiny, crowded tent, likely would have tested the patience of them all. Finally, the storms abated and conditions greatly improved. The climbers quickly exploited the window of superb weather to push upward and establish their next camp at 15,000 feet in the Grand Basin. Here they toiled upward over hard-packed, relatively level snow and ice. The laborious step cutting was behind them.

In the Grand Basin, which Stuck later re-named the Harper Glacier, in Walter and Arthur Harper's honor, the doubt that had dogged Stuck momentarily evaporated. "With the exception of [Karstens] ridge, Denali is not a mountain that presents special mountaineering difficulties of a technical kind," he proclaimed. "Its difficulties lie in its remoteness, its size, the great distances of snow and ice its climbing [involves,] the burdens that must be carried over those distances. We estimated that it was twenty miles of actual linear distance from [McGonagall] pass ... to the summit ... But the Northeast Ridge, in its present condition, adds all the spice of sensation and danger that any man could desire."[15]

Altitude sickness quickly destroyed his renewed confidence and optimism. In the Grand Basin, severe headaches and acute shortness of breath debilitated him. In his preparations for the climb, Stuck, age 50, had cut his smoking down to two pipes a day and had given up smoking altogether once he had reached the ridge. None of this helped. The effects of thin air at high altitude vary from climber to climber. A number of issues, age, conditioning, proper hydration, and medical history come into play. Karstens, 32, a smoker, and Harper, 21, a nonsmoker, had the best wind of the four men. Smoking was only part of the Archdeacon's respiratory problems. He had already survived a bout with pneumonia, a lung inflammation that would one day kill him.

Just when the weather turned ideal, Stuck's failing health slowed the ascent. "When it was evident that the progress of the party was hindered by the constant stops on my account," he wrote, "the contents of my pack were distributed amongst the others and my load reduced . . ."[16]

Leading the way to their next camp at 16,600 feet, a spot near Browne and Parker's highest camp, Karstens and Harper halted in amazement to stare at the footsteps of their predecessors still scratched in the ice.

The North Peak loomed over the new camp. While the four climbers sat resting during a relay to the camp, "(we) began to talk about the flag staff that was supposed to have been put up on the north peak of Denali by Anderson," wrote Harper, "and as we were talking about it I suddenly looked up to the ridge that was running down from the north peak and to our great surprise I saw it standing out against the blue sky!"[17]

Karstens got out his binoculars and everyone had a clear view of the spruce pole. Instead of downcast, the party rejoiced, happy to confirm their cohorts' claims. As they progressed upward the climbers found that the pole was visible from only certain points on the upper glacier, perhaps explaining why Parker and Browne had missed it.* "To Lloyd belongs the honor of conceiving and organizing the attempt," Stuck said later, "To McGonagall belongs the credit of discovering the pass . . . and the credit for climbing to nineteen thousand five hundred feet . . . but to Pete Anderson and Billy Taylor . . . belongs the honor of the first ascent of the North Peak." Throughout his life, Karstens lauded the

---

*When Stuck and Karstens returned to Kantishna and reported seeing the flagpole, some of the miners believed that Browne, Parker, and LaVoy must have seen it the previous summer but kept it secret. Mountain experts claim that no one else but the 1913 expedition saw the flagpole. In late spring 1910, however, Northern Commercial Company fur buyer J.E. Baker said he saw the flagpole twice through his binoculars from two different places in the Kantishna. An even more credible witness, Woodbury Abbey, who surveyed the park boundaries in 1921, said he spotted it several times through his transit from various prominences in the Kantishna District. His family members saw it as well. "McKinley reared up cloudless before us, the base a dozen miles away, the peak perhaps twenty," his daughter Denise said. "Through Dad's transit . . . we believed that once or twice we glimpsed the cairn and pole erected by Billy Taylor and his companions."

near superhuman feat of Anderson and Taylor, and that of his old pal McGonagall, whom he had never doubted.[18]

Buoyed by this discovery, the climbers pushed on to camp. On June 6 they forged ahead to set up their final camp at 17,400 feet. They had two full weeks of food and fuel with them, which they could stretch to three weeks. If need be, they could wait out an extended storm, or even establish yet another, higher camp. Everything seemed primed for success but as others had learned on Mt. McKinley, there is no sure thing.

Archdeacon Stuck, so near his cherished goal, was failing. For days, he had been convulsed by choking and shortness of breath, even blackouts. The altitude smothered him and "the medicine chest held no remedy for blind staggers." That he had even gotten this high was a powerful testament to both his extraordinary will and the excellence of his companions. At one point, Karstens wrote in his journal, "Deacon having hard time breathing but we will get him there somehow."[19]

On the evening of June 6, the eve of the summit attempt, Harper cooked a dinner of noodles and pemmican that quickly wrought internal havoc on everyone but the cook. After a few hours of rest, the weary, distressed men arose at three a.m. and headed for the summit. The temperature was -21°F. "My stomach was bad and I had one of the most severe headaches," Karstens wrote. "I put Walter in lead and kept him there all day with never a change. I took 2nd place on the rope so I could direct Walter and he worked all day without a murmur."[20]

Above 20,000 feet a strafing, sub-zero wind slashed at the four exhausted climbers inching up an icy slope. They wore multiple layers of clothing, enough to sustain them in mid-winter at -50°F, but they were still cold. The wind was brutal. They stopped often to pound warmth into their hands and feet. Karstens stomped his feet so often and hard that later he lost two toenails. Altitude sickness pummeled them all. They labored upward with pounding headaches, churning stomachs, and shortness of breath.

They measured their progress this way: two steps, pause for rest, a few more paces, stop again. Stuck, the last climber on the rope, and dangerously near his limits, was pulled upward like a balky horse. He thought of failure and death but prayed for life and triumph.

Things looked bleakest for the Archdeacon when Harper reached the top of a rise which the men thought to be the summit but instead reported yet another, higher rise. Staggering along at the end of the rope the news hammered Stuck's confidence. "I confess my heart sank, for I had realized all day that I was very near my altitude limit," he said, "and had been apprehensive that I might be physically unable to get to the top." Harper returned to where Stuck knelt in the snow and took the mercury barometer, the last item in the Archdeacon's pack. Now all Stuck had to do was keep moving.[21]

Just past mid-day, Harper stopped. He could go no higher. After weeks of toil, he had reached the summit of North America's tallest mountain. Karstens and Tatum came seconds behind. Stuck, the last man on the rope, "in enthusiasm and excitement somewhat over passing [my] narrow wind margin," was literally hauled up the last few feet before he collapsed unconscious on the floor of the little basin that forms the summit. "Have I climbed a mountain?" Stuck would write after the climb. "I climbed it largely by [Harper's] legs. Have I made memorable journeys? I made them largely by his powers."[22]

Despite the stabbing cold and pounding fatigue, the climbers exulted in the panorama below them. "To the south and east . . . the near-by peaks and ridges stood out with dazzling distinction," Stuck wrote, ". . . and the beautiful crescent curve of the Alaskan range exhibited itself from Denali to the sea." On one side of the range, the great drainages rolled south to Cook Inlet and the North Pacific; on the other the rivers pulsed to the Yukon and on to the Bering Sea. No other humans had ever seen these stupendous sights and, not surprisingly, the Archdeacon of the Yukon beheld the power of his God. "Yet the chief impression was not of our connection with the earth so far below, its rivers and its seas," he said, "but rather of detachment from it . . . Above us the sky took a blue so deep that none of us had ever gazed upon a midday sky like it before . . . 'it seemed like special news of God.'"[23]

In full sunlight, the temperature was just 7°F and the cruel wind relentless. "The miserable limitations of the flesh gave us continual warning to depart," Stuck recalled, "we grew . . . still more wretchedly cold." The men spent an hour-and-a-half on the summit reading instruments and holding a brief prayer service before the remorseless wind drove them down. Before leaving, they planted a small cross and unfurled a handmade American flag.

On the weary descent to their high camp, the full enormity of their triumph began to sink in. "Only those who have for long years cherished a great and almost inordinate desire," Stuck explained, "and have had that desire gratified to the limit of their expectation, can enter into the deep thankfulness and content that filled the heart upon the descent of this mountain . . . I remember no day in my life so full of toil, distress, and exhaustion, and yet so full of happiness and keen gratification."[24]

In camp that night, Stuck fully recognized that he never would have achieved the summit without Karstens and Harper. "There seemed no reason why Karstens and Walter . . . should not go another ten thousand feet, were there mountains in the world ten thousand feet higher than Denali," he said, "but the writer [Stuck] knows that he himself could not have gone much higher."[25]

The next day, the weary climbers took advantage of a brilliant, calm day to head down. During a rest break and after a pot of tea, Stuck placed a thermometer at 14,600 feet and carefully described its location. When found two decades later, the thermometer had recorded an un-calibrated minimum of -90°F, with an estimated minimum of -106°F.

Late that night, after negotiating the tortured ridge, the four men stumbled into their high camp on the Muldrow. Karstens had led the descent and in one long day had put the worst behind them. "One feels upon reflection that we took more risk in descending that ridge than we took at any time in the ascent," Stuck recalled. "But Karstens was most cautious and careful, and in the long and intensive apprenticeship of this expedition had become most expert."[26]

Two days later, the haggard and battered climbers approached base camp. "We began to be very anxious about Johnny . . . What had happened to the boy? Had he grown alarmed at our prolonged absence, and sought to make his way to the nearest men, fifty miles away?" Stuck fretted, conjuring numerous harrowing possibilities. Instead of two weeks, Fredson had been alone for 31 days.[27]

"It was a joy and an enormous relief to find the boy well and happy. He had faithfully fulfilled his task," Stuck exulted, "both the dogs and Johnny were fat and well-favored. I shall never forget the great load that was lifted from my heart as we approached the base camp . . . when at last we saw him . . . He a gave great shout . . . and

The Summit at Last 177

DENALI PARK AND PRESERVE, MUSEUM COLLECTION, #2805

Teenager John Fredson tended base camp while the other members of the Stuck-Karstens expedition of 1913 assaulted the summit. His loyalty and dedication during his month alone in the wilderness testified to his steadfast character.

came running, and never stopped until he had reached us and taken the pack from my back and put it on his own."[28]

Fredson's fidelity and thoughtfulness awed them all. In camp the men dined on a feast of fresh sheep steak, biscuits, and coffee laced with sugar and milk. The selfless boy ". . . had not touched a spoonful of either [milk or sugar] that on our return we might enjoy what we had been so long deprived of!" Stuck recalled. Fredson's unselfishness, rather than a fluke, genuinely indicated his true character. Stuck had brought down from 19,000 feet a small piece of granite, which he had Tiffany's in New York make into four scarf pins, one for each climber. Weeks later, the grateful Archdeacon gave his to Fredson.[29]

In sharp contrast to the world of ice and snow, the piedmont blazed with flowers and green grass. If the summit was "like looking out the windows of Heaven," as Tatum later said, then the cross-country trek to Glacier City was Hell. Merciless clouds of mosquitoes tormented the dogs and men without relief. During the climb, Tatum had suffered much—altitude sickness and tonsillitis—but, while crossing the McKinley River, he nearly perished. While fighting the icy current, he tangled in the dog chains and plunged into a deep hole. Karstens pulled the drowning Tatum to shore.[30]

The climbers stopped briefly in Eureka where Jack Hamilton fed them a lavish meal. On Caribou Creek they visited with the Quigleys and McGonagall. It must have gratified Karstens to deliver the news of his friend's vindication first-hand.

On June 20, three months and six days after they left Nenana, the party reached Tanana and the next morning Stuck telegraphed the triumphant news to a Seattle newspaper. The story was soon wired back to Alaskan towns and sparked a celebration. "There was unanimous rejoicing but no trace of surprise," the newspapers exulted, "it has remained for true Alaskans to clinch and to win."[31]

13

DOWN THE TRAIL

"SHELDON 'O' SHELDON why dident [sic] you come in and make the trip as you suggested doing ... why souldent [sic] I have a man with me one worthy of the ascent and not an absolute Paresite [sic] and liar," Harry Karstens wrote to Charles Sheldon. "I told you about the deacon trying for years to get me to go on this trip, and how fine he was to me now I understand to my sorrow."[1]

The glow of the summit triumph quickly dissolved into rancor. Karstens fumed over what he perceived as Hudson Stuck's intentional slights. The barrage of newspaper references to the "Stuck Expedition" and to "Stuck's companions" had inflamed Karstens even prior to the climb. Initial headlines had read, *Archdeacon Stuck to Climb McKinley*," and "*All Fairbanks Wishes Success for Archdeacon Hudson Stuck.*" In the press, Karstens was merely one member of the "*Hudson Stuck Mount McKinley expedition.*" Afterward, he viewed similar statements as intolerable insults.[2]

"We were equal partners he was to finance the expedition it was not to cost me a cent. I was to furnish the experience," Karstens said later. He saw the Archdeacon's public accounts of his exploits as exaggerations. Hudson Stuck "would talk of his hardships and long trips to show what a good man he was, I took it for granted he was surely as traveled enough (I woke up after the first day) ..." Karstens later explained.[3]

Clearly Karstens felt duped. Not only was he broke but overlooked as well. The fairest newspaper report of the climb appeared in the tiny, boomtown *Ruby Record-Citizen*. After parting with Stuck in Tanana, Karstens went downstream to Ruby to retrieve his launch and begin his summer freighting operations. In an interview, he divided expedition honors equally. For the first time, the headlines—*Stuck-Karstens Expedition*—gave equal credit to both men.[4]

Karstens simply did not believe that Stuck had upheld his end of their bargain. He believed that a man's word was his bond. A handshake was good as a written contract. He believed that because Stuck had not paid him promptly, and published accounts focused on Stuck rather then his team members, the man was a liar. He considered Stuck a parasite for the manner in which he shifted most of his chores during the climb to his assistants. He also believed the "Preacher" to be shamelessly self-aggrandizing. In sharp contrast, Karstens reportedly carried "his laurels unassumingly."[5]

If mountain climbing tests endurance, strength, and ability, the endeavor also teaches lessons of ego, ambition, loss, and loneliness. On the slopes and glaciers, and in the storms and high camps, the very fiber of a person's being is laid open for his companions' examination. No fault goes unexposed or unexplored. During the climb, both Stuck and Karstens had revealed their individual strengths and weaknesses. In the aftermath, instead of glory Karstens felt betrayed. He and Walter Harper had done the work, carried Stuck to the top, and now seemed ignored.

When Karstens finally returned to Fairbanks he gave several interviews, largely controlling his pique. "The successful explorer is very modest about the marvelous feat performed by the party, yet he felt a little aggrieved at the local papers for characterizing the party as the 'Stuck' expedition," wrote one reporter. He told the reporter he preferred the "Stuck-Karstens Expedition." He only asked the press for equal credit.[6]

Archdeacon Stuck did not learn of the extent of his partner's displeasure until late July. He first found out from a newspaper he read while on board the steamer *St. Michael* bound for the States. Immediately he wrote the editor of the *Fairbanks Daily Times*.

"In your issue of 10th July is a communication from Mr. Harry Karstens in which he takes a very natural exception to the continual reference to our expedition as the 'Stuck' expedition. I desire to join my protest to his. Before leaving on that enterprise I explained to your reporter that Mr. Karstens and I were partners in the affair.

Various transportation and mining interests occupied Harry Karstens in the years following his successful climb of Mt. McKinley. Here he and some friends take a break on his gas launch far up an Interior river.

The telegram sent to you from Tanana (and a copy thereof) sent to the *Seattle Times* is the only statement made by me about the ascent," Stuck explained. "I am not in any way responsible for the (headlines) . . . I feel perfectly free to say that without Mr. Karstens we should have never reached the top to the mountain . . . Karstens was always the real leader . . .

"Neither Karstens nor I had any ulterior money-making in view when we set about this undertaking," he went on, "but were actuated by a real desire to climb the mountain for the sake of climbing the mountain. I have already declined a lecturing tour that would have tied me up all the winter, for I am a missionary first and a mountain climber afterwards, and my visit Outside is primarily in the interests of missionary work in Alaska."[7]

To Karstens it appeared that Stuck was saying that he did not care if either of them made any money. In hindsight it appears that Stuck neither grasped Karstens' financial sacrifice in undertaking the trip nor his expectations after its success. By the time the party had reached Tanana on June 20, Karstens had missed a full month of lucrative river freighting. "Before I promised to go [on the climb,]" Karstens wrote, "I had a nice little sum of money now I am broke and in debt working my head off to get even so I can go on the new stampede at the head of the Tanana."[8]

Karstens obviously believed that a successful climb would result in handsome remuneration. On more than one occasion he had listened to Stuck bemoan Cook's financial windfall. He also knew that Tom Lloyd had been paid well for the full story of his fanciful climb. Stuck also made statements that encouraged Karstens' expectations of monetary return. "The expedition will not be without the likelihood of financial value, and that these will be returned to you for the time and the labor," Stuck assured Karstens prior to the trip, "It will be satisfaction enough to me to have made the ascent." Stuck also added a subsequent caveat. ". . . but it will not be my fault if there is not compensation to you . . ."[9]

Stuck's comment about money seems a little disingenuous. Perhaps the statement is accurate if he meant personal reward but from the very beginning he had calculated the financial gain for the church. The winter following the climb, Stuck toured the lower 48, writing, lecturing, and lobbying for Alaska missions. His appearances drew large and enthusiastic crowds. He was feted as guest of honor at the annual dinner of the American Alpine Club in Boston. He spoke at the Explorers Club and the American Geographical Society, the recipient of his climbing records. He also met with Charles Sheldon in Woodstock. His fame spread around the world and he was named a Fellow of the Royal Geographical Society.

In fairness, this trip was no grand "victory lap." The fund-raising trip Outside had been planned well before the climb and would have occurred regardless of its outcome. Bishop Rowe loathed fund raising and passed the load on to Stuck whenever he could. Rather than a triumphant tour, as many Alaskans—including Karstens—saw it, church business came first. Nonetheless, Stuck's enhanced prestige attracted generous donations. He easily met his primary goal, enhanced funding for the church, and came home with money for hospitals at Tanana and Ft. Yukon.

Forsaking personal profit, Stuck rebuffed a climbing lecture tour as it conflicted with his established schedule. Without such a tour, personal financial reward for the climb would be nil. "I think I should not bother with [profiting from the climb] were it not for you, but I have made up my mind to try to make at least $1,000 for you," Stuck wrote Karstens. In the end Stuck paid Karstens half of the $2,300 in engagement fees and royalties he earned, a far cry from the tens of thousands Cook had received.[10]

Stuck tried time and again to publicly credit Karstens for their success and redress the original oversight. "I have noticed that many newspapers have referred to the expedition as the 'Stuck expedition,'" he told the *New York Sun*. "It could be more properly called the Stuck-Karstens expedition . . . Karstens was my colleague to the very top . . . Some of the papers referred to Mr. Karstens as my guide, which wasn't fair to him." Nonetheless, the *Sun* called Stuck the "first man to reach the summit of Mount McKinley."[11]

On another occasion, Stuck again reiterated his position. "Mr. Karstens, who was my partner in this enterprise, organized the whole expedition of six men and boys and fourteen dogs so that every person in the party had his own special duties to perform," Stuck wrote, "without Harry Karstens' leadership and ability we would not have succeeded."[12]

The inaccurate newspaper headlines also miffed Charles Sheldon and prompted him to write Stuck's publisher, Charles Scribner's Sons, to ask that Karstens be given equal credit in their forthcoming article and book. In response, Scribner's contacted Stuck who agreed that Karstens deserved equal credit and that his book, *The Ascent of Denali*, should acknowledge that fact.[13]

A close reading of Stuck's book gives scant evidence of any acrimony during the climb. At that point in history expedition memoirs routinely failed to mention the conflicts and personality clashes that are an essential part of human nature in times of challenge and stress. That Stuck made no mention of conflict was merely a matter of following custom. Perhaps his book would have been more compelling if he had detailed the personal turmoil overcome, thus adding to the luster of this outstanding achievement.

The constant public reference to "Stuck's triumph" also aggrieved many Fairbanks residents. When his book, came out, a Fairbanks paper termed it a "Novel" and re-named it *Stuck's Ascent of "Damlie,"* a reference to the Glen Creek boys' ascent. The story contained an imaginary dialogue between the "Archstuckon," and an "Innocent."

"Archstuckon—I stood on the top of Mt. McKinley, where the foot of white man had never trod and what do you think—I found the whole top of the mountain staked!
Innocent—Who had staked it?
Archstuckon—O, the darned Sourdoughs."[14]

In Fairbanks, where Stuck had never been very popular with many miners and merchants, Karstens' growing anger was further fueled by the "boys" who told him that's "what you get for befriending a preacher."[15]

Stuck seemed genuinely baffled by Karstens' displeasure and could not understand why he failed to answer his conciliatory letters. "I am altogether at a loss to understand why you should cherish any but the kindest feeling to me. I have given you . . . the fullest credit for your great part in our joint enterprise," Stuck wrote. He tried to explain about the money. "I could have made much more [than $2 300] if I had been content to give up everything else and devote myself exclusively to lecturing; but I am a missionary first and mountain climber afterwards."[16]

Included in his letter, however, was a particularly patronizing and insulting statement. "I saw you hailed in the local paper the other day as 'the world-famous explorer' I have no quarrel with the description whatever, but I would point out that if you are 'world-famous' it is I who have made you so . . . I have sung your praises . . . whoever heard of you before? Sheldon has written nothing of you. You must remember that in this matter of fame it is not enough to be able to do things, it is also necessary to be able to tell about them."[17]

Despite Stuck's repeated attempts at reconciliation, Karstens never forgave him. "I have never written to him at any time since we were on the mountain, as he had entirely disgusted me with his untruthfulness from the time I first joined in the enterprise with him," Karstens wrote fifteen years after the climb.[18]

For all his days, Karstens regretted not making the climb with Charles Sheldon. "'O' Why, 'O' Why . . . didn't you take a chance at that hill," he wrote Sheldon, ". . . we would have had one of the grandest trips ever made on a hill for you know me and my failings and I know you we could have taken Mrs. Sheldon and made it easy . . ."[19]

In spite of their feud, both men deserve due credit; their inability to reconcile does a disservice to their grand success. To sum up in the same language and manner that Stuck had used to laud the Glen Creek boys: To Hudson Stuck belongs the honor of conceiving and organizing the attempt. To Harry Karstens belongs the honor of instituting the plan, leading the expedition, and enabling all team members to summit and return safely. To Robert Tatum belongs the credit of hard work and accomplishment far beyond his experience. And to Walter Harper goes the credit for being the first person to reach the top of North America's highest peak.

The summer following the climb, Karstens kept busy with river freighting and guiding. He hauled supplies to the diggings and brought the gold back to town. In September, he, and his three assistants, including Harry Lucke, guided Dr. Holmes of the Territorial Bureau of Mines on his inspection trip to the Nenana coal fields. An early, severe blizzard in the mountains dumped 18 inches of snow on them. A horse stepped on Holmes' ankle but the "prince . . . never murmured during the whole trip," Karstens reported.[20]

Over the winter of 1913–14, Karstens led Dem Wheeler of Indiana on an epic 70-day, 1,500-mile circuit of the upper Kuskokwim River drainage. They went by dogteam, in temperatures to -40°F, from Fairbanks to Ruby, Ruby to Takotna, Takotna to the base of Mt. Foraker and back to Fairbanks via Kantishna. Scotty Dalton of Seward drove the second team while Karstens led the way with his bundled passenger. "The long trip was without incident of particular note or hardship," Karstens said. Judging by Karstens' comments concerning the Holmes and Wheeler expeditions, it is obvious that he was more than willing to assume most of the work if his companions refrained from "whining" and pitched in as best they could with the chores.[21]

Karstens' reputation soared in the wake of this trip. "Among the youngest of the old pioneers, [Karstens] has won an enviable reputation for himself as a trailblazer and true Alaskan," a reporter intoned.[22]

On his return from the Wheeler trip, Karstens received word that his father had died in Chicago. Weeks later, his grief turned to joy when he married Frieda Louise Gaerisch on July 31, 1914, in a small ceremony in the Fairbanks home of his old friend and partner, R.C. Wood.

Frieda Louise was born in Benton, Minnesota, and came to Alaska in 1905, from Portland, Oregon. She was a nurse and her skills were in high demand in the Territory. A few months later, an illness forced her to return to Portland but "ever after that [first visit] I had a great desire to return to Alaska and see more of that great country." She got her wish in June 1909 when Father Monroe gave her a nursing job at Fairbanks' St. Joseph's Hospital.[23]

If after their marriage Louise had expected Harry to settle into the role of a stay-at-home businessman, she was mistaken. Karstens would later tell Sheldon "[My] wife is trying to civilize me but it is a hard job every once in a while I take a trip for a month or so and when I get back she is glad to see me when she remembers she has a job on hand I'm off on another trip but she says she hasn't lost hope yet."[24]

The hunting season opened one day after the wedding. Just prior to his marriage, Karstens had been preparing for a four-to-five month hunting trip to the Toklat River. On August 9, Karstens and his three hunters left town on the launch *Doman* bound for Diamond. "Say Sheldon, this is tough luck," he wrote his friend. "Married 10 days and off up here [on the Toklat] for four or five months."[25]

Morgan Belmont, C. Oliver Iselin, Jr., and H. Carey Morgan, all recent Harvard graduates, and members of some of America's wealthiest families, had contacted Karstens on the recommendation of Charles Sheldon. The trio came north prepared to shoot "everything from mice to moose," both for themselves and for Cambridge's Museum of Comparative Zoology.[26]

When the two horse packers Karstens had hired for the cross country journey to the Toklat returned to Fairbanks at the end of September, they reported that the New Yorkers had settled in to Sheldon's old cabin on the Toklat, and "showed no inclination to return for several months." Already the hunters had seen a band of 600 sheep, killed numerous rams, and two big grizzlies. The hunt was off to a rousing start.[27]

An unseasonably warm winter, with the Toklat and Nenana Rivers running almost ice-free, delayed by two and one-half weeks the party's planned mid-winter return to Fairbanks. With each passing day, Louise grew increasingly worried. Her husband's prolonged absences were something she'd never get used to.

On January 7, 1915, Karstens and Morgan mushed into Fairbanks with a giant load of furs, hides, horns, and caribou antlers, one of which measured 69 inches across. The bewhiskered Morgan, decked

COURTESY OF CANDY WAUGAMAN COLLECTION

*When the federal government began construction of the Alaska Railroad in 1916, Karstens, like many of his peers, contracted to haul freight and passengers. Pictured here is Frank Tondro, the famed "*Malemute Kid*," just one of many dog mushers and horse freighters who one day would be put out of business by the railroad they helped build.*

in his trail gear, looked more like a trapper than an heir to a fortune. After a brief reunion with Louise, Karstens left for the Toklat to bring back his other two hunters and the remaining trophies.

Two weeks later, he returned with Belmont and Iselin, and two heavily loaded freight sleds. The happy hunters exulted to reporters that theirs had been the best-equipped and guided hunting party ever afield in Interior Alaska. They credited Karstens for their success and safe return. In all, the six-month-long trip went smoothly, a remarkable achievement since seven people had shared the little Toklat cabin. Belmont, forced home by business obligations, expressed one regret, "I am obliged to go east." His friend Morgan, entranced by the mining potential of the Kantishna, engaged a mining engineer to examine the Quigleys' properties. He eventually declined to invest.[28]

In the summer of 1915, Louise accompanied her husband on a river trip. They started out from Fairbanks in Karstens' gas-powered launch, pushing several barges of freight bound for Diamond City. Louise received immediate introduction to the joys of river travel— mosquitoes, sweepers, hidden sandbars, and three straight weeks of rain. When Harry contracted to take a load of freight up the Tolovana River, Louise returned to Fairbanks on the steamer *Delta*.

In 1916, with construction of the Alaska Railroad booming, Karstens inaugurated an express passenger service between Fairbanks and Nenana. Over the course of the next five years, dozens of dogteam freight haulers and horse packers worked on the railroad, the first massive public works project in Interior Alaska. We will never know how many of these pioneer transporters realized at the time that the completed project would end their careers, the railroad helping to bring the old frontier era to a rapid close.

Following the climb, the other members of the expedition carried on in relative anonymity. Shortly after the climb, Stuck enrolled Harper in Mount Hermon Academy in Massachusetts. Harper said that he wanted to become a physician and tend his people. After Harper went south to school, Fredson took his place as the Archdeacon's field assistant. In winter, Fredson mushed dogs with Stuck, and in summer, piloted the *Pelican*. He "was proud he'd been chosen to do the job Walter Harper had done so well for nearly ten years," his biographer wrote. Fredson was the first of his tribe to graduate from eighth grade and in 1916 went off to high school at Mount Hermon High School where he formalized his name as Fredson. Tatum returned south and spent his years preaching the Gospel.[29]

When Stuck died in 1920, headlines hailed him as "the first white man to scale Alaskan heights." Years later, Karstens made a telling remark about the Glen Creek boys' climb which could also have referred to him. "The old timers are not mentioned . . . Such is life for those who accomplish things but have no influence."[30]

The cataclysmic world events of 1917 would forever change the lives of millions of people, even those living in the Alaska wilderness. In far-off Washington, D.C., where the Nation's leaders braced for the coming storm, Charles Sheldon was engaged in a remarkable effort that would impact Harry Karstens' life in a dramatic way, and forever alter the region's dynamics.

14

Mt. McKinley National Park

Tension and urgency permeated the White House. Military aides and advisers bustled in and out of President Woodrow Wilson's office. In January 1917, Germany had declared unrestricted submarine warfare in critical zones of the North Atlantic, voiding an agreement with Wilson to preserve the peace. Exploding ships took Americans to the bottom of the sea. "The man who kept us out of the war" confronted the inevitable—the United States and Germany would collide in war.

Newspapers brimmed with stories of the Bolshevik Revolution, German plots against the United States, U-boat sinkings, and the slaughter on the fields of Flanders. A New York headline blared, *"Only Miracle Can Prevent War Now."* The establishment of a new national park in the far north was hardly a main concern, just another low-priority item to be considered later. For its anxious supporters, a delay in passing Senate Bill 5716, *A Bill to Establish a Mount McKinley National Park, in the Territory of Alaska*, might mean the ruin of the wildlife that they so ardently wished to protect.

Both Charles Sheldon and Belmore Browne greatly feared that construction of the Alaska Railroad would spur unlimited market hunting. To America's fledgling conservationists, railroads were synonymous with wildlife destruction. Enter the railroad—gone the buffalo; gone the frontier.

Lack of dependable year-round transportation had long hindered the Interior's development, especially gold and coal mining. The same act of Congress that had granted Alaska territorial status in 1912 created a commission to study the feasibility of building a railroad from the tidewater to the Interior. Two years later, Congress authorized the President to construct the railroad. Wilson ordered the new Alaska Engineering Commission (AEC) to locate a route for the railroad and report to the Interior Secretary.

Fieldwork was completed by mid-October, and on April 10, 1915, President Wilson selected the western route from Seward to Fairbanks via the 2365 foot Broad Pass in the Alaska Range. Here was the route that would connect Interior's vast resources with an ice-free port and bring hundreds of workers close to the wildlife of the McKinley region.

Browne and Sheldon saw their worst fears materializing. Although railroad construction camps received beef and poultry deliveries, game meat was served regularly. The Alaska Engineering Commission (AEC), builders of the railroad, believed their project to be exempt from the law prohibiting commercial sales of game meat because it was not a "dealer." Consequently, the AEC let contracts to supply game meat and, to skirt the law, sold meals to employees below cost. Very quickly, the market hunters blasted the large herds of Dall sheep found on the rolling bluffs along the Nenana canyon into oblivion.

"[The AEC] had bought, up to December 21, 1916, 5,013 pounds of sheep meat... [which] is used in the mess house [at Nenana] where the men are charged 33.3 cents per meal, or $1.00 per day," wrote game warden R.S. McDonald in a report to Governor J.A. Strong. He also stated his fears that "the sheep will be practically exterminated before the railroad is completed." Already the population of the new railroad center at Nenana numbered 4,000.[1]

Geologist Stephen R. Capps was one of those lobbying for the creation of a park to protect the wildlife from market hunters. "With the establishment of a town at Nenana a market for wild meat is brought closer to the game ranges," Capps reported, "and the completion of the railroad will make accessible to visitors a famous game country which so far has been preserved only by its inaccessible location."[2]

Many pioneer Alaskans viewed wildlife protection as part of what they derided as the "conservation fad," and entirely unreasonable. Years later, Alaska Governor Thomas A Riggs Jr. summed up attitudes about market hunting in a letter he wrote to a park supporter. "You can tell Dr. [William T.] Hornaday [then a leading conservationist] that I was not only a party to feeding railroad laborers on legally killed game but instigated it. I fed three tons or 6,000 pounds of game to some 1,000 laborers . . . and tell him to quote me further as saying that I consider that the laboring man is as much entitled to an occasional luxury as I am . . . This idea that only the sportsmen financially able to hunt big game shall taste it, does not make a hit with me. It is just this 'I-am-better-than-thou' attitude . . . that is stirring up class hatred in our country."[3]

During his time on the Toklat River, Sheldon had viewed first hand the effects of market hunting and knew what would happen if it went unchecked. He possessed the means, the character, and political connections to do something about it. His connections with pioneer conservationists assured his views would be heard in the highest seats of power. His concern on the eve of World War I was whether his goal could be accomplished before the complete decimation of his beloved wildlife.

Sheldon was anything but a conservation dilettante. Throughout his adult life, he campaigned for protection of migratory birds, forests, and parks. At one time or another, he served on the boards of directors of the Boone and Crockett Club, National Parks Association, American Forestry Association, and National Geographic Society. He was a member of the Explorers Club, American Ornithological Union, and the New York Zoological Society, all organized and dominated by influential and wealthy eastern sportsmen. With Teddy Roosevelt in the White House until 1909, and a force long afterward, these groups enjoyed immense influence.

Sheldon's first priority on his return home from Alaska in 1908 was his faltering financial situation. The stay on the Toklat had cost him dearly and it would be some time before he recouped his losses. Once he had stabilized his fortunes, and married, the Sheldon family spent winters in Washington, D.C., where Sheldon could lobby for creation of the park and other conservation issues, and summers in Nova Scotia.

Upon his return from the Toklat, Sheldon began laying the foundation for the park by winning key but elusive Alaskan support. Alaskans deeply resented the "tyranny" of a distant government that seemed bent on stifling Alaska's development and channeling its resources into the hands of rich easterners. Many Alaskans believed

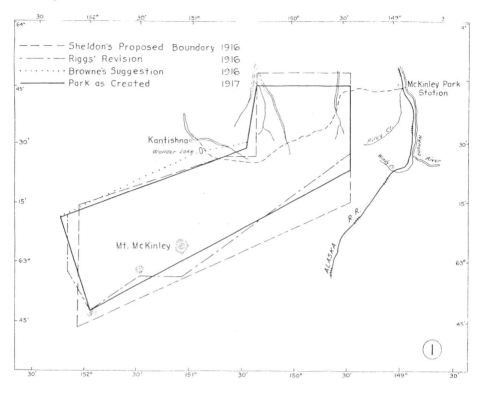

COURTESY OF NATIONAL PARK SERVICE

Three different boundary variants were drawn for the proposed park. Wildlife range, topography, mining, and politics decided the final boundary decisions.

that the lack of development within the Territory had been due "to the numerous reserves" established. A typical headline read: *"Conservation Fadists Arrest Progress and seek to Supplant Self-Government with Bureaucracy."*[4]

The wave of Alaska–Yukon gold strikes and stampedes had attracted tens of thousands of people seeking wealth and a better life. "Those who decided to stay in the north country prized freedom, independence, and individual achievement above all else," explained historian Frank Norris. "Alaskans of every stripe were furious at this spate of laws and regulations. To them, the territory was a vast storehouse of riches, just beginning to be tapped." To this day, many Alaskans hold that same view and wrestle with the same ideologies.[5]

To win support for the establishment of a park, advocates would have to certify that the park had no agricultural potential, few resources, and no timber. In essence, Sheldon and his allies would have to persuade Congress that, except for scenery and wildlife, the real estate was worthless. In another of many ironic twists, park proponents would also need to convince Congress of the danger of the railroad but at the same time promote the park as a lure for rail passengers and profits.

Sheldon was not alone in his desire to establish a northern park. When Belmore Browne returned home from his 1912 climb, he visited the Secretary of the Interior, a family friend, and became the first person to propose the establishment of a national park on the northern flank of Mt. McKinley. The country and wildlife enthralled him and his stories extolled the beauty and wonder of his "God's Country." His numerous public appearances focused on the mountain and his climbs, but he often got in his licks for protection. He also made the point that the name McKinley was inappropriate. He echoed the sentiments of many when he wrote, ". . . in looking backward over the history of the big mountain, it seems strange and unfortunate that the name of Mt McKinley should have been attached to it. Any of the Indian names . . . would have been far more appropriate. . . ." He added that the Russian name *Bulshaia*, or even *Densmore*, the prospector, would have been better.[6]

Sheldon, Browne, Harry Karstens, and Hudson Stuck all championed the Athabascan name for the mountain. "Forefront in the author's heart and desire must stand a plea for the restoration . . . of its immemorial native name," wrote Stuck, "if there be right and reason in these matters [the name McKinley] should not have been placed there at all." In the end, partisan politics resulted in adoption of the name Mount McKinley National Park.[7]

Browne and Sheldon were initially unaware of each others' efforts to establish a park. After Sheldon made his first public pronouncements in mid-1915 the two men met and forged a powerful partnership. Not only did Browne know the mountain intimately, he also knew the wildlife on the south side of the Alaska Range, information that Sheldon lacked. As chairman of the Conservation Committee of the prestigious Camp Fire Club, Browne was a public figure who enjoyed the respect of mountain climbers, explorers, hunters, and

WILLIAM SHELDON COLLECTION, #76-42-2, ARCHIVES, UNIVERSITY OF ALASKA, FAIRBANKS

The establishment of Mt. McKinley National Park is probably the crowning achievement of Charles Sheldon's varied and storied career as a pioneer conservationist. He and Belmore Browne deserve equal billing for the arduous but successful battle to create Alaska's first national park.

members of the art world. His celebrity helped make him an effective advocate for the park. Over the years, his role in the fight to establish the park has been somewhat over-looked.

"Prior to 1912, Interior Secretary Franklin K. Lane had been opposed to an Alaskan park on account of its remoteness," Belmore

Browne explained, "but with the encouragement of Stephen Mather I was able to win him over to the idea of a Mt. McKinley National Park by convincing him that the region was the fountainhead of the game supply in the Yukon and Tanana Rivers, and that the game was being ruthlessly killed off."[8]

The support of Stephen Tyng Mather, then Assistant to the Secretary of the Interior, was crucial. Mather, an avid climber and mountaineer, became involved in park issues after a visit to Yosemite and Sequoia in 1914. What he saw on that trip appalled him. Conflicting patterns of land ownership and use, combined with miniscule park budgets, had resulted in resource damage and shoddy visitor services. Mather, whose activism was stirred by a meeting with John Muir, complained to Washington. Secretary Lane responded, in essence saying that "if you don't like what you see, come to Washington and do something about it." In December, the independently wealthy Mather moved to Washington to oversee the national parks, then a minor division of the Interior Department.[9]

Mather spent much of his first two years in the Interior Department working for the creation of an independent and fully funded parks department. Although he faced strong congressional resistance to yet another new bureaucracy, in 1916 the President signed the National Park Service Act, and appointed Mather the agency's first director

In September 1915, Sheldon publicly presented his plan for the park to the Boone and Crockett Club, the most powerful sportsmen's association of the day. Browne immediately added his support, and that of the Camp Fire Club. The American Game Protective Association, another sporting fraternity, also pledged backing for a *Denali* National Park.

After obtaining Boone and Crockett's formal endorsement, Sheldon next laid out his plan to Dr. Edward W. Nelson, Chief of the U.S. Biological Survey. Together, they roughed out boundaries that would include all of the Dall sheep's winter range and portions of moose and caribou habitat. He excluded the Kantishna mining district and located the eastern boundary 30 miles from the railroad. Three factors influenced the boundary decisions: wildlife ranges, topography, and mining activity. Politics was an important fourth factor.

Sheldon first officially proposed the park to Mather in a letter dated December 15, 1915. Mather enthusiastically embraced the idea. Thomas

Riggs, then head of the Alaska Boundary Survey—and future Governor—was assigned to draft a bill with the boundaries suggested by Sheldon. Riggs adjusted the proposed boundaries based on topography and his interest in protecting mining concerns. His revision lopped 700 square miles off Sheldon's version. Browne met with Riggs and offered his own proposal.

"The southern side [of the central Alaska Range] is a region which protects itself," Browne explained, "The northern side is the region that is going to need protection by the Government, and for that reason we have drawn this park entirely on the north side."[10]

When the bill was finally introduced in Congress, the boundary lines had been re-written a third time, based largely on the desire for straight lines rather than inclusion of habitat or scenic features. (Browne's initial boundary proposal was the most complete. In 1922, the boundaries were extended to coincide with his original sketch.)

Now came the tough part, gaining key political support for the bill. Sheldon sorely needed the help of his friend James A. Wickersham, Alaska's Delegate to Congress, and then publicly opposed to the park's creation. Although Wickersham recognized the park's tourism potential, he strongly resisted any attempt to inhibit mining activity. Sheldon argued, perhaps half-heartedly, that the two uses were not exclusive. Wickersham demanded that the borders of the proposed park exclude the Kantishna mining district and that language be inserted that guaranteed the rights of miners to locate claims within the park. He also demanded hunting rights in the park for all miners and prospectors. Sheldon reluctantly agreed. Many parks in the lower 48 provided for mining activity but McKinley would be the first to give miners hunting privileges.

Wickersham adopted the compromise proposal, which was spelled out in the park's first regulations. "For necessary development it is permitted that prospectors and miners engaged in prospecting and mining within the park may take and kill while in the park what game or birds are needed for their actual necessities when short of food . . . but in no case shall animals or birds be killed in the park for sale or for removal there from or wantonly . . . No animals shall be killed within the park limits primarily for the purpose of dog food, except with prior permission . . . but when animals are killed for food by prospectors, or miners the excess portions may be fed dogs

ALASKA STATE LIBRARY, PCA-20-21

Alaska's lone Delegate to Congress, James Wickersham, opposed establishment of the park for nearly two years. He championed the effort only after his concerns for "miners' rights" were addressed via special provisions allowing mining and hunting within the new park.

without such prior permission." In addition, prospectors could stake new claims, develop existing ones, build cabins, and cut firewood.[11]

"My objection to including this area in a park has been very largely overcome by the provision in the bill which extends the mineral-land laws there," Wickersham testified during Congressional hearings. "[I support] the freest use of the said park for recreation purposes by the public and for the preservation of animals, birds, and fish, and . . . provided that prospectors and miners engaged in mining may take and kill therein so much game or birds as may be needed for their actual necessities when short of food . . . I prepared that section myself . . .

"The situation is this," he added, "You have now so many restrictions upon the development of the Territory that I regret very much to see another large area withdrawn and rules and regulations adopted which will by their severity exclude the miners." (Wickersham owned claims in the Kantishna, and his views may have been slightly self-serving.)[12]

Park supporters spilt over these hunting exemptions. The fiery Hornaday, of the New York Zoological Society, adamantly opposed the special privileges. He could not be mollified and supporters feared that he might derail the park effort. In these tense times, Sheldon employed all of his considerable charm and diplomatic skills to keep things from falling apart.

Although sportsmen's groups, miners, and railroaders all had some comment to make on the bill, the Athabascans who lived in the park area were not consulted. The concept of a park, with inviolate boundaries, had no meaning to them. The language that exempted miners from the ban on hunting in the park, made no reference to Natives at all. Without any input from them, they were denied their traditional hunting grounds.

On April 16, 1916, Delegate Wickersham and Senator Key Pittman of Nevada introduced identical park bills. "It is particularly fitting that Mr. Wickersham, who was the first man to attempt to climb Mt. McKinley in 1903, should have introduced the bill . . . and it is fitting also that the bill should bear his name."[13]

"Everyone . . . should realize what a wonderful country—a country of impressive mountain scenery and big game—we have in that northern territory, and how seriously the wild life of that region is menaced . . . The Mount McKinley region now offers a last chance for the people of the United States to preserve, untouched by civilization, a great primeval park in its natural beauty," wrote geologist Capps. "I have tried to make plain the fact that the area within the proposed national park is a game country without rival in America . . . but unless this game refuge is immediately reserved a few years may see these great herds destroyed beyond hope of reestablishment. Even today the encroachments of the market hunter are serious . . . many sled-loads of wild meat are carried into the towns during the winter . . . even from a region so difficult of access. How much more rapidly will the game disappear when the railroad is completed to a point within 15 miles of this game paradise! . . . The scenery will keep indefinitely, but the game will not, and it must be protected soon or it will have been destroyed."[14]

If the McKinley climbers, with all their claims and counter-claims, accomplished anything, it was to bring notice of this great mountain to the public eye. Instead of a hazy, distant place, Mt. McKinley had become a household name, a place to care about. Park advocates traded on the mountain's stories of defeat and triumph to gain the notice of Congressmen and the public. Browne used his celebrity to promote the park.

The actual campaign through Congress was entrusted to the American Game Protective Association, spearheaded by its President John B. Burnham, who had successfully championed the landmark Federal Migratory Bird Law. Burnham would be a key player, freeing Sheldon and Browne to testify in the Congressional public hearings.

"I think it would be safe to say that the interior would be an unknown waste if it was not for the game. This great region could not have been opened up without the aid of the wild animals," Browne said during the hearings. "With the opening of the railroad you are

DENALI NATIONAL PARK AND PRESERVE, MUSEUM COLLECTION, #16-1.7

After World War I mineral strikes within the new park boundaries spawned a small stampede. Here some of these newcomers gather at a hydraulic mining operation on Moose Creek. Seated at the top left of the group is John Busia, a Croat, who in 1918 joined his father Marko and uncle Tom, veterans of the 1905 stampede, at Eureka camp, then experiencing a renaissance. Busia went on to spend nearly 40 years in the Kantishna. His father, Marko, 58, died on March 28, 1923.

going to get a class in there that is not going to protect the game . . . and you are going to have repeated over again the slaughter of the big game animals that has followed our march westward . . . The real necessity is to preserve it as a game refuge to insure a supply of meat in the years to come.

"There is no peril from the prospector. All peril would be from the poachers and hunters of meat to sell. There is no peril in allowing the bona fide prospector to secure such meat as he wants; he could never deplete the supply."[15]

Next, the veteran climber offered an eloquent plea. "Giant moose still stalk the timberline valleys; herds of caribou move easily across the moss-covered hills; bands of white 'big-horn' sheep look down on the traveler from frowning mountains, while at any time the powerful form of the grizzly bear may give the crowning touch to the wilderness picture. But while the Mount McKinley region is the fountainhead from which come the herds of game that supply the huge expanse of south-central Alaska, that fountainhead is menaced. Slowly but surely the white man's civilization is closing in, and already sled loads of dead animals from the McKinley region have reached the Fairbanks market. Unless a refuge is set aside, in which the animals that remain can breed and rear their young unmolested they will soon 'follow the buffalo.'"[16]

"Follow the buffalo." Many in the fledgling conservation movement envisioned a similar fate for Alaska's wildlife. "The great good that has come with our national expansion has always been followed by evils," Browne continued, "Are we as a nation able to profit by our mistakes? Can these tragedies be prevented? Yes: but our last and only chance lies in the Mount McKinley region."[17]

Browne promoted the widely held belief that this game refuge would incubate large numbers of animals that would then pulse out into the surrounding countryside, benefiting hunters of all stripes. Whether he actually believed his pronouncement or not, the argument had proven valuable in the creation of several American parks and refuges.

Explosive world events delayed the bill's passage. The decisive moment came in early 1917, when Secretary Lane addressed the National Park conference and advocated that both Mt. McKinley and the Grand Canyon be made national parks.

Events now moved swiftly. The House swept aside troublesome amendments and passed the park bill. The motion by Senator Pittman setting aside the 2,200-square-mile reserve sailed through the Senate with little or no opposition. After the Secretary of the Interior signed the bill, Sheldon hand-carried it to the White House. On February 24, 1917, President Wilson signed into law the act establishing Mt. McKinley National Park "for the benefit and enjoyment of the people." Six weeks later the United States Congress declared war on Germany.

Two days after the signing, the pen used by the President was presented to Sheldon. This singular conservation act, passed in a tumultuous time, remains a tribute to the vision of Charles Sheldon. Typically he made no boasts. "When you write about the McKinley Park project for the Forest and Stream [Magazine] I hope that you will keep my name out of it," Sheldon told a supporter, "it is sufficient to say that I have been among those interested in passing it. The Camp Fire Club came into it independently and it was they who combined all elements . . . the Park should be considered to have been created by us all equally together with Mather—The Boone and Crockett Club should be substituted for my personal efforts."[18]

Because Belmore Browne was the first to publicly propose the national park, and worked tirelessly for it, many of his contemporaries argued that he deserved the title "Father of Mt. McKinley National Park." The article in *Forest and Stream* appropriately hailed the park's creation as a monument to the perseverance of Browne and Sheldon and their two organizations. The shared credit was much deserved.[19]

Reaction in Alaska was mixed, and at first largely muted by the mining exemption. Some railed against the "lock-up" of public lands, while a few visionaries saw "a vast tract of land in Alaska which some day will be recognized as America's greatest scenic attraction."[20]

The establishment of the park did not end the threats to Sheldon's paradise. In fact, the boundaries were ignored and commercial and sport hunting continued largely unchecked. One wealthy Californian, for example, would spend the next two years trophy hunting in the Kantishna.

Conservationists were outraged in the spring of 1917 when the National Food Commission recommended a general relaxation of game laws throughout the country for the "period of the war." Sheldon pointed to the situation in Alaska as an example of "relaxed" regulations. "In the Fairbanks district the [current] law has been the

TOM WALKER PHOTO

The large herds of Dall sheep that wandered the mountain ranges near DENALI *did not receive complete protection until the early 1920s when Harry Karstens took his post as the park's first Chief Ranger.*

greatest farce," Sheldon fumed. "Instead of public co-operation to enforce, we have had complete co-operation including judges, juries, marshals, *all the people unanimously,* to ignore it. Since the first law was passed the killing and selling meat for the Fairbanks market has gone on unrestricted . . ."[21]

The act creating the park contained no funding provisions and, without a ranger force, the park would be a park in name only. Although Sheldon pushed to secure an appropriation in the Sundry Account for protection and surveying of the park, urgent world affairs dominated the Government and the funding request went nowhere.

At the end of 1918, Sheldon, then a Colonel in the Office of Naval Intelligence, again succeeded in placing a $10,000 park appropriation request in the annual budget "for salaries of range keepers and for the establishment of range stations," but again the funds were not allocated.[22]

A Boone and Crockett Club resolution in early 1919 urged Congress to protect the park's wildlife and appropriate funds for rangers and equipment. With the demobilization of American forces after the Armistice, Kantishna's mineral resources, and a new strike at Copper Mountain in the park, attracted the attention of returning veterans. The influx of miners and prospectors led to an increase in hunting. Alarmed by reports of the wholesale slaughter of the region's wildlife, the Club chided Congress for its dawdling.

After four long years, money for a ranger force was finally appropriated for the 1921 fiscal year. Several different names surfaced as potential park superintendents and rangers. Most of the nominees were completely unacceptable to Sheldon, a few downright laughable. He knew Alaska and the sometimes-desperate men wandering the tundra and taiga. Whoever would become the first superintendent needed courage, tenacity, and indomitable will. For Sheldon, the choice was clear, his old friend, Harry Karstens.

EPILOGUE

Like the State of Alaska itself, Mt. McKinley National Park grew out of its gold rush antecedents to become a world treasure. The national park owes a debt to many of the gold rush era pioneers who helped build it. In 1921, after lengthy debate at the local and national level, Henry P. "Harry" Karstens was appointed the first Superintendent of Mt. McKinley National Park. In many respects his efforts to carve out a park and wildlife reserve in a territory amid people completely opposed to the concept would be the greatest challenge of his life. In the planned second and final volume of this two volume history, his arduous struggle will be told.

APPENDIX

The Last Stampede

Pete Anderson was born in Sweden on April 9, 1867, and came to Alaska in 1906. Later in his life he lived in Nenana and worked as a tinsmith and metal worker. Anderson mined gold on the Totatlanika River and seldom spoke of his climbing exploits. He was 80 years old when he died on March 2, 1947.

Belmore Browne achieved great success as a wildlife and landscape artist. During World War II, he was a special consultant on mountaineering and survival to the armed forces of the United States and Great Britain. He never lost his interest in Mt. McKinley National Park and involved himself, for both good and bad, in its politics throughout his life. Works by Browne are owned by the Smithsonian Institution, the National Gallery, and the National Academy of Design, among others. Numerous museums, including the American Museum of Natural History in New York, commissioned him to paint dioramas, often featuring scenes from the park region. He finished his last major project—a habitat group at the Boston Museum of Science—two months before his death, at 74. He passed away on May 2, 1954 in Rye, New York.

On August 22, 1945, **John Fredson**, "Wolf Smeller," died of pneumonia, a complication of influenza, at the Hudson Stuck Memorial Hospital in Ft. Yukon. The man who once wrote, "What is a man created for but to serve God and his country?" would be sorely missed. He was buried in Ft. Yukon near the Archdeacon's grave, but in 1996, his remains were disinterred and taken home to Venetie for reburial. Years after his death, Walter John, Jr., secretary of the Venetie Tribal Council, described Fredson as the "George Washington" of the Gwich'in.

ARTHUR HARPER suffered from that the era's dread disease, "consumption" (in other words, tuberculosis). His family and friends urged him to go the desert southwest where they hoped the warm and dry climate would alleviate his pain and prolong his life. The trip proved too much for his enfeebled system, and at age 63, he died in Yuma, Arizona, on November 24, 1897. A 2,000 foot peak southwest of Eagle, Alaska, honors his memory.

After three years of school Outside, **WALTER HARPER** returned north in 1917 to rejoin his patron on one last epic journey. On his return, Harper fell gravely ill with typhoid. A multi-day fever as high as 105° sorely tested his constitution. The long-planned Arctic winter trek seemed dashed but to Stuck's "great joy," Harper, now 20 pounds lighter, made a rapid recovery. Only nine days after Harper sat up in bed, the two men left Ft. Yukon at -38° F. The ensuing six-month, 2,500-mile trip by dog team took them from Ft. Yukon west to Kotzebue Sound, then north along the coast to Point Barrow, and east to Herschel Island, before circling back to Ft. Yukon.

On September 4, 1918, in the Ft. Yukon chapel, Archdeacon Stuck presiding, Harper married Frances Wells his nurse during his bout with typhoid. For a honeymoon, the couple borrowed a boat and went hunting up the Porcupine River. On their return to Ft. Yukon, they packed for a trip Outside to join the war effort, she in the Red Cross, he in the Army. En route to national service, they planned to visit Frances' father, living near Philadelphia. In late October 1918, the newlyweds went by river steamer to Dawson, where they took the train to Skagway. Just before their departure from Skagway they learned of Germany's military collapse. Now Harper could go directly to college, funded in part by his bride.

On October 23, 1918, the S.S. *Princess Sophia* left Skagway loaded with passengers, freight, and gold. In a heavy south wind and blowing snow, she ran aground at 2:00am on Vanderbilt Reef, about 30 miles northwest of Juneau. Rescue attempts failed. On October 25, 1918, more than 350 people drowned when the steamer slipped off the reef in a storm and sank. The tragedy stunned both Karstens and Stuck. "I will not believe it at present," Stuck said, but on the last day of October the territorial governor notified Stuck that Harper's body had been recovered. "The most terrible thing that has happened in my experience," Stuck mourned.

In the same chapel where Walter and Frances had married less than two months earlier, the Archdeacon presided over a memorial service for the victims. Frances Wells' estate donated $2500 to the Ft. Yukon mission, which built a solarium for patients. With his own funds Stuck purchased a stone to mark their graves in Juneau's Evergreen Cemetery: "Here lie the bodies of Walter Harper and Frances Wells his wife drowned on the Princess Sophia 25th Oct. 1918. May light perpetual shine upon them. 'They were lovely and pleasant in their lives and in death they were not divided.' II Samuel 1:23."

Tom Lloyd came to America from Wales in 1888, and at age 18 went to work in the Pennsylvania coalfields. In the Yukon, he gained considerable wealth managing "Arkansas Jim" Hall's fabulous claims. Like a lot of others who struck it rich, Lloyd lost all of his personal wealth Outside before returning to Alaska to try again. He stampeded to the Kantishna early on, becoming the first to stake quartz claims there. In 1917, Tom Lloyd died in St. Joseph's hospital in Fairbanks of apoplexy. "He was awful fat. Had kind of a nervous breakdown and just keeled over," Billy Taylor remembered. In fact, Lloyd had suffered for more than a year from liver and heart trouble. In heavy rain, hundreds attended Lloyd's funeral. Among his honorary pallbearers were Bill McPhee and Dave Petree, the two men whose bet had spurred the 1910 climb. He left behind a loyal wife, three sons, and a daughter.

Charles McGonagall, 83, died of a heart attack in Eugene, Oregon, in 1953. He always said that he got nothing from the 1910 climb but a lot of hard work. He also said that he didn't want to go on it in the first place.

When General **William L. "Billy" Mitchell** died of influenza on February 17, 1936, in Middleburg, Virginia, he was recognized as a visionary military mind and the "father of the U.S. Air Force."

Henry Carey Morgan, who Karstens guided on a hunting trip to the Toklat River in 1915, died near New York on July 24, 1923, in the wreck of a "flying boat." He was 31.

Herschel Clifford Parker, born July 9, 1867, died in Los Angeles, California, on March 12, 1944, and was buried in Inglewood Cemetery.

After **Charles Sheldon** died on September 21, 1928, in Nova Scotia, the story of his McKinley adventures was edited by C. Hart

Merriam and Edward Nelson and posthumously published by his wife as *Wilderness of Denali*. "He was a man of much force and determination and possessed a great devotion to the right," wrote conservationist George Grinnell, "a strong common sense in pushing forward good measures."

The cabin that **THOMAS STRAND**, a.k.a., Tom Savage, built for his family and lived in near Ferry, north of Healy, has been washed away by the Nenana River. Strand is buried on a rise a few hundred yards west of the Ferry bridge. An inscription on a concrete slab near a white cross reads *Tom Strand, November 28, 1860, to June 12, 1953*.

On October 10, 1920, three years after Walter Harper's tragic death, Archdeacon **HUDSON STUCK** died of bronchial pneumonia in the hospital in Ft. Yukon that he helped establish. He was one month shy of his 58th birthday. According to his wishes, villagers buried him in the native graveyard adjacent to the final resting place of William Loola, the longtime Native deacon at Ft. Yukon. A huge crowd turned out for a memorial service at St. John the Divine's in New York City.

Ft. Yukon's aging Chief Jonas addressed the memorial gathering at Fort Yukon, "My relatives; with weeping and great sorrow I speak to you again of the Big Preacher; for we loved him. What great work he did so that our future might be good! ... My relatives, a man who loved us greatly has labored among us; so let us truly seek to live as he did."

Eight years after the 1913 climb, the newly ordained Reverend **ROBERT G. TATUM** returned to spend another year in Alaska from Tennessee, where he had become a local legend. Tatum died on January 26, 1964, at Knoxville, Tennessee, ending 43 years of ministry. He was 72.

WILLIAM "BILLY" TAYLOR (a.k.a., Honest Bill) was born in Canada in 1883, and came to Alaska from Dawson in either 1901 or '02. A teamster in Dawson, with a livery of horses and mules, he kept busy until selling out and heading for Alaska. He died in August 1944, at age 61. According to his obituary, "William Taylor, member of the party that made the widely-disputed ascent of the mountain passed away in Fairbanks this morning after a lengthy illness that kept him in the hospital since May 14." Previous to his death he still held claims on Glacier, Eureka, and Moose creeks, and owned a cabin at Healy. At the time of his death he was living in Fairbanks in a $25 tent. "He was not married and had no surviving relatives in this area. The climbing expedition was at first discredited because Lloyd's claim that all four had reached the top of the unscaled mountain was disputed by Taylor . . ."

Backed by friends such as Bill McPhee, **JAMES A. WICKERSHAM** campaigned for and won election as Alaska's Delegate to the U.S. Congress, serving from 1909 to 1921, and again from 1931 to 1933. During his tenure as Delegate, he introduced legislation to create Alaska's first national park, provide home rule for Alaska, to build the Alaska Railroad, develop the Alaska Agricultural College and School of Mines, and introduced the first bill to call for Alaska statehood. During his time as delegate, Wickersham was described as ". . . one of the most forceful members of the House. When he speaks Congress listens . . ."

In 1921, Wickersham opened a law office in Juneau and maintained it until his death on October 4, 1939. His beloved first wife Deborah died in 1926. "No other man has made as deep and varied impression on Alaska's heritage," wrote Wickersham's biographer." Alaska is deeply in debt to him."

NOTES

PROLOGUE

1. Brooks, Alfred H., *Blazing Alaska's Trails*, University of Alaska Press, Fairbanks, 1953.
2. Brooks, Alfred H., Annual report of the Smithsonian Institution, 1903.
3. Brooks, Alfred H., *An Exploration to Mt. McKinley America's Highest Mountain*, GPO, Washington, D.C., 1904.
4. *Alaska Weekly*, January 23, 1925.
5. Smith, Philip S., *Memorial of Alfred Hulse Brooks*, Bulletin of the Geological Society of America, Volume 37, 1926.
6. Brooks, Alfred H., *An Exploration to Mt. McKinley America's Highest Mountain*, GPO, Washington, D.C., 1904.
7. Brooks, Alfred H., *The Mt. McKinley Region, with description of the igneous rocks of the Bonnifield and Kantishna Districts*, GPO, Washington, D.C., 1911.

CHAPTER ONE

1. *Fairbanks Daily News-Miner*, February 20, 1913.
2. Slemmons, Mary Anne, *James Wickersham, U.S. District Judge of Alaska, Transcripts of Diaries 1–13, January 1, 1900–February 13, 1908*, Alaska State Library, Juneau 2000.
3. *New York Sun*, 1896; Dickey, W.A., "The Sushitna River, Alaska," *National Geographic Magazine*, November 1897.
4. Wickersham, James, *Pioneering Around McKinley*, Charles Sheldon Collection, Box 5, Folder 3, Archives, Alaska and Polar Regions Department, Rasmuson Library, University of Alaska, Fairbanks.
5. Ibid.
6. Ibid.
7. Wickersham, James, Diary May 16, 1903 through September 17, 1903, James Wickersham papers, MS 107, Box 1, Diary 6, Alaska State Library, Juneau.
8. Ibid.
9. *Dawson Daily News*, August 8, 1905.
10. Wickersham, James, Diary May 16, 1903 through September 17, 1903, James Wickersham papers, MS 107, Box 1, Diary 6, Alaska State Library, Juneau.
11. Ibid.
12. Ibid.
13. Ibid.
14. Ibid.

15. Ibid.
16. Wickersham, James, *Old Yukon: Tales-Trails-and Trials*, Washington Law Book Co, Washington, D.C. 1938.
17. Wickersham, James, Diary May 16, 1903 through September 17, 1903, James Wickersham papers, MS 107, Box 1, Diary 6, Alaska State Library, Juneau.
18. Ibid.
19. *Skagway Alaskan*, letter, S.H. Young to L.S. Keller, May 31, 1911.
20. Wickersham, James, Diary May 16, 1903 through September 17, 1903, James Wickersham papers, MS 107, Box 1, Diary 6, Alaska State Library, Juneau.
21. Ibid.
22. Ibid.
23. Ibid.
24. Wickersham, James, *Old Yukon: Tales-Trails-and Trials*, Washington Law Book Co, Washington, D.C. 1938.
25. Wickersham, James, Diary May 16, 1903 through September 17, 1903, James Wickersham papers, MS 107, Box 1, Diary 6, Alaska State Library, Juneau; Slemmons, Mary Anne, *James Wickersham, U.S. District Judge of Alaska, Transcripts of Diaries 1–13, January 1, 1900–February 13, 1908*, Alaska State Library, Juneau, 2000.

Chapter Two

1. *Dawson Record*, October 27, 1903; *Nome Nugget*, September 9, 1903.
2. *Fairbanks Evening News*, September 27, 1906; *Alaska Weekly*, May 11, 1928.
3. *Fairbanks Evening News*, August 24, 1905.
4. Ibid.
5. *Fairbanks Evening News*, July 22, 1905.
6. *Fairbanks Evening News*, August 24, 1905.
7. *Fairbanks Evening News*, July 22, 1905; *Fairbanks Evening News*, August 15, 1905.
8. *Fairbanks Evening News*, September 26, 1905.
9. *Yukon World*, Dawson City, Sept. 29, 1905.
10. Ibid.
11. *Fairbanks Evening News*, September 26, 1905.
12. Burford, Virgil, *North to Danger*, Robert Hale Ltd, London, 1955.
13. *Yukon World*, Dawson City, Sept. 29, 1905; Sheldon, Charles. *The Wilderness of Denali*, Charles Scribner's Sons, New York, 1930.
14. Capps, S. R. *The Kantishna Region Alaska*, USGS Bulletin #687, 1919; Diane Gudgel-Holmes papers, Box 4, University of Alaska, Anchorage.
15. Karstens, H.P., Memoirs of Henry P. Karstens, Dartmouth College Library.
16. Letter Van Slyke to Wickersham, September 11, 1905, James Wickersham papers, Alaska State Library; *Fairbanks Weekly News*, March 17, 1906.
17. *Tanana Semi-Weekly Miner*, September 21, 1906.
18. *Fairbanks Evening News*, February 21, 1906.
19. *Fairbanks Daily News-Miner*, September 20, 1907.
20. *Fairbanks Daily Times*, March 25, 1908.
21. *Fairbanks Daily Times*, December 4, 1906.

22. Service, Robert, *The Spell of the Yukon*, Dodd, Mead, & Company, New York, 1953; *Yukon Valley News*, Rampart, July 4, 1906; *Douglas Island News*, July 18, 1906.
23. *Fairbanks Evening News*, August 27, 1906.
24. *Fairbanks Evening News*, August 25, 1906.
25. Karstens, H.P., letter to Bradford Washburn, February 7, 1951, "Highlights of My Existence in the North," Dartmouth College Library.
26. *Fairbanks Weekly News*, March 17, 1906.
27. Sheldon, Charles, *The Wilderness of Denali*, Charles Scribner's Sons, New York. 1930.

CHAPTER THREE
1. *Dawson Daily News*, March 30, 1904.
2. Stuck, Hudson, *Ten Thousand Miles with a Dog Sled*, Charles Scribner's Sons, New York, 1914.
3. Ibid.
4. Shuenemann, Joan Karstens, July 5, 1984, Oral History Tape #517; Unfiled documents folder, Grant Pearson Collection, Museum Archives Denali National Park and Preserve.
5. Ibid.
6. Karstens, Henry P., letter to Bradford Washburn, February 7, 1951, "Highlights of My Existence in the North," Dartmouth College Library.
7. Berton, Pierre, *The Klondike Fever*, Alfred A. Knopf, Inc., New York, 1958.
8. Ibid; Karstens, Henry P., Memoirs of Henry P. Karstens, Dartmouth College Library.
9. Radio Interview KFAR, "*Here's a Pioneer*;" Karstens, Henry P., Memoirs of Henry P. Karstens, Dartmouth College Library.
10. Karstens, Henry P., Memoirs of Henry P. Karstens, Dartmouth College Library.
11. Radio Interview KFAR, "*Here's a Pioneer;*" Karstens, Henry P., Memoirs of Henry P. Karstens, Dartmouth College Library.
12. Karstens, Henry P., letter to Bradford Washburn, February 7, 1951, "Highlights of My Existence in the North," Dartmouth College Library.
13. Karstens, Henry P., Memoirs of Henry P. Karstens, Dartmouth College Library; Karstens letter to Francis Farquhar in Terris Moore's *Mt. McKinley: The Pioneer Climbs*, University of Alaska Press, Fairbanks, 1962.
14. Karstens, Henry P., Memoirs of Henry P. Karstens, Dartmouth College Library.
15. *Fairbanks Daily News-Miner*, July 2, 1951
16. Karstens, Henry P., letter to Bradford Washburn, February 7, 1951, "Highlights of My Existence in the North," Dartmouth College Library.
17. Karstens, Henry P., Memoirs of Henry P. Karstens, Dartmouth College Library; Letter Elva Scott, Eagle Historical Society, to Tom Walker, January 7, 1992.
18. Karstens, Henry P., letter to Bradford Washburn, February 7, 1951, "Highlights of My Existence in the North," Dartmouth College Library.
19. Karstens, Henry P. Memoirs of Henry P. Karstens, Dartmouth College Library; Karstens, Henry P., letter to Bradford Washburn, February 7, 1951,

"*Highlights of My Existence in the North,*" Dartmouth College Library; Karstens letter to Francis Farquhar in Terris Moore's *Mt. McKinley: The Pioneer Climbs*, University of Alaska Press, Fairbanks, 1962.

20. The Eagle-Valdez Trail, Bureau of Land Management, Pamphlet BLM-AK-GI-92-036-8351-080.

21. Karstens, Henry P., letter to Bradford Washburn, February 7, 1951, "*Highlights of My Existence in the North,*" Dartmouth College Library.

22. Moore, Terris, *Mt. McKinley: The Pioneer Climbs*, University of Alaska Press, Fairbanks, 1962.

23. Karstens, Henry P., Memoirs of Henry P. Karstens, Dartmouth College Library; Karstens, Henry P., letter to Bradford Washburn, February 7, 1951, "*Highlights of My Existence in the North,*" Dartmouth College Library.

24. *Jessen's Weekly*, December 6, 1951.

25. *Valdez News*, September 19, 1903.

26. Karstens, Henry P., Memoirs of Henry P. Karstens, Dartmouth College Library; Moore, Terris, *Mt. McKinley: The Pioneer Climbs*, University of Alaska Press, Fairbanks, 1962.

27. Karstens, Henry P., Memoirs of Henry P. Karstens, Dartmouth College Library.

28. Ibid.

29. Ibid.

30. Ibid; Moore, Terris, *Mt. McKinley: The Pioneer Climbs*, University of Alaska Press, Fairbanks, 1962.

31. Ibid.

32. Ibid.

33. Karstens, Henry P., Memoirs of Henry P. Karstens, Dartmouth College Library.

34. Pearson, Grant, "The 70-Mile Kid," *Alaska Sportsman*, June 1950; Moore, Terris, *Mt. McKinley: The Pioneer Climbs*, University of Alaska Press, Fairbanks, 1962; Karstens, Henry P., Memoirs of Henry P. Karstens, Dartmouth College Library.

35. *Dawson Daily News*, May 20, 1904, Rex Fisher Collection.

36. Pearson, Grant, "The 70-Mile Kid," *Alaska Sportsman*, June 1950.

37. Moore, Terris, *Mt. McKinley: The Pioneer Climbs*, University of Alaska Press, Fairbanks, 1962; *Jessen's Weekly*, December 6, 1951; *Fairbanks Semi-Weekly News*, March 25, 1905.

38. Karstens, Henry P., letter to Bradford Washburn, February 7, 1951, "*Highlights of My Existence in the North,*" Dartmouth College Library.

CHAPTER FOUR

1. Sheldon, Charles, Journal entry July 11, 1906, Charles Sheldon Collection, Archives, Alaska and Polar Regions Department, Rasmuson Library, University of Alaska, Fairbanks; Sheldon, Charles, *Wilderness of Denali*, Charles Scribner's Sons, New York, 1930.

2. Scull, E. Marshall, *Hunting in the Arctic and Alaska*, John C. Winston, Co., Philadelphia, 1914

3. Sheldon, Charles, *Wilderness of Denali*, Charles Scribner's Sons, New York, 1930.

4. Ibid.
5. Karstens, H.P., Memoirs of Henry P. Karstens, Dartmouth College Library; Jean Karstens Shuenemann, July 5, 1984, Oral History Tape #517, Museum Archives, Denali National Park & Preserve.
6. Sheldon, Charles, *Wilderness of Denali*, Charles Scribner's Sons, New York, 1930.
7. Ibid.
8. Grinnell, George Bird, Personal Collection of William Sheldon.
9. Pearson, Grant, *My Life of High Adventure*, Prentice-Hall, New York, 1962.
10. Ibid.
11. *Fairbanks Evening News*, September 25, 1906.
12. Ibid.
13. Letter Karstens, H.P., to Bradford Washburn, February 7, 1951, "Highlights of My Existence in the North," Dartmouth College Library.
14. Karstens, H.P., Memoirs of Henry P. Karstens, Dartmouth College Library; Letters, various, Boxes 4 and 5, Charles Sheldon Collection, Archives, Alaska and Polar Regions Department, Rasmuson Library, University of Alaska, Fairbanks; *Fairbanks Daily Times*, May 10, 1907.
15. *Tanana Miners' Record*, March 18, 1907, Rex Fisher Collection; *Tanana Weekly Miner*, April 12, 1907.
16. Sheldon, Charles, *Wilderness of Denali*, Charles Scribner's Sons, New York, 1930.
17. *Fairbanks Daily News*, September 3, 1907, Rex Fisher Collection.
18. Sheldon, Charles, *The Wilderness of Denali*, Charles Scribner's Sons, New York, 1930.
19. Ibid.
20. Ibid.
21. Ibid.
22. Ibid.
23. Sheldon, Charles, journal entry, February 13, 1908, Box 3, Charles Sheldon Collection, Archives, Alaska and Polar Regions Department, Rasmuson Library, University of Alaska Fairbanks.
24. Sheldon, Charles, *The Wilderness of Denali*, Charles Scribner's Sons, New York, 1930.
25. Ibid.
26. Undated letter, Karstens to Sheldon, Charles Sheldon Collection, Archives, Alaska and Polar Regions Department, Rasmuson Library, University of Alaska Fairbanks.
27. Sheldon, Charles, *Wilderness of Denali*, Charles Scribner's Sons, New York, 1930.
28. Ibid.
29. Ibid
30. Ibid.
31. *Fairbanks Daily News*, June 20, 1908; *Alaska-Yukon Magazine*, January, 1909.
32. *Fairbanks Daily News, June 10, 1908*; *Fairbanks Daily News*, June 17, 1908.
33. Sheldon, Charles, *The Wilderness of Denali*, Charles Scribner's Sons, New York, 1930.

34. Sheldon letter to F.C. Selous, August 11, 1908, Charles Sheldon Collection, Box 3, Folder 12, Archives, Alaska and Polar Regions Department, Rasmuson Library, University of Alaska, Fairbanks.

35. *Fairbanks Daily News-Miner*, October 27, 1913; *Fairbanks Daily News-Miner*, November 24, 1913; November 24, 1913; December 1, 1913.

36. *Fairbanks Daily Times*, August 17, 1915.

CHAPTER FIVE

1. Mitchell, William L., *The Opening of Alaska*, Cook Inlet Historical Society, Anchorage, 1981.

2. *Fairbanks Daily News-Miner*, November 5, 1908.

3. Ibid.

4. Biological Survey Circular #39, August 22, 1903, U.S. Department of the Interior, Washington, D.C.

5. Alaska Game Law of 1902, 32 Statute 328, Library of Congress, Washington, D.C.

6. Gudgel-Holmes, Dianne, "Steven Foster of the Kantishna River," *Native Place Names of the Kantishna Drainage, Alaska*, Oral History Project, Department of the Interior, National Park Service, Alaska Region, 1991.

7. Murie, Adolph, *The Wolves of Mt. McKinley*, Fauna of the National Parks of the United States, Fauna Series #5, GPO Washington, 1944.

8. *Fairbanks Daily News-Miner*, May 8, 1919; *Nenana News*, December 27, 1921.

9. Frank Glaser Interview Tapes, Jim Rearden Collection, recorded 1953.

10. Ibid.

11. Beach, William N., *In the Shadow of Mt. McKinley*, Derrydale Press, New York, 1931.

12. William G. Stroecker Interview, June 12, 1992.

13. Luckey, Harry, "Hunting in Alaska," *Hunter-Trapper-Trader*, December, 1920.

14. Nellie Strand Atwater Interview, August 1993; *Fairbanks Daily News-Miner*, June 13, 1953; Nenana Recording District General Records, Box 2, page 199.

15. Dixon, Joseph S., *Birds and Mammals of Mt. McKinley National Park*, Fauna Series No. 3, 1938, GPO, Washington, D.C.

16. Capps, Stephen R., *National Geographic Magazine*, January, 1917; Letter Stephen R. Capps to Stephen T. Mather, December 22, 1916, RG 79, CCF, Box 111, Folder: Proposed National Parks, National Archives and Records Administration, Washington, D.C.

17. Letter, R.S. McDonald to Territorial Governor John F.A. Strong, 20 May 1917, Roll 42, Governor of Alaska General Correspondence, National Archives and Records Administration, Washington, D.C.

CHAPTER SIX

1. Pearson Grant, "Joe Quigley, Sourdough," *Alaska Sportsman*, March 1950; *Fairbanks Daily News-Miner*, September 19, 1937.

2. Brooker, Edgar, Manuscript, RG-08, DENA 5462, Folder B-12, 1984, Museum Archives, Denali National Park and Preserve; Meyers, Bill, Oral History Tape #508, Archives, Denali National Park and Preserve.

3. Pearson, Grant, "Joe Quigley, Sourdough," *Alaska Sportsman*, March 1950.

4. *The Klondike Nugget*, December 14, 1901; Haigh, Jane G. and Murphy, Claire Rudolf, *Gold Rush Women*, Alaska Northwest Books, Portland, 1999; http://www.rootsweb.com/ ~akdenali/debio.html.

5. Browne, Belmore, *The Conquest of Mt. McKinley*, G.P. Putnam's Sons, New York, 1913; Patty, Ernest N., *North Country Challenge*, David McKay Co., New York, 1969.

6. McGarvey Lois, *An Old Sourdough. Along Alaskan Trails*, Vantage Press, 1960.

7. *Fairbanks Daily Times*, January 30, 1915.

8. Sheldon, Charles, *The Wilderness of Denali*, Charles Scribner's Sons, New York, 1930.

9. Pearson, Grant, *My Life of High Adventure*, Ballantine Books, New York, 1962; Pearson, Grant, "Joe Quigley, Sourdough," *Alaska Sportsman*, March 1950.

10. Burford, Virgil, *North to Danger*, Robert Hale Ltd, London, 1955; Myers Harry M. and William A., *Back Trails*, Lapeer County, 1932.

11. *The Alaska Sportsman*, "From Ketchikan to Barrow," July 1940.

12. Wold, Joanne, "Fannie the Hike," *Alaska Magazine*, October 1990. This may be an apocryphal story as similar tales involving either a steer or a bison circulate in the American West.

13. Letter, Quigley to Sheldon May 2, 1913, Historical Letters File, Museum Archives, Denali National Park and Preserve; Burford, Virgil, *North To Danger*, Robert Hale, Ltd, London, 1955; Myers Harry M. and William A., *Back Trails*, Lapeer County, 1932.

14. Letter Fannie Quigley to C. Sheldon, May 2, 1913, Historical Letters File, Museum Archives, Denali National Park and Preserve.

15. Ibid.

16. Haigh, Jane G., "Searching for Fannie Quigley, A social, prosperous time of life," *Fairbanks Daily News-Miner*, June 20,1999; www.rootsweb.com/~akdenali/debio.html; Burford, Virgil, *North to Danger*, Robert Hale Ltd, London, 1955.

17. McGarvey Lois, *An Old Sourdough, Along Alaskan Trails*, Vantage Press, 1960.

18. Ibid.

19. Patty Ernest N., *North Country Challenge*, David McKay Co, New York, 1969; Fritz Nyberg Oral History Tape 509A, Museum Archives, Denali National Park and Preserve.

20. Nyberg, Fritz, and Meyers, Bill, Oral History, Tape 509B, Museum Archives, Denali National Park and Preserve; Pearson, Grant, "Fannie Quigley, Frontierswoman," *Alaska Sportsman*. August 1947.

21. *Fairbanks Daily News-Miner*, July 21, 1920.

22. McGarvey Lois, *An Old Sourdough. Along Alaskan Trails*, Vantage Press, 1960.

23. Ibid.

24. Denise Abbey Interview, April 8, 1998; Abbey, Denise, Original MSS, 1927, *Campfire Girls Magazine*; Pete Bagoy Interview, March 30, 1996.

25. Burford, Virgil, *North to Danger*, Robert Hale Ltd, London, 1955.

26. Stewart, John, Oral History Tape #507, Museum Archives, Denali National Park and Preserve; Denise Abbey Interview, April 8, 1998; Brooker, Edgar, Letter, February 25, 1984, RG-08, DENA 5462, Folder B-12, Museum Archives, Denali National Park and Preserve.

27. www.rootsweb.com/~akdenali/debio.html.

28. McGarvey Lois, *An Old Sourdough. Along Alaskan Trails*, Vantage Press, 1960.

29. Browne, Belmore, *Outing Magazine*, Volume 62, Number 4, July 1913.

30. Burford, Virgil, *North to Danger*, Robert Hale, Ltd., London, 1955; Hall, George L., *Sometime Again*, Superior Publishing Company, Seattle, 1945.

31. Saleeby, Becky M, Quest for Gold, C.R.I.M.M., National Park Service, Alaska Region, 2000.

32. Denise Abbey Interview, November, 1994.

33. Norma Hoyt Oral History Tape #513, Museum Archives, Denali National Park and Preserve; *Fairbanks Daily News-Miner*, July 21, 1920; Patty Ernest N., *North Country Challenge*, David McKay Co, Inc., New York, 1969.

34. McGarvey Lois, *An Old Sourdough. Along Alaskan Trails*, Vantage Press, 1960.

35. All spellings as they appeared in the original letter. Alaska State Probate Records, RG 509, Box 17370.

36. Burford, Virgil, *North to Danger*, Robert Hale Ltd, London, 1955.

37. Patty, Ernest N., *North Country Challenge*, David McKay Co, New York, 1969.

38. *Fairbanks News-Miner*, June 25, 1914.

39. *Iditarod Pioneer*, July 4, 1914; *Alaska Gazetteer and Directory* (1915–16); *Fairbanks Daily News-Miner*, April 6, 1920.

CHAPTER SEVEN

1. Probate Records, Box 18029, Alaska State Archives, Juneau.

2. Letter, Knute Lind to brother, 1916, Dianne Gudgel-Holmes Collection, University of Alaska, Anchorage.

3. Brooker, Edgar, History Manuscript, RG-08, DENA 5462, Folder B-12, Museum Archives, Denali National Park and Preserve.

4. Probate Records, Boxes 10277, 17371, Alaska State Archives, Juneau.

5. Ibid.

6. Collins, Florence, Firm, Jo Ann, and Thiede, Diane, "Slim Carlson," *Alaska Magazine*, June, 1970.

7. *Fairbanks Daily Times*, May 26, 1912; *Fairbanks Daily Times*, June 25, 1913; *Fairbanks Daily News-Miner*, October 9, 1926.

8. Gudgel-Holmes, Dianne, *Ethnohistory of Four Interior Alaskan Waterbodies*, State of Alaska, Department of Natural Resources, Division of Research and Development. Anchorage, 1979.

9. *Fairbanks Times*, December 19, 1914.

10. Stuck, Hudson, *The Ascent of Mt. McKinley*, Charles Scribner's Sons, New York, 1913.

11. *Fairbanks Daily News-Miner*, April 29, 1910.

12. Stuck, Hudson, *The Ascent of Mt. McKinley*, Charles Scribner's Sons, New York, 1913.

13. Hudson Stuck Diary, February 22, 1915, MF 91, Reel 2, Archives, Alaska and Polar Regions Department, Rasmuson Library, University of Alaska Fairbanks.
14. *Fairbanks Daily News-Miner*, October 9, 1926.
15. Farrell, Ed., *Biographies of Alaska-Yukon Pioneers 1850–1959*, Volume 3, Heritage Books, Inc. Juneau.

CHAPTER EIGHT
1. *Fairbanks Daily News-Miner*, April 20, 1910.
2. *Fairbanks Daily News-Miner*, April 22, 1910.
3. Cook, Frederick, *To the Top of the Continent: Discovery, Exploration and Adventure in Sub-arctic Alaska. The First Ascent of Mt McKinley, 1903–1906*, Doubleday, Page, and Co., New York, 1908.
4. *The New York Sun*, June 5, 1910; *Jessen's Weekly*, December 6, 1951.
5. Kantishna Recording District, General Records; Mining Locations, Volume 1, 1905–1919; Kantishna Recording District, Deed Book, 1905–1919.
6. *The New York Times*, June 5, 1910.
7. *Fairbanks Daily Times*, Dec. 22, 1909.
8. Ibid.
9. Sheldon, Charles, *Wilderness of Denali*, Charles Scribner's Sons, New York, 1930.
10. Washburn, Bradford, *Mount McKinley: The Conquest of Denali*, Harry N. Abrams, Inc. New York, 1991; *The New York Times*, June 5, 1910.
11. *The New York Times*, June 5, 1910; Bright, Norman, Billy Taylor Interview, *American Alpine Journal*, 1939; *Jessen's Weekly*, December 6, 1951.
12. *The New York Times*, June 5, 1910.
13. Bright, Norman, Billy Taylor Interview, *American Alpine Journal*, 1939; *The New York Times*, June 5, 1910.
14. *The New York Times*, June 5, 1910.
15. Cole, Terrence, *The Sourdough Expedition*, Alaska Northwest Publishing Company, Anchorage, 1985.
16. *The New York Times*, June 5, 1910.
17. Ibid.
18. Ibid.
19. Ibid.
20. Ibid.
21. Ibid.
22. Bright, Norman, Billy Taylor Interview, *American Alpine Journal*, 1939.
23. Ibid.
24. *The New York Times*, June 5, 1910.
25. Bright, Norman, Billy Taylor Interview, *American Alpine Journal*, 1939.
26. Ibid.
27. *The New York Times*, June 5, 1910.
28. Ibid.
29. *Fairbanks Daily Times*, April 12, 1910; *Fairbanks Daily News-Miner*, April 12, 1910, April 14, 1910, April 15, 1910, April 19, 1910.
30. *The New York Times*, June 5, 1910.

31. Ibid.
32. *Fairbanks Daily News-Miner*, April 14, 1910.
33. *Fairbanks Daily Times*, April 12, 1910.
34. *Fairbanks Daily News-Miner*, April 15, 1910.
35. *The New York Times*, April 16, 1910, April 19, 1910.
36. *The New York Times*, April 16, 1910; *Arizona Gazette, Phoenix*, November 14, 1912.
37. Letter Sheldon to E.W. Nelson, April 15, 1910, Folder 7, Box 9, RU 7364, Series 1, Edward W. Nelson Collection, Smithsonian Institution, Washington, D.C.
38. *The New York Times*, April 16, 1910; *Arizona Gazette, Phoenix*, November 14, 1912.
39. *Fairbanks Daily News-Miner*, April 15, 1910.
40. Ibid.
41. *Fairbanks Daily News-Miner*, April 14, 1910.
42. *Fairbanks Daily Times*, June 9, 1910; Washburn, Bradford, *Mount McKinley: The Conquest of Denali*, Harry N. Abrams, Inc., New York, 1991.
43. Bright, Norman, Billy Taylor Interview, *American Alpine Journal*, 1939.
44. Ibid.
45. Browne, Belmore, *The Conquest of Mount McKinley*, G.P. Putnam's Sons/The Knickerbocker Press, New York, 1913.
46. *Fairbanks Daily News-Miner*, April 9, 1929.
47. Bright, Norman, Billy Taylor Interview, *American Alpine Journal*, 1939; Stuck, Hudson, *The Ascent of Denali*, Charles Scribner's Sons, New York, 1913.
48. Nyberg and Myers Oral History Tape #509B, Museum Archives, Denali National Park & Preserve.
49. *The New York Times*, June 5, 1910.
50. Washburn, Bradford, *Mount McKinley: The Conquest of Denali*, Harry N. Abrams, Inc. New York, 1991; *Jessen's Weekly*, December 6, 1951.
51. Pearson, Grant H. with Philip Newell, *My Life of High Adventure*, Ballantine Books, New York, 1962.
52. *New York Times*, June 5, 1910.

CHAPTER NINE
1. *Dawson Daily News*, December 3, 1910.
2. *Fairbanks Daily Times*, December 3, 1910.
3. *Fairbanks Daily News-Miner*, December 2, 1910.
4. *Fairbanks Daily News-Miner*, April 2, 1909.
5. A "mission Indian" was a term used to describe a Native raised and educated at a mission school such as St. Mark's. *Fairbanks Daily News-Miner*, December 9, 1910.
6. *Fairbanks Daily News-Miner*, December 9, 1910.
7. *Fairbanks Daily Times*, December 17, 1910; Letter, Gunter Scheidmann, to Tom Walker, March 22, 2001, Politisches Archiv, Berlin; *The Alaska Weekly*, March 11, 1927.
8. *Fairbanks Daily News-Miner*, December 17, 1910.
9. Ibid.

10. Ibid.
11. Ibid.
12. Ibid.
13. *Fairbanks Daily News-Miner*, December 17, 1910; *Fairbanks Daily Times*, December 17, 1910.
14. Ibid.
15. *Fairbanks Daily News-Miner*, December 17, 1910.
16. *Fairbanks Daily Times*, January 14, 1911; Probate Records, Box 17371, Alaska State Archives.
17. Ibid.

Chapter Ten

1. Browne, Belmore, *The Conquest of Mount McKinley*, G.P. Putnam's Sons/The Knickerbocker Press, New York, 1913.
2. Bates, Robert H., *Mountain Man: The Story of Belmore Browne, Hunter Explorer, Artist, Naturalist*, The Amwell Press, Clinton, New Jersey, 1988.
3. Browne, Belmore, *The Conquest of Mount McKinley*, G.P. Putnam's Sons/The Knickerbocker Press, New York, 1913.
4. Dunn, Robert, *The Shameless Diary of an Explorer*, Modern Library, New York, 2001.
5. Browne, Belmore, *The Conquest of Mount McKinley*, G.P. Putnam's Sons/The Knickerbocker Press, New York, 1913.
6. Ibid.
7. Cook, Frederick A., *To the Top of the Continent*, Doubleday, Page & Company, 1908.
8. Browne, Belmore, *The Conquest of Mount McKinley*, G.P. Putnam's Sons/The Knickerbocker Press, New York, 1913.
9. Ibid.
10. Ibid.
11. Ibid.
12. *Fairbanks Daily Times* April 12, 1909; Wickersham, James A., *Old Yukon—Tales, Trails, and Trials*, Washington Law Book Co., Washington, D.C. 1938.
13. Browne, Belmore, *The Conquest of Mount McKinley*, G.P. Putnam's Sons/The Knickerbocker Press, New York, 1913.
14. Ibid.
15. Ibid.
16. Ibid.
17. Browne, Belmore, *The Conquest of Mount McKinley*, G.P. Putnam's Sons/The Knickerbocker Press, New York, 1913; Rusk, Claude E. "On the Trail of Dr. Cook," *Pacific Monthly*, October, November, and December 1910.
18. Browne, Belmore, *The Conquest of Mount McKinley*, G. P. Putnam's Sons/The Knickerbocker Press, New York, 1913.
19. Ibid.
20. Ibid.
21. Ibid.
22. Ibid.
23. Ibid.

24. Ibid.
25. Ibid.
26. Browne, Belmore, "Hitting the Home Trail from Mt. McKinley," *Outing Magazine*, 1913, Vol. LXII, No.4.
27. Ibid.
28. Ibid.
29. Ibid.
30. Ibid.
31. Browne, Belmore, *The Conquest of Mount McKinley*, G.P. Putnam's Sons/The Knickerbocker Press, New York, 1913.
32. Ibid.

Chapter Eleven

1. Stuck, Hudson, *The Ascent of Denali*, Charles Scribner's Sons, New York, 1914.
2. Letter Stuck to Karstens, 12 December 1911, Henry P. Karstens Papers, Dartmouth College Library; *The Spirit of Missions*, July 1915, Archives of the Episcopal Church, Austin, Texas; Washburn, Bradford, and Peter Cherici, *The Dishonorable Dr. Cook*, The Mountaineers Books, Seattle, 2001.
3. Thompson Paul E, "Who Was Hudson Stuck?", *Alaska Journal*, Winter, 1980.
4. *Fairbanks Daily News-Miner*, May 8, 1923; *The Spirit of Missions*, July 1915, Archives of the Episcopal Church, Austin, Texas.
5. *The Spirit of Missions*, July 1915, Archives of the Episcopal Church, Austin, Texas.
6. Dean, David M., *Breaking Trail, Hudson Stuck of Texas and Alaska*, Ohio University Press, Athens, 1988.
7. Ibid.
8. *The Spirit of Missions, Alaska Number*, September 1912, Archives of the Episcopal Church, Austin, Texas.
9. Dean, David M., *Breaking Trail, Hudson Stuck of Texas and Alaska*, Ohio University Press, Athens, 1988.
10. *Fairbanks Daily News-Miner*, October 13, 1912.
11. Letter, February 7, 1951, Karstens to Bradford Washburn, "Highlights of My Existence in the North," Dartmouth College Library.
12. Letter Stuck to Karstens, December 12, 1911, Henry P. Karstens Papers, Dartmouth College Library; Letter Stuck to Karstens, March 25, 1912, Henry P. Karstens Papers, Dartmouth College Library.
13. *Fairbanks Evening News*, 1906; *Fairbanks Daily News-Miner*, June 29, 1908; *Fairbanks Daily News-Miner*, May 11, 1909; *Fairbanks Daily News-Miner*, May 12, 1909.
14. Stuck, Hudson, *The Ascent of Denali*, Charles Scribner's Sons, New York, 1914.
15. Pamphlet, Manuscript 4, Box 11, #2, Alaska State Library; Mozee, Yvonne, in *The Ascent of Denali: Containing the Original Diary of Walter Harper, First Man to Achieve Denali's True Summit*, The Mountaineers, Seattle, 1977.
16. *Fairbanks Daily News-Miner*, December 4, 1918.

17. *The Spirit of Missions, Alaska Number*, September 1912, Archives of the Episcopal Church, Austin, Texas.

18. From *Stories Told By John Fredson to Edward Sapir*, Alaska Native Language Center, University of Alaska, Fairbanks, 1982; Mackenzie, Clara Childs, *Wolf Smeller, A Biography of John Fredson, Native Alaskan*, Alaska Pacific University Press, Anchorage, 1985.

19. Stuck, Hudson, "Johnny and the Sugar," *The Spirit of Missions*, February, 1914, Archives of the Episcopal Church, Austin, Texas.

20. *The Spirit of Missions, Alaska Number*, September 1912, Archives of the Episcopal Church, Austin, Texas; Undated letter to Sheldon, Box 2, Folder 2, Charles Sheldon Papers, Archives, Alaska and Polar Regions Department, Rasmuson Library, University of Alaska, Fairbanks.

21. Letter Stuck to Karstens, 15 September 1912, Henry P. Karstens Papers, Dartmouth College Library.

Chapter Twelve

1. Stuck, Hudson, "Johnny and the Sugar," *Spirit of Missions*, February, 1914.
2. Ibid.
3. Ibid.
4. Ibid.
5. Browne, Belmore, *The Conquest of Mount McKinley*, G.P. Putnam's Sons/The Knickerbocker Press, New York, 1913; Terris Moore Collection, Box 2, File 6, Harry Karstens' Diary of the 1913 McKinley Expedition, May 9, 1913, Archives, Alaska and Polar Regions Department, Rasmuson Library, University of Alaska, Fairbanks.
6. Stuck, Hudson, *The Ascent of Denali*, Charles Scribner's Sons, New York, 1914.
7. Ibid.
8. Letter Karstens to Sheldon, Charles Sheldon Collection, Box 2, Folder 2, Undated Correspondence, Harry P Karstens, 1914–1923, Archives, Alaska and Polar Regions Department, Rasmuson Library, University of Alaska, Fairbanks.
9. Mozee, Yvonne, in *The Ascent of Denali: Containing the Original Diary of Walter Harper, First Man to Achieve Denali's True Summit*, The Mountaineers, Seattle, 1977; Stuck, Hudson, *The Ascent of Denali*, Charles Scribner's Sons, New York, 1914; Terris Moore Collection, Box 2, File 6, Harry Karstens' Diary of the 1913 McKinley Expedition, May 9, 1913, Archives, Alaska and Polar Regions Department, Rasmuson Library, University of Alaska, Fairbanks.
10. Dean, David M., *Breaking Trail, Hudson Stuck of Texas and Alaska*, Ohio University Press, Athens 1988.
11. Letter Karstens to Sheldon, Charles Sheldon Collection, Box 2, Folder 2, Undated Correspondence, Harry P Karstens, 1914–1923, Archives, Alaska and Polar Regions Department, Rasmuson Library, University of Alaska, Fairbanks.
12. Ibid.
13. Dean, David M., *Breaking Trail: Hudson Stuck of Texas and Alaska*, Ohio University Press, Athens, 1988; Stuck, Hudson, *The Ascent of Denali*, Charles Scribner's Sons, New York, 1914; *Fairbanks Daily News-Miner*, Karstens Obituary, November 29, 1955.

224 NOTES

14. Stuck, Hudson, *The Ascent of Denali*, Charles Scribner's Sons, New York, 1914.
15. Ibid.
16. Ibid.
17. Mozee, Yvonne, in *The Ascent of Denali: Containing the Original Diary of Walter Harper, First Man to Achieve Denali's True Summit*, The Mountaineers, Seattle, 1977.
18. Stuck, Hudson, *Ascent of Denali*, Charles Scribner's Sons, New York, 1914.
19. Terris Moore Collection, Box 2, File 6, Harry Karstens' Diary of the 1913 McKinley Expedition, June 6, 1913, Archives, Alaska and Polar Regions Department, Rasmuson Library, University of Alaska, Fairbanks.
20. Ibid.
21. Stuck, Hudson, *The Spirit of Missions*, July, 1915, Archives of the Episcopal Church, Austin, Texas.
22. Letter, Stuck to John Wood, November 24, 1917, Alaska Papers, Archives of the Episcopal Church, Austin, Texas.
23. Stuck, Hudson, *Ascent of Denali*, Charles Scribner's Sons, New York, 1914.
24. Ibid.
25. Ibid.
26. Ibid.
27. Stuck, Hudson, "Johnny and the Sugar," *Spirit of Missions*, February, 1914.
28. Ibid.
29. Ibid.
30. *Knoxville News-Sentinel*, May 22, 1932; Terris Moore Collection, Box 2, File 6, Harry Karstens' Diary of the 1913 McKinley Expedition, June 12, 1913, Archives, Alaska and Polar Regions Department, Rasmuson Library, University of Alaska, Fairbanks.
31. *Fairbanks Daily Times*, June 21, 1913.

CHAPTER THIRTEEN
1. Letter Karstens to Sheldon, Charles Sheldon Collection, Box 2, Folder 2, Undated Correspondence, Harry P Karstens, 1914–1923, Archives, Alaska and Polar Regions Department, Rasmuson Library, University of Alaska, Fairbanks.
2. *Fairbanks Daily Times*, April 12, 1913.
3. Letter Karstens to Sheldon, Charles Sheldon Collection, Undated Correspondence, Harry P Karstens, 1914–1923, Box 2, Folder 2, Archives, Alaska and Polar Regions Department, Rasmuson Library, University of Alaska, Fairbanks.
4. *Ruby Record-Citizen*, July, 1913, Rex Fisher Collection.
5. Ibid.
6. *Fairbanks Daily Times*, July 10, 1913; *Alaska Citizen*, July 14, 1913.
7. *Fairbanks Daily Times*, August 3, 1913.
8. Letter Karstens to Sheldon, Charles Sheldon Collection, Box 2, Folder 2, Undated Correspondence, Harry P Karstens, 1914–1923, Archives, Alaska and Polar Regions Department, Rasmuson Library, University of Alaska, Fairbanks.
9. Letter Stuck to Karstens, September 18, 1912, Henry P. Karstens Papers, Dartmouth College Library.
10. Letter Stuck to Karstens, September 29, 1913, Henry P. Karstens Papers, Dartmouth College Library.

11. *The New York Sun*, Sept 6, 1913.
12. Stuck, Hudson, "Johnny and the Sugar," *Spirit of Missions*, February, 1914; Stuck, Hudson, *The Ascent of Denali*, Charles Scribner's Sons, New York, 1914.
13. Letter Scribner to Sheldon, October 2, 1913, Charles Sheldon Collection, Box 3, File 11, Archives, Alaska and Polar Regions Department, Rasmuson Library, University of Alaska, Fairbanks.
14. *Fairbanks Daily News-Miner*, March 14, 1914.
15. Letter, Karstens to Sheldon, Charles Sheldon Collection, Box 2, Folder 2, Undated Correspondence, Harry P Karstens, 1914–1923, Archives, Alaska and Polar Regions Department, Rasmuson Library, University of Alaska, Fairbanks.
16. Letter Stuck to Karstens, February 8, 1915, Henry P. Karstens Papers, Dartmouth College Library.
17. Ibid.
18. Letter Karstens to Farquhar, April 10, 1928, Francis P. Farquhar Collection, Box 1, Folder 1, Archives, Alaska and Polar Regions Department, Rasmuson Library, University of Alaska, Fairbanks.
19. Letter Karstens to Sheldon, Charles Sheldon Collection, Box 2, Folder 2, Correspondence, Harry P Karstens, 1914–1923, Archives, Alaska and Polar Regions Department, Rasmuson Library, University of Alaska, Fairbanks.
20. Ibid; *Alaska Sportsman*, December 1963.
21. Letter Karstens to Sheldon, Charles Sheldon Collection, Box 2, Folder 2, Correspondence, Harry P Karstens, 1914–1923, Archives, Alaska and Polar Regions Department, Rasmuson Library, University of Alaska, Fairbanks; *Fairbanks Daily Times*, March 20, 1914; *Fairbanks Daily News-Miner*, March 20, 1914.
22. *Fairbanks Daily Times*, August 1, 1914.
23. Memoirs of Mrs. H.P. Karstens, Henry P. Karstens Papers, Dartmouth College Library; *Alaska Magazine*, F.L. Karstens Obituary, February 1975.
24. Letter Karstens to Sheldon, Charles Sheldon Collection, Box 2, Folder 2, Correspondence, Harry P Karstens, 1914–1923, Archives, Alaska and Polar Regions Department, Rasmuson Library, University of Alaska, Fairbanks.
25. Letter Karstens to Sheldon, September 14, 1914, Charles Sheldon Collection, Box 2, Folder 2, Correspondence, Harry P Karstens, 1914–1923, Archives, Alaska and Polar Regions Department, Rasmuson Library, University of Alaska Fairbanks.
26. *Fairbanks Daily Times*, September 25, 1914.
27. Ibid.
28. *Fairbanks Daily News-Miner*, January 7, 1915.
29. Mackenzie, Clara Childs, *Wolf Smeller, A Biography of John Fredson, Native Alaskan*, Alaska Pacific University Press, Anchorage, 1985.
30. *Washington Post*, October 12, 1920; Memoirs of Henry P. Karstens, Henry P. Karstens Papers, Dartmouth College Library.

Chapter Fourteen

1. Joseph A. Strong, Alaska Governor, to Secretary of the Interior, February 13, 1917, RG 79, CCF, Box 111, Folder: Proposed National Parks, National Archives and Records Administration, Washington, D.C.
2. Capps, Stephen R., The Kantishna Region, Alaska, USGS Bulletin 687, GPO, Washington, D.C. 1919.

3. Letter T.A. Riggs to Edmund Seymour, October 12, 1920, Edward W. Nelson Collection, RU 7364, Series 9, Box 40, Folder 1, Smithsonian Institution.

4. *Alaska-Yukon Magazine*, February, 1912.

5. Norris, Frank, *A Lone Voice in the Wilderness, The National Park Service in Alaska 1917–1969*, Environmental History, Volume 1, No 4, October 1996.

6. Browne, Belmore, *The Conquest of Mount McKinley*, G.P. Putnam's Sons/The Knickerbocker Press, New York, 1913.

7. Stuck, Hudson, *The Ascent of Denali*, Charles Scribner's Sons, New York, 1914.

8. Browne, Belmore, *The Backlog*, Camp Fire Club, May 1938.

9. Albright, Horace M., *The Birth of the National Park Service, the Founding Years, 1913–33*, Howe Brothers, Salt Lake City, 1985.

10. Testimony of Belmore Browne, Senate Committee on Territories, May 5, 1916.

11. Charles Sheldon Collection, Box 2, Folder 8, Department of Interior, Rules and Regulations, signed Stephen T. Mather, Director National Park Service, Archives, Alaska and Polar Regions Department, Rasmuson Library, University of Alaska, Fairbanks.

12. Testimony of James Wickersham, in A Bill to Establish the Mount McKinley National Park, in the Territory of Alaska, Government Printing Office, May 5, 1916.

13. Wadsworth, W.A., President, and Roosevelt, Kermit, Secretary, Boone and Crockett Club Resolution, 1916.

14. Capps, Stephen R., "A Game Country Without Rival in America," *National Geographic Magazine* January 1917.

15. Testimony of Belmore Browne in A Bill to Establish the Mount McKinley National Park, in the Territory of Alaska, Government Printing Office, May 5, 1916.

16. Ibid.

17. Ibid.

18. Undated letter from Sheldon to G.B. Grinnell, Charles Sheldon Collection, Box 4, File 46, Archives, Alaska and Polar Regions Department, Rasmuson Library, University of Alaska, Fairbanks.

19. *Forest and Stream Magazine*, #87, April, 1917.

20. *Nenana News*, February 24, 1917.

21. Letter Sheldon, Charles to Grant, Madison, June 9, 1917, E.W. Nelson Collection, RU 7364, Series 9, Box 40, Folder 2, Smithsonian Institution.

22. *Fairbanks Daily News-Miner*, December 7, 1917.

BIBLIOGRAPHY

Interviews by Author

Abbey, Denise, November, 1994, August 1998.
Abbey, Woodbury "Bud," August 1998.
Bagoy, Peter, November 23, 1995, March 21, 1996, February 20, 1996.
Coghill, Jack, October, 1995.
Ketzler, "Bear," April 2005.
Mercer, Berle, March 1994.
Morino, Joe Jr., October 1990.
Morino, Jim, July 1999.
McCutcheon, Steve, March 1991.
Nancarrow, William, numerous.
Nyberg, Fritz, October 1974.
Onka, Oliver, November 23, 1995.
Plumb, Earl, April 19, 1998.
Stroecker, William G., January 3, 1992.
Strand, Sally Atwater, August 1993.
Teeland, Walter, April 23, 1991.
Vogel, Oscar, October 1978, November 1978.
Waugaman, William, Sr., numerous.
Wear, Jean Simmons, November 2, 1992.
Wright, Jesse, February 9, 2002.

Periodicals

Alaska Gazetteer and Directory (1915–16)
Alaska Journal
Alaska Magazine
Alaska Sportsman Magazine
Alaska-Yukon Magazine
American Alpine Journal
Backlog, Camp Fire Club
Campfire Girls Magazine
Forest and Stream Magazine
Hunter-Trapper-Trader Magazine

National Geographic Magazine
Outing Magazine
Pacific Monthly Magazine
Pathfinder
Spirit of Missions

Newspapers

Alaska Citizen
Alaska Weekly
Dawson Daily News
Dawson Record
Fairbanks Daily News-Miner
Fairbanks Daily Times
Fairbanks Evening News
Fairbanks Miner
Fairbanks Weekly News
Iditarod Pioneer
Jessen's Weekly
Klondike Nugget
Knoxville News-Sentinel
Nenana News
New York Sun
New York Times
Nome Nugget
Ruby Record-Citizen
Skagway Alaskan
Tanana Miners' Record
Tanana Semi-Weekly Miner
Tanana Weekly Miner
Valdez News
Washington Post
Yukon World, Dawson

Archival Sources

Alaska State Library, Juneau.
Alaska State Probate Records, Alaska State Archives, Juneau.
Archives of the Episcopal Church, Austin, Texas.
Denali National Park and Preserve, Museum Archives.
Dartmouth College Library, Rauner Special Collections.
Eagle Historical Society.
Jim Rearden Collection.
National Archives and Records Administration, Washington, D.C.
Nenana Recording District Mining Records, Fairbanks, Alaska.

Smithsonian Institution, Charles Sheldon Papers, Edward W. Nelson Collection.
University of Alaska, Fairbanks, Rasmuson Library, Archives, Alaska and Polar Regions Department.
University of Alaska, Anchorage, Consortium Library, Dianne Gudgel-Holmes Collection.

BOOKS/REPORTS

Albright, Horace M. *The Birth of the National Park Service: The Founding Years, 1913-1932*. Howe Brothers, Salt Lake City, 1985.
Baker, Marcus. *Geographic Dictionary of Alaska*. G.P.O. Washington, 1906.
Bates, Robert H. *Mountain Man: The Story of Belmore Browne, Hunter Explorer, Artist, Naturalist*. The Amwell Press, Clinton, New Jersey, 1988.
Beach, William N. *In the Shadow of Mt. McKinley*. Derrydale Press, New York, 1931.
Beeman, Marydith. *Lost and Found in Alaska and Yukon and Klondike*, Volume 1 and 2. Eagle River, 1995.
Bernhardt, J. The *Alaska Engineering Commission*. D. Appleton & Company, New York, 1922.
Berton, Pierre. *The Klondike Fever*. Alfred A. Knopf, Inc., New York, 1958.
Brooks, Alfred H. *Blazing Alaska's Trails*. University of Alaska Press, Fairbanks, 1953.
Brooks, Alfred H. *An Exploration to Mt. McKinley America's Highest Mountain*. Journal of Geography, Washington, DC, 1903.
Brooks, Alfred H. *The Mt. McKinley Region, with description of the igneous rocks of the Bonnifield and Kantishna Districts*. GPO, Washington, DC, 1911.
Brown, William E. *Denali, Symbol of the Alaskan Wild*. The Donning Company/Publishers, Virginia, 1993.
Browne, Belmore. *The Conquest of Mt. McKinley*. G.P. Putnam's Sons, New York, 1913.
Burford, Virgil. *North to Danger*. Robert Hale Ltd, London, 1955.
Buzzell, Rolfe G. *Drainage Histories of the Kantishna Mining District. 1903-1968*. National Park Service, Alaska Region, Anchorage, 1989.
Capps, S. R. *The Kantishna Region Alaska*. USGS Bulletin #687, 1919.
Coates, Ken & Morrison, Bill. *The Sinking of the Princess Sophia, Taking the North Down With Her*. University of Alaska Press, Fairbanks 1991.
Cohen, Stan. *The Klondike Centennial Scrapbook: The Great Klondike Gold Rush*. Pictorial Histories Publishing Company, Missoula, 1997.
Cohen, Stan. *The Streets were paved with Gold. A Pictorial History of the Klondike Gold Rush, 1896-1899*. Pictorial Histories Publishing Company, Missoula, 1977.
Cole, Terrence. *The Sourdough Expedition*. Alaska Northwest Publishing Company, Anchorage, 1985.
Cole, Terrence. *Crooked Past. The History of a Frontier Mining Camp: Fairbanks, Alaska*. University of Alaska Press, Fairbanks, 1991.
Cook, Frederick. *To the Top of the Continent: Discovery, Exploration and Adventure in Sub-arctic Alaska. The First Ascent of Mt McKinley, 1903-1906*. Doubleday, Page, and Co., New York, 1908.
Davis, Mary Lee. *We Are Alaskans*. W.A. Wilde Co., 1931.

Dean, David M. *Breaking Trail, Hudson Stuck of Texas and Alaska*. Ohio University Press, Athens, 1988.
Dixon, Joseph S. *Birds and Mammals of Mt. McKinley National Park*. Fauna Series No. 3, GPO, Washington, DC. 1938.
Dunn, Robert. *The Shameless Diary of an Explorer*. Modern Library, New York, 2001.
Farrell, Ed. *Biographies of Alaska-Yukon Pioneers 1850-1959*, Volume 3. Heritage Books, Inc. Juneau.
Gates, Michael. *Gold at Fortymile Creek, Early Days in the Yukon*. University of British Columbia Press, Vancouver, 1994.
Gudgel-Holmes, Dianne. "Steven Foster of the Kantishna River," *Native Place Names of the Kantishna Drainage, Alaska*. Oral History Project, Department of the Interior, National Park Service, Alaska Region, 1991.
Gudgel-Holmes, Dianne. *Ethnohistory of Four Interior Alaska Waterbodies*. State of Alaska, Department of Natural Resources, 1979.
Haigh, Jane G. and Murphy, Claire Rudolf. *Gold Rush Women*. Alaska Northwest Books, Portland, 1999.
Hales, David A. *An Index to the Early History of Alaska as Reported in the 1903-07 Fairbanks Newspapers*. Rasmuson Library, Fairbanks.
Hunt, William. *Golden Places, History of Alaska-Yukon Mining*. National Park Service, Anchorage, 1990.
Hunt, William. *North of 53°, Wild Days of Alaska-Yukon Mining Frontier, 1870-1914*. McMillan Company, New York, 1974.
Hunt, William. *Whiskey Peddler. Johnny Healy, North Frontier Trader*. Mountain Press Publishing Company, Missoula, 1993.
Johnson, James Albert. *Carmack of the Klondike*. Epicenter Press and Horsdale & Schubert Publishers, Seattle and Ganges B.C., 1990.
Mackenzie, Clara Childs. *Wolf Smeller, A Biography of John Fredson, Native Alaskan*. Alaska Pacific University Press, Anchorage, 1985.
McGarvey Lois. *An Old Sourdough. Along Alaskan Trails*. Vantage Press, 1960.
Mitchell, William L. *The Opening of Alaska*. Cook Inlet Historical Society, Anchorage, 1981.
Moore, Terris. *Mt. McKinley: The Pioneer Climbs*. University of Alaska Press, Fairbanks, 1962.
Mozee, Yvonne. In *The Ascent of Denali: Containing the Original Diary of Walter Harper, First Man to Achieve Denali's True Summit*. The Mountaineers, Seattle, 1977.
Murie, Adolph. *The Wolves of Mt. McKinley*. Fauna of the National Parks of the United States, Fauna Series #5, GPO Washington, 1944.
Myers Harry M. and William A. *Back Trails*. Lapeer County, 1932.
Patty, Ernest N. *North Country Challenge*. David McKay Co, New York, 1969.
Pearson, Grant. *A History of Mount McKinley National Park, Alaska*. National Park Service, 1953.
Pearson, Grant, and Newell, Philip. *My Life of High Adventure*. Ballantine Books, New York, 1962.
Prindle, L.M. *Bonnifield and Kantishna Regions*. U.S. Geological Survey Bulletin 314, Washington 1907.
Rand McNally and Company. *Rand McNally Guide to Alaska and Yukon*. New York, 1922.

Ricks, M.B. *Directory of Alaska Post Offices and Postmasters, 1867–1963*. Tongass Publishing, Ketchikan, 1965.

Rouch, Peggy Dodson. *Girl in the Gold Camp: A True Account of an Alaska Adventure 1909–10*. Epicenter Press, Seattle, 1996.

Saleeby, Becky M. *Quest for Gold*. C.R.I.M.M., National Park Service, Alaska Region, 2000.

Schneider, William; Gudgel Holmes, Dianne; Dalle-Molle, John. *Land Use in the North Additions of Denali National Park and Preserve: An Historical Perspective*. National Park Service, Anchorage, 1984.

Scull, Marshall E. *Hunting in the Arctic and Alaska*. John C. Winston, Co., Philadelphia, 1914.

Service, Robert. *The Spell of the Yukon*. Dodd, Mead, & Company, New York, 1953.

Sheldon, Charles. *The Wilderness of Denali*. Charles Scribner's Sons, New York, 1930.

Sherwood, Morgan B. *Big Game in Alaska: A History of Wildlife and People*. Yale University Press, New Haven, 1961.

Slemmons, Mary Anne. *James Wickersham, U.S. District Judge of Alaska, Transcripts of Diaries 1–13, January 1, 1900–February 13, 1908*. Alaska State Library, Juneau 2000.

Stuck, Hudson. *The Ascent of Mt. McKinley*. Charles Scribner's Sons, New York, 1913.

Stuck, Hudson. *Ten Thousand Miles with a Dog Sled*. Charles Scribner's Sons, New York, 1914.

Washburn, Bradford, Peter Cherici. *The Dishonorable Dr. Cook*. The Mountaineers Books, Seattle, 2001.

Washburn, Bradford. *Mount McKinley: The Conquest of Denali*. Harry N. Abrams, Inc. New York, 1991.

Wickersham, James. *Old Yukon: Tales-Trails-and Trials*. Washington Law Book Co, Washington, DC. 1938.

INDEX

Abbey, Denise: 91–92, 173.
Abbey, Woodbury: 173.
Abramskey, Billy: 26, 28.
Aiken, Butte: 8.
Alaska Boundary Survey: 196.
Alaska Commercial Co.: 40–41.
Alaska Engineering Commission: 190.
Alaska Game Law of 1902: 72.
Alaska Game Law of 1908: 73.
Alaska Game Law of 1912: 75.
Alaska Natives: 128, 133, 153, 155–156, 161.
Alaska Peninsula: 137.
Alaska Railroad: 187–191, 193, 195, 198–199, 209.
Alaska Range: x–xi, 4–5, 8–9, 34, 45–46, 66, 68–69, 75–77, 80, 113–114, 129, 134, 138–139, 142–146, 149–151, 175, 190, 193, 196.
Alaska Territorial Bureau of Mines: 185.
Alaska-Yukon Pacific Expo, 1909: 67.
Albert, Jennie (*Seyn-dahn*): 161.
alcohol: 86, 92, 102, 156–157.
Alder Creek: 140.
Allakaket, town: 156.
Alma Lake (Roosevelt/Wonder Lake): 9.
altitude sickness: 118, 171–172, 174–175, 178.
American Alpine Club: 141, 182.
American Altitude Record: 148, 151, 175.
American Forestry Assn: 191.
American Game Protective Assn.: 191, 199.

American Geographical Society: 141–142, 182.
American Museum of Natural History: 5, 137, 205.
American National Bank: 35.
American Ornithological Union: 191.
Amundsen, Raold: 139.
Anderson Pass: 114, 145.
Anderson, Pete: 100, 112–120, 122–126, 128, 144, 148, 151, 168, 173–174, 205.
"*Archdeacon of the Yukon*": 153, 175.
Arctic: 5, 137.
Armistice: 203.
Ascent of Denali: 183.
Aten, Arthur: 145–147, 149.
Athabascans: xii, 2, 4, 8, 24, 53, 69, 77, 79, 103, 107, 125, 127–128, 131, 134, 153, 161–163, 198.
"*Natsit gwich'in*": 162, 205.
Athabascan Place Names:
 "Dee-na-thy (Mt. McKinley): 8.
 "Chet-siah" (Heart Mountain): 8.
 "Chid-zey-ah" (Chitsia Hills): 8.
 "Chid-zi-ah-na" (Moose Creek): 8.
 "Hun-teth-na" (Kantishna River): 8.
 "Toot-tlat" (Toklat River): 8.
Aubert, Mrs.: 160.
Auk, The: 65.

Bagoy, Pete: 91.
Baker, J.E.: 173.
Barnette, E.T.: 27, 122.
Barrill, Edward: 113, 121, 140–142
bear, black: 86, 88, 90.

Index

bear, grizzly: xii, 9, 55, 60, 67, 75, 77–78, 127, 137, 146, 186, 200.
Bearpaw River: 17, 19, 20–21, 61–62, 67, 81, 98, 108, 125, 167.
Bearpaw, town: 21.
Beauchamp, Clarence (aka Boatman): 105–06.
beaver: 105.
Bcbc shipyard: 35.
Bell, Alexander Graham: 57.
Belmont, Morgan: 186–187.
Belt & Hendricks Trading Post: 13.
BenBenneck, A.J. "Gus": 16, 28.
Benson, Joseph. H.: 16, 28.
Bergman, town: 24.
berries: 88–89, 102, 130.
Berry, Clarence: 39.
Berry, Richard T.: 130–134.
Bettis, Titus: 133.
Bettles, Gordon C.: 24–25, 28, 101, 134.
Bettles Group: 25.
Bettles, town: 24, 156
Bevington, V.E.: 39.
Beyadatenna, village: 133.
Big Creek: 69.
Billings, Montana: 34.
Birch Creek: 104.
Bolshevik Revolution: 189.
Bonanza Creek, Yukon: 39.
Bone-Dry Law, 1918: 156.
Bonnifield Mining District: 18.
Bono, Louis: 30.
Boone and Crockett Club: 63, 191, 195, 201–203.
Boss, William: 20.
bounty, wolf: 105.
Bowman, John: 101–102, 104.
Bradley, John: 122.
Brelle, Fred: 103.
Bremner, John: 24.
Broad Pass: 129, 133, 145, 190.
Brochu, Joseph: 27, 98–99.
Bronx Zoo: 55.
Brooker, Edgar Jr.: 84.
Brooker, Edgar Sr.: 108.
Brooks, Alfred Hulse: x–xii, 5, 9–11, 61, 115, 120, 139, 144.
Brooks Range: 160.

Brown, John, U.S. Attorney: 134.
Brown, market hunter: 63.
Browne, Belmore: 13, 91, 123, 135–153, 155, 163, 167–170, 173, 189–190, 193–196, 199–201, 205.
Browne's Tower: 172.
Bryce, market hunter: 63.
Bulshaia, Russian for Mt. McKinley: 193.
Bunch, E.S.: 159.
Burnham, John B.: 199.
"*Burning Daylight*": 39.
Burns, Joe: 91.
Burns, Robert: 102.
Burrell, Lyman: 39.
Busia, John: 199.
Busia, Marko (Old Marko): 81, 105, 199.
Busia, Tom: 199.

Cache Creek: 114–115, 168.
Cairns, Ralph: 123, 145.
Calderhead & Hall: 20, 95.
Calhoun, C.H.: 132–134.
Camp Fire Club: 193, 195, 201.
Canadian Pacific Railway: 137.
Cantwell River: xi, 18.
Cantwell, town: 129.
Capps, Henry: 63.
Capps, Stephen R.: 80, 190, 198.
caribou: xii, 3, 5, 7, 22, 55, 58, 60, 63, 70–78, 86, 88, 91, 115, 127, 168, 186, 195, 200
Caribou Creek: 19, 27, 28, 178.
Carlson, Haljmar "Slim": 76, 104–105, 123.
Carlo Creek: 130, 133.
Carmack, George: 39.
Carnegie Hall: 155.
Carr, E.M.: 108.
Carson City, Nevada: 30.
Cascades Mts: 2, 10, 158.
Cavanaugh, Irish Tom: 35–38, 40.
"Che-ah": 8.
Cheechako: 5, 24, 51, 109, 111, 113, 120, 132, 156, 163.
Chena River: 4, 27, 45, 70, 77, 86.
Chena, town: 6, 30, 71, 93, 113.

Chicago, Ill.: 34, 44, 129, 158, 160, 185.
Chief Jonas: 208.
Chihuahua and Pacific Exploration: 53.
Chihuahua and Pacific Railroad: 53.
child labor: 155.
Chilkoot Pass: 36, 84–85.
Chilkoot Trail: 36
Chitsia Creek: 9, 11, 15, 21.
Chitsia Mountain/Range: 1, 21, 23, 74.
Chronister, James: 28, 160.
Chulitna River: 114, 143, 145.
Chute, Jerome: 49.
Circle City: 5, 43, 84, 94, 156, 162.
Clay Street cemetery: 133.
Clearwater Fork, Toklat: 23, 67.
Coast Mountains: 36.
Coldfoot, town: 156.
commercial fishing threat: 156–157.
conservation: 51, 63, 80, 189–192, 194, 200–201.
Conwyl Mining Co.: 62.
Cook, Frederick A.: 11, 51, 77, 113, 115, 120–122, 136–137, 139–144, 151, 155.
  remuneration: 155, 182–183.
Cook Inlet: x, 139, 143, 175.
Copper Mountain: 203.
Copper River: 33, 45, 48.
Courtney, Anna: 30.
Courtney, Grant: 30.
Crossley, James District Attorney: 132.
cyanide: 85.
Czech: 85.

Dall, William H.: 74.
Dalton, Jim: 20, 28, 74.
Dalton, Joseph: 15–17, 19–20, 27–28, 94, 150.
Dalton, Scotty: 185.
Davidson, Charles A.: 113–114, 116.
Dawson City: xii, 36–40, 44, 53, 70, 84–86, 101, 108, 125, 206, 208.
Dawson gold: 15.
Deadhorse Trail: 36.
Deadmen's Valley, N.W.T.: 127.
Delta River: 33–34, 45–46, 48, 159.
Denali: 4, 56, 62, 65, 114, 153, 172–173, 175–176, 202.

Denali, naming: 193.
Denali National Park: xi, 31, 65, 79, 195.
Denali Park road: 79.
Densmore, Frank: xi, 39, 193.
Densmore's Mountain: xii.
Densmore, Spencer and McPhee: xii.
Diamond, town: 21, 25, 31–32, 61, 163, 167, 186, 187.
Dickey, William: 4.
Dillon, John: 133.
diphtheria: 128.
Disston, Henry: 139–140.
distemper, dogs: 103.
Dixon, Joseph: 80.
Dogs/dogteams: 23, 25, 33–35, 42–49, 58, 60–63, 65, 67, 71, 75, 77, 81–83, 85, 92–93, 103, 105, 107, 109, 114, 117–118, 120, 124, 128–132, 134, 145, 147, 159–160, 165–169, 172, 176, 178, 183, 188, 196.
Doherty, J.E.: 20.
Dome Creek nugget: 32.
duck, Labrador: 80.
Dugan River (aka Kantishna): 6.
Duke's Trading Post: 65–66, 102, 129, 132.
Dyea: 36.

Eagle, Alaska: 2–4, 39–44, 156–157, 206.
eagle, bald: 73.
Eagle Gorge: 12.
Eagle Trail: 43.
earthquake: 150, 169–170.
Edmonton, Alberta: 127.
"Egghead Expedition": 136, 143, 151.
El Dorado: 84.
Eldorado Creek, Kantishna: 103–104.
Eldorado Creek, Yukon: 39.
Episcopal Church: 66, 153–156, 158, 161–163.
  25th Alaska Anniversary: 153, 163.
  Anniversary Climb: 155.
Ester Creek: 39.
Ester Hill: 120.
Eureka camp: 21–22, 32, 94, 108, 178.
Eureka Creek: 16–17, 19–20, 22–26, 28–29, 63, 74, 91, 99, 103, 107, 167, 208.

Eureka Group: 19, 28.
Evan, John: 104.
Explorer's Club: 141–142, 182, 191.

Fairbanks: 2, 4, 6, 15, 17, 19–20, 22, 23, 25–28, 30–33, 39, 45–46, 48–49, 53, 55, 58–63, 65–67, 70–72, 74–75, 77, 80, 83–86, 89, 91–92, 94–96, 100, 102, 104–105, 111, 113, 115, 119–120, 122–123, 125–134, 155–160, 163, 167–168, 180, 183–188, 190, 200–202, 207–208.
Fairbanks Daily News: 67.
Fairbanks Daily Times: 95, 145, 180.
Fairbanks Miner: 6.
"Fake Peak": 143, 144.
Farrar, Mason (Mace): 160.
Federal Migratory Bird Law: 199.
Ferry: 78, 132, 208.
feud, violent: 103.
Finlay River, B.C.: 127.
First National Bank, Fairbanks: 159.
Fish, James "Jim": 41, 44–46.
Five Finger Rapids: 37.
Flat, town: 83.
Fleming, H.T.: 29–30.
food prices: 22, 27, 38.
Foraker River: 105.
Fort Egbert: 3, 41–43.
Fort Gibbon: 44, 46, 48, 128.
Fort Reliance: 39.
Fort Yukon: 5, 44, 156, 182, 205–208.
Fortymile: 3, 39, 44, 84, 87, 94, 101.
Fortymile River: 43, 84.
Fortymile River, Mosquito Fork: 43.
Foster, Addison G., U.S. Senator: 2.
Foster, Elizabeth: 31.
Foster, Ernest, Commissioner: 30–31, 62, 103–104, 108, 125–126, 128.
Foster, Gertrude: 31.
Foster, Steven R.: 73, 107.
foxes: 60, 64, 75, 77, 89, 105–107.
Fredson (aka Fred), John: 162–163, 165, 167–169, 176–178, 188, 205.
    father, "Fred": 162.
    mother, "Louise": 162.
    "George Washington": 163, 205.
    Zhoh Gwatsan: 162, 205.

Friday Creek: 17–26, 86–88, 99.
frontier justice: 24, 125, 134.
frost injuries: 27, 33, 41, 46–47, 49, 81–83, 96, 98, 109, 117, 159, 169.
fur-farming: 106.
fur prices: 105.

Gaerisch, Freda Louise: 185–188.
Gakona, town: 47.
gambling: 22, 25, 37, 157.
game populations: 71–72, 74, 107, 186.
game wardens: 73, 79.
    appointment of: 73.
game violation fines: 74, 79.
gardens: 88, 102, 106.
"Gay '90s": ix.
George, Esaias: 162, 167–168.
German/Germany: 128, 129, 132, 189, 201.
"Gilded Age": ix.
Giles, Frank: 105.
"Ginkhii choo," translation: 156.
Glacier City: 21–22, 29–30, 32, 49, 51, 61, 63, 65, 125–126, 128, 151, 178.
Glacier Creek: 16, 18, 19–21, 25–26, 28–31, 81–82, 86, 88, 93, 103, 108, 116, 208.
Glacier Peak: 100.
Glaser, Frank: 75.
"Glen Creek boys": 111–112, 114, 120, 124, 129, 134, 146–147, 151, 158, 164, 183, 185, 188.
Glen Creek/camp: 94, 100–102, 108, 110, 112–115, 119–121.
Glen Prospect: 100.
gold rush: 13, 34, 70, 84, 99, 134.
Goldstream valley: 160.
gold strikes: ix, x, 3, 9, 35–37, 39, 44, 71, 84, 145, 160, 182, 189.
"Golden Beaches," Nome: 44.
"Golden Stairs": 36.
Goodpaster Trail: 70.
Grand Basin: 118, 122, 147, 172.
Grand Canyon National Park: 200.
Granite Creek: 102.
grayling: 88.
Great Bear Bar: 40.

236 INDEX

Great Icefall: 165.
Greely, Adolphus W.: 43.
Griffin, E.W.: 113, 118, 122.
Grinnell, George Bird: 57, 208.
Gulliver, Louisa Walter (Sheldon): 158.
Gulkana: 47.

Hagel, Frank: 32.
Hall, "Arkansas Jim": 207.
Hall's Bookstore: 55.
Hamilton, Jack or John: 25, 30, 178.
Hamilton & Ott's claim: 30.
Hamilton's store: 21, 31.
Harnish, Elam: 39–40.
Harper, Arthur: xi, 161, 172, 206.
Harper Glacier: 172.
Harper, Walter: 153–154, 160–163, 165, 167–176, 180, 188, 206–208.
Harvard: 186.
Hauselmann, Fred: 67, 84, 98.
Haydon, Horace "Jack": 51, 53, 55, 60.
Haydon, Wilbur: 53.
Headless Creek, N.W.T: 127.
Healy Fork (river): 71, 130.
Healy, town: 71, 208.
Healy, J. J.: 36.
Heilig, Albert A.: 2, 4.
Helena, Montana: 35.
Henderson Creek: 39–40.
Henry, Eva: 79.
Herman, "Big": 75.
Herman, "Little": 75.
Hess, market hunter: 63.
Hicks, Boedak: 79.
Hogatza River: 24, 134.
Holmes, Dr., Bureau of Mines: 185.
Holy Cross, town: 157.
"hootch": 102.
Horn, Jack: 16, 17, 84.
Horn, Robert: 113–114, 116.
Hornaday, William T.: 190.
horses: 34–36, 41, 45, 53, 55, 61–63, 143, 185, 208.
Hudson Bay Co.: 5.
Hudson Stuck Memorial Hospital: 205.
Humboldt Prospect: 100.
Hunker Creek, Yukon: 86.

hunting: xii–xiii, 43, 51, 53–64, 66–68, 73, 83, 86–88, 91–92, 103–104, 109, 137–138, 140, 146, 162, 167–168, 186–187, 191, 193, 196.
miners' exemption: 196–198, 200–201, 203.

Iditarod: 32, 83, 109, 160.
"Indian Uprising": 125–128.
influenza: 128, 205, 207.
Ingersol, Charles: 106.
insanity: 98, 104, 128.
Inupiaqs: 2.
Iselin, C.O. Jr.: 186–187.
isolation: 31, 98–99, 101, 103–104, 109, 127–128, 159, 163.

Jake Wade, camp: 43.
Jeffery, George A.: 2, 5, 6, 10, 12.
Jeffery Glacier: 10.
Jenny Creek: 77.
John, Walter Jr.: 25.
Johnson, Jim: 115.
Johnson, John W.: 27.
Juneau: 84, 206–207, 209.

Kachemak Bay: 137.
Kaltag, town: 160.
"Kantish-i-naw": 20.
Kantishna gold:
  clean-ups: 31–32.
  placer: 16–18, 27, 30, 84, 100.
  quartz: 18, 30, 84–85, 100, 114, 207.
  shape/texture: 26.
  value: 17, 20, 28–30, 32, 88.
Kantishna gold stampede, *1905*: 17–24, 27, 32, 85–86, 95, 101, 106, 108, 111, 113–114, 121–122, 124.
Kantishna gold stampede, *1906*: 32.
Kantishna gold strike: 15–17, 32, 75, 83–84, 101, 106.
Discovery claims:
  Eureka Cr: 15.
  Friday Cr: 17.
  Glacier Cr: 16.
  Yellow Pup: 16.
Kantishna Hills: 13–14, 83, 96, 106.
Kantishna King: 28, 160.

Kantishna mining district: 15, 17, 20–32, 34, 49–51, 54, 63, 65, 68, 73–80, 83–84, 93, 95, 98–99, 101, 104, 106–109, 125–126, 128–129, 134, 146, 150, 159, 163, 168, 173, 185, 187, 195–196, 198–199, 201, 203, 207.
Kantishna River: xi, 6, 11–13, 17–18, 21, 24, 29, 53, 55, 61, 67, 75, 95, 97, 103, 105, 145, 163.
Kantishna trail: 19, 22–23, 77, 81–82, 129.
Karstens, Freida Louise: 185–188.
Karstens, Henry P.: 23, 29, 33–51, 53–68, 102, 123, 154, 158–161, 163, 179–188, 193, 202–203, 206.
Karstens' Ridge: 169–172.
"Kar-steins": 58.
Katmai eruption, 1912: 150.
Keeler, Dan: 108–109.
Keim, Alois Charles: 98.
Kenai Mts.: 137.
Ketchumstuck Flat: 43.
Klondike: ix–x, 3, 17–20, 23, 32, 34–35, 37, 39, 45, 53, 79, 84–85, 94, 96, 101, 105, 108, 161.
Klondike Kings: 38.
Klondike River: ix, 37, 38.
Kluane Lake: 53.
Knight's Roadhouse: 23.
Knight, T.J.: 130–134.
Knik, town: 145.
Koch, Daniel: 103.
Kollm, Max: 129.
Koyukuk District: 24, 101, 157, 161.
Koyukuk River: 24, 156, 160.
Kuhn, William: 103–104.
Kuskokwim River: xx, 8, 73, 185.

Lake Bennett: 36, 84.
Lake Lindemann: 36.
Lake Mansfield: 43.
Lake Minchumina: 8, 73, 105, 107.
Lake Shore & Michigan Railroad: 53.
Lambert, Rudolph: 98.
Lane, Franklin K.: 194–195, 200.
lay/layman: 30.
Lavoy, Merl: 135–136, 145–147, 150–151, 169–170, 173.

Lewes, The: 37.
Lewis, George: 145.
Liard River: 5.
Lind, Knute: 101.
Little Moose Creek: 98.
Livengood, town: 32.
Lloyd, William R. "Billy": 94–96, 101, 108, 113–115.
Lloyd, Thomas: 30, 62, 94, 100, 111–124, 143–145, 167, 173, 182, 207, 209.
London, England: 105, 155.
London, Jack: 39–40.
Loola, William: 208.
Lousetown, Yukon: 37.
Lucke, Harry: 69–70, 75, 77–79, 185.
"Lucky Gulch," Eureka Creek: 19.
Lundeen, C.G.: 8.
lynx: 65, 90, 105, 106.

Mackenzie River: 5.
magazines: 102, 117, 139.
   Atlantic Monthly: 102.
   Century: 102.
   Forest and Stream: 201.
   Harper's Monthly: 102, 139.
   North American: 102.
   Scribner's: 102, 183.
mail-carriers: 23–34, 41, 43–49, 51, 77, 79, 114, 157.
mail service, Kantishna: 23, 49, 57, 93, 102, 104.
Manley Hot Springs: 13.
Mann, Bob: 28.
market hunting: 22, 43, 63–64, 68–80, 128, 189–191, 198, 200–202.
   game killed:
      by numbers: 69, 71, 73–80, 200.
      by weight: 71, 78, 80, 190.
      game meat: 73, 74, 190, 198, 200, 202.
      prices: 70, 71, 190.
Marko, Johnny (Busia): 199.
Marko, Old (Busia): 81, 105, 199.
Marko, Tom (see Busia): 199.
marten: 105–106.
Mather, Stephen Tyng: 195, 201.
Maurer, Emil: 128–134.
Maurer, Mrs. Emil: 128–134.
Maurice, Albert: 97–99.

Mayo, Al: xi, 101.
Mazama Mountaineering Club: 143.
McClean, Mary Catherine: 92.
McDonald, R. S.: 190.
McGarvey, Lois: 89–91.
McGlaughlin, market hunter: 63.
McGonagall, Charles: 23, 44–49, 100, 112–124, 146, 151, 158, 165, 169, 173–174, 178.
McGonagall Pass: 114, 115, 145, 146, 150, 165, 168, 172, 207.
McKenzie, Angus: 86.
McKenzie, Fannie (Quigley): 21, 63, 67, 81, 85, 87, 93, 151.
  "Fannie the Hike": 86.
  "Mother McKenzie": 86, 100.
  Sedlacek, Frances: 85.
McKenzie Roadhouse, Yukon: 86.
McKinley Bar: 85.
McKinley City: 24, 95.
McKinley River: 11, 19–21, 102, 115, 145, 178.
McLeod Creek: 9.
McLeod, Frank: 127.
McLeod, John: 5–13, 59–60, 125–128, 130–132.
McLeod, Laura: 5.
McLeod, Murdock: 5, 127.
McLeod, Willie: 127.
McPhee, Bill: 38–39, 101, 111, 113, 118, 122, 207, 209.
McPhee Pass: 115.
McQuesten, Jack: 101.
Means, Sam: 63, 67.
measles: 128.
medical/medicine: 100, 157, 163, 172, 175.
Mentasta Lake: 43.
mercury: 85, 104.
Merrifield, Billy: 60–62, 64, 67, 114.
Merriam, C. Hart: 53, 207–208.
Mexico: 20, 53.
Middle River (also Teklanika): 77–78.
Miles Canyon: 37.
Miles City, Montana: 105.
Milich, George: 74.
miners' meetings: 3, 39.
Mission Creek: 39, 43.

Mitchell, Alexander ("The Bard"): 67, 102, 105.
Mitchell, William "Billy" Lt.: 41–44, 70, 207.
Monroe, Father: 186.
Moore, William: 35.
Moose: xii, 3, 11–13, 22, 58, 70–71, 74–75, 78, 81, 86, 88, 93, 162, 186, 195.
Moose Creek (Kantishna): 15–17, 19, 21–23, 25, 27, 57, 84–85, 94, 100, 102, 107, 146, 167, 199, 200, 208.
Moose Creek (Nenana): 132.
Morgan, H. Carey: 186–187, 207.
Morningside Hospital, Oregon: 98.
mosquitoes: 11, 57, 66, 178, 197.
Mount Herman Academy: 188.
Mt. Brooks: 149.
Mt. Deborah: 9.
Mt. Foraker: 9, 185.
Mt. McKinley: x, xii, 1, 4–5, 8–9, 11, 51, 54, 64–65, 68, 70, 74–76, 106, 109, 126, 137, 145–146, 153–155, 158, 167, 173–174, 179–181, 183–184, 193, 198, 199.
  "Central Northeastern ridge": 117–118, 147, 169, 172.
  Climb histories:
    1903, first attempt: 10–11, 139, 198.
    1903, second attempt: 2, 11, 139.
    1906 climb, Cook: 113, 120–122, 137, 139–142, 155.
    1910 climb, Cairns: 123.
    1910 climb, Lloyd: 111–124, 146.
    1910 Maurer fiasco: 128–129.
    1910 climb, Parker Expedition: 136, 142–144, 163.
    1912 climb, Browne-Parker: 135–136, 138, 144, 149–151, 153, 155, 163.
    1913 climb, Karstens-Stuck: 158, 161, 165–178.
    1913: first ascent: 175.
  North Peak: 119, 122–123, 134, 144–151, 173.
Mt. McKinley National Park: 14, 58, 70, 74, 80, 101, 205.
  act: 189.

appropriations: 202–203.
boundary decision: 192, 195–186, 198
establishment: 189–203.
naming: 193, 195.
Muddy River: 64.
Mudlark: 6, 13.
Muir, John: 195.
Muldrow Glacier: 114, 116–118, 123, 145–146, 165–168, 176.
mules, Mark and Hannah: 6, 10, 12–13.
Mulville, James: 32.
Munson, Billie: 45.
Murie, Adolph: 74.
Murrow, Joe: 68.
Myrtle Creek: 23.

Nagita, Chief: 131–134.
children, Sophia, William: 133.
Nahanni River, NWT: 127.
Nash, Martin: 145.
National Food Commission: 201.
National Parks Association: 191.
National Park Service: 195.
National Park Service Act of 1916: 195.
Nelson, Edward W.: 53, 195, 205.
Nelson, Gust: 113.
Nenana Canyon: 131, 190.
Nenana coal fields: 185.
Nenana River: x, 18, 49, 61, 65–66, 71, 74–75, 78–79, 84, 129–130, 134, 161–162, 186, 206.
Nenana, town: 18, 66, 79, 91, 102, 134, 167–168, 178, 188, 190, 205.
New York: 67, 111, 113, 122, 137, 141, 158, 178, 183, 189, 205, 207–208.
New York Sun: 4, 186.
New York Zoological Society: 191, 198.
Nikolai, town: 75.
Nome: 4, 15, 17, 109.
Nordale Hotel: 132.
Normile, trail-breaker: 46–47.
Norris, Frank: 192.
Northern Commercial Co.: 24, 173.
Northern, saloon: 55.
North Pole: 139, 141.
Northwest Mounted Police: 36–37, 108.
Northwest Territories (NWT): 127.
Nova Scotia: 191, 207.

Noyes, Arthur H.: 4.
Nyberg, Fritz: 90.

Old Yukon: Tales-Trails-Trials: 5.
Olympic Mountains: 2.
Olympic National Park: 2.
Order of Alaska Pioneers: 94, 113, 118, 120, 122.
Osgood, Wilfred H.: 57.
Ott, Phil: 30, 122.

Palace, saloon: 55.
"Panic of 1893": ix.
Panorama Mountain: 130.
Parker, Herschel: 111, 123, 135–137, 139–151, 153, 155, 163, 167–170, 173, 207.
partnership of necessity: 99.
passenger pigeon: 80.
Patty, Ernest: 90, 92, 94.
Pearson, Grant: xi, 124.
Peary-Cook controversy: 142.
Peary, Richard, Admiral: 141–142.
Pedro, Felix: 4, 70.
pemmican: 147, 166, 168, 174.
Peters Glacier (aka Hannah): 10–11, 65, 139.
Peterson, Gust (Lloyd sponsor): 118.
Peterson, Frank: 8.
Petree, Dave: 113, 207.
Pickarts, Bettles & Pickarts: 24.
Pinchot, Gifford: 57.
Pioneer Hotel: 113.
Pioneer Ridge: 145.
Pioneer saloon: xii, 39.
Pittman, Key, U.S. Senator: 198, 200.
pneumonia: 173, 205, 208.
poison: 63–64, 75, 77–78, 106–107, 128.
Polychrome Mountain: 87.
population: x, 2, 21, 25, 32, 37, 99, 100, 190.
porcupine: 90, 99.
Porcupine River: 5, 157, 206.
"Portland Bench," Nome: 17.
Potasi, mine: 53.
"Pothole Camp": 116.
Prince William Sound: 145.
Prindle, Louis M.: 18.

prospector described: 151–152.
prostitution: 22, 35, 157.

"Queen of Eureka," nugget: 28.
Quigley, Fannie (McKenzie): 21, 63, 67, 81–96, 100, 105, 178.
   cooking: 86–87, 90–91.
   nicknames: 86, 90, 91, 93.
Quigley Gulch, Yukon: 84.
Quigley, Joe: 16–17, 21, 51, 63, 67, 81–96, 178.
Quigley Ridge (aka mineral): 86.

Rabbit Creek, Yukon: ix.
Radovich, Eli, "Bill the Turk": 75–77.
Rainy Pass: x.
Rampart, Alaska: 4, 13, 15, 156.
Rat Portage: 5.
ravens: 64.
R.C. Wood, Co.: 159.
Reaburn, D. L.: x, xi, 5.
recorder's office/recorders: 17, 25, 39, 94, 100.
Regan, Matt: 15, 19.
Rhinehart, William: 84, 103–104.
Rice, miner: 62.
Richardson Trail: 48.
Riggs, Thomas: 190, 196.
Riverboats, steam and gas:
   "*Delta*": 188.
   "*Doman*": 186.
   "*Dusty Diamond*": 21, 55.
   "*Florence S.*": 20, 30, 62, 67.
   "*Jennie M.*": 19.
   "*John Cudahy*": 3.
   "*Luella*": 60–61.
   "*Minneapolis*": 95.
   "*Pelican*": 157, 161, 163, 188.
   "*Snoqualmie*": 160.
   "*St. Michael*": 180.
   "*Tanana Chief*": 6, 19.
   "*White Seal*": 108.
   "*Wilbur Crimmin*": 61.
roadhouses: 28, 31, 41, 45, 47, 75, 86, 107–109.
robbery: 29–30, 125, 128, 130–131, 160.
Rodman's Roadhouse: 109.

Romanov, John: 74.
Roosevelt: 21, 24–25, 30, 32, 108–109.
Roosevelt, Theodore: 21, 57, 191.
Rowe, Peter Trimble: 48–49, 155–157, 182.
Royal Geographical Society: 182.
Ruby, town: 32, 180, 185.
Ruby Record-Citizen: 178.
Rungius, Carl: 57.
Rusk, Claude: 143–144.
Ruth Glacier: 143–144.

saloon: 12, 21–22, 35, 37, 39, 55, 94, 100, 101, 111, 113.
Samson's Hardware, Fairbanks: 115.
Sanctuary River: 77, 80.
Savage Fork (river): 75, 77–79, 80.
Savage, Tom (see Strand)
Scales, The: 36.
Schaup Creek (aka Friday): 86.
scurvy: 88.
Seattle Times: 181.
Seattle, Wa.: ix, xii, 35, 43–44, 60, 67, 111–112, 121, 143, 178.
"Seventymile Kid": 39, 49, 58, 159.
Seventymile River: 39–41.
Seward, town: 145, 185, 190.
Sheenjek River: 162.
Sheep Camp: 36.
sheep, Dall: xii, 22–23, 51, 53–55, 58–65, 67–71, 73–78, 80, 87, 93, 115, 127, 138, 145, 178, 186, 190, 195, 200, 202.
sheep, bighorn: 80.
sheep, desert: 53.
sheep, Stone: 5, 53, 55, 137.
Sheldon, Charles: xiii, 32, 51–68, 73–74, 80, 87–88, 102, 109, 114, 121, 144, 155, 159, 171, 179, 182–184, 186, 188–191, 193–199, 201–203, 207–208.
shooting, assault: 98, 103, 127, 131–134.
Silas, dog: 63, 65.
Skagway: 35–36, 44, 60, 129, 206.
Skookum Hill: 39.
Slate Creek: 102.
smallpox: 44, 157.

Smith, Charley: 59.
Smith, J. R., "Soapy Smith": 35.
Smithsonian Institution: 120, 205.
Smythe, Captain: 67.
snow-blindness: 46–47, 147, 149, 169.
snowshoes: 115–116, 121.
Sorensen, Soren: 39.
"Sourdough Expedition": 113, 123–124
sourdough flagpole: 118, 122–124, 151, 170, 173.
Sourdough Gully: 118, 122.
South Pole: 137.
Spruce Creek: 23, 29.
Square Deal, town: 21.
Squaw Rapids: 37.
St. John's in the Wilderness: 156.
St. John the Divine's, NY: 208.
St. Joseph's Hospital, Fairbanks: 186, 207.
St. Mark's Mission, Nenana: 134, 161–163.
St. Mathew's Cathedral, Dallas: 155.
St. Patrick's Day: 167.
staking a claim, how-to: 16–17.
Steamships, coastal: 35.
 "*Al-Ki*": 35.
 "*Portland*": ix.
 "*Princess Sophia*": 206–207.
Steele Fork (river): 77.
Steele, Tom: 75, 77.
Stendahl, John: 100, 124.
Stevens, Morton: 5, 9–10, 12–13.
Stevens Village: 162.
Stiles, Joe: 15–17, 19–20, 28, 94.
Stiles, Simon: 28.
Stone, Andrew Jackson: 5, 137.
Stony River: 76.
Strand, Edward: 79.
Strand, Tom, (aka Tom Savage): 75, 79, 103, 208.
Strong, Governor John F. A.: 73, 190.
Stuck, Hudson Archdeacon: 75, 123, 153–163, 165–178, 179–185, 188, 193, 206–208.
Stuck-Karstens controversy: 179–184.
sugar, Fredson and: 178.
suicide: 41, 97–98, 104.
Susitna ("Sushitna") River: 4, 139.
Susitna District: 130.

Sutton, Al: 68.
Swanson, Charlie: 29.
Swift, Calvin: 30.

Tacoma, Wa.: 1–2, 3, 137.
Takotna, town: 76, 185.
Tanacross: 41.
Tanana Crossing: 41, 43, 48.
Tanana Restaurant: 159.
Tanana River: xi–xii, 4, 6, 13, 17, 22, 29, 43–44, 48, 53, 57, 60–61, 65, 67, 71, 75, 95, 159, 163, 178, 182, 195.
Tanana, town: 29, 153, 180–182.
Tanana Trading Co.: 21.
Tanana Valley: 4, 27, 28.
Tansy, Samuel: 30.
Tatum, Robert G.: 163–165, 167–169, 171, 175, 178.
taxonomy: 55.
Taylor, William "Billy": 30, 62, 94, 100, 108, 112–124, 144, 148, 151, 168, 173–174.
Teklanika ("Techlanika") River: 69, 74–75, 77, 80.
Tenderfoot Creek: 159.
Texas: 155–156.
Third Judicial District: 2.
Thirtymile: 37.
Thompson Pass: 45.
Thorofare: 102.
"*Toklat*," horse: 65–66, 160.
Toklat River: 6, 16, 23, 49, 52, 55, 59–61, 64–66, 68, 75, 77, 80, 87, 186–187, 191, 207.
Tokositna River: 139.
Tolovana River: 188.
Totatlanika River: 205.
Tondro, Frank (aka "Malemute Kid"): 187.
Topkok: 44.
Tortella (see St. Mark's): 18.
To the Top of the Continent: 141.
tourist, first: 67.
trailbreakers: 33, 46–47.
Trapper Creek: 16.
trapping: 8, 26, 29, 32, 60, 63, 67, 75–79, 83, 89–90, 97, 103, 105–108, 125, 127–128.

Trundy, Charles: 108.
tuberculosis: 3, 97, 161.
Tucker, Herman: 143–144.
"Tunnel Camp": 117–118, 119, 124, 147.
Two-Bull Moose Gulch: 9.
typhoid: 37, 206.

Una Creek: 130–131.
University of the South: 155, 163.
U.S. Air Force: 207.
U.S. Army: x, 41, 43–44.
U.S. Army Signal Corps: 43, 163.
U.S. Biological Survey: 53, 56, 58, 65, 195.
U.S. Commissioner: 25, 30, 73, 86, 100, 103, 108, 125, 133, 134.
U.S. Geological Survey: x–xi, 61, 80.
U.S. Interior Department: 193–195, 201.
U.S. Office of Naval Intelligence: 220.

Valdez: 41–46, 48.
Valdez Creek: 130, 134.
Valdez Hotel: 41.
Van Chobin: 125.
Van Orsdel, J.C., Commissioner: 86, 108.
Van Slyke, Lee, Commissioner: 25, 30, 108.
Vanderbilt Reef: 206.
Vaugnes Restaurant: 34.
Vautier, U.S. Deputy Marshall: 30.
Venetie Tribal Council: 205.

Wahoo, Nebraska: 85.
"Wall Street Glacier": 115.
Washington-Alaska Military Cable and Telegraph Service (WAMCATS): 43–44, 70.
Washington, D.C.: 5, 188, 191, 195.
Washington saloon: 111, 113.
Washington State: 1, 30, 79, 92–93, 137.
Walton, Izaak: 7.
Webb, Bert: 53.

Webb, Charley: 5–7, 10, 12–13.
Webb Creek (Moose Cr.): 8–9.
Wells, Francis: 206–207.
West Point: 43.
Wheeler, Deming: 109, 185.
whipsaw lumber: 37, 84.
Whitehorse: 60.
White House: 189, 191, 20.
Whitely-Karstens Co.: 160.
Whitely, W.F.: 68, 159.
White Pass Railroad/Trail: 36, 53.
Wickersham, Deborah: 1, 4, 13, 209.
Wickersham, Howard: 3–4.
Wickersham, Judge James: xiii, 1–15, 21, 25, 30, 53, 56, 75, 100, 120, 123, 127, 139, 142, 144, 159, 196–198, 209.
Wickersham Wall: 14, 144.
Wilderness of Denali: 208.
Wilderness of Upper Yukon: 53.
"Willows Camp": 115, 117–118.
Wilson, C. Herbert: 108.
Wilson, Jim: 60, 61.
Wilson, Woodrow: 189, 190, 201.
"Windy Bill": 34–35.
"Windy Bills": 34, 127.
Wiseman: 32.
wolf: 64, 75–78, 105, 109.
wolverine: 64–65, 189, 191.
Wonder Lake: 9.
Wood, Richard C.: 159, 185.
Wood River: 71.
World War I: 57.
Wright, Arthur: 163.

Yale: 52.
Yanert Fork (River): xi.
Yellow Pup Creek: 16, 28, 31.
Yukon: ix, 33, 36, 53, 58, 71, 207.
Yukon Order of Pioneers: 94, 101, 108.
Yukon River: 4, 36–37, 39, 41–44, 53, 60, 70, 84, 153, 160, 175, 195.
Yukon sled: 131, 165.

Zielke, Charles: 132.